CCBC

Choices
1998

Kathleen T. Horning
Ginny Moore Kruse
Megan Schliesman

Cooperative Children's Book Center
School of Education
University of Wisconsin–Madison

CCBC Choices was produced by University Publications, University of Wisconsin–Madison. Cover design: Lois Ehlert

For information about other CCBC publications, send a self-addressed, stamped envelope to: Cooperative Children's Book Center, 4290 Helen C. White Hall, School of Education, University of Wisconsin–Madison, 600 N. Park St., Madison, WI 53706–1403 USA. Inquiries may also be made via fax (608/262–4933) or e-mail (*ccbcinfo@mail.soemadison.wisc.edu*). See the World Wide Web (*http://www.soemadison.wisc.edu/ccbc/*) for information about CCBC publications and the Cooperative Children's Book Center.

Contents

Acknowledgments

Thank you to Friends of the CCBC member Tana Elias for creating the index for this edition of *CCBC Choices*. Thank you also to Friends member Lois Ehlert, who created the cover design four years ago.

We value the responses and insights of participants in CCBC Book Discussions throughout 1998.

Cheers to all participants in the annual CCBC Award Discussions of books published during 1998: the Mildred L. Batchelder, Randolph Caldecott, John Newbery, Coretta Scott King Author and Coretta Scott King Illustrator award discussions during November and December, 1998. Special thanks to Madge Klais, who coordinated Madison Metropolitan School District staff participation in the Coretta Scott King discussions and the Américas Award Discussion, held in March, 1999.

Many thanks to participants in the *CCBC-Net* community for sharing comments about some of their favorite books of the year and outcomes of regional or local award book discussions.

Great appreciation to the individuals with specialized interests and expertise who—at our request—evaluated or volunteered their comments about one or more books, especially Anne Altshuler, Julie Causton, Tzu-chang Chang, Jami Davis, Joseph Elder, Lisa M. Frink, Kirsten Hartman, David Herrmann, Marie Horning, Margaret Jensen, Helen Julius, John Kruse, Heidi Oliversen, Jeanne Audrey Powers, Debbie Reese, and Jean Reinbold.

CCBC student staff members Jolen Neumann and Stephanie Steinwedel assisted with the meticulous job of proofreading.

The Friends of the CCBC, Inc., is a membership organization that sponsors programs to develop public appreciation for children's literature and supports special projects at the CCBC. Membership is open to all. Information about membership can be found in Appendix V.

The Friends of the CCBC underwrote the professional design, typesetting, layout, printing and binding of *CCBC Choices 1998*. Members of the 1998–99 Friends of the CCBC, Inc., Board of Directors are: President Mary Petersen, Vice-President Kate Odahowski, Recording Secretary Renée Hoxie, Treasurer Julie Fingerson, and Directors-at-Large Tana Elias, Margaret Jensen and Pamela Wittig. Committee chairs include Nancy Beck, Don Crary and Kathy Tessmer (1998). The *Newsletter* editor is Tana Elias.

We appreciate the Friends' ongoing commitment to providing university students and faculty, teachers, school library media specialists, public librarians and others with an attractive, easy-to-use edition of this publication. All of our reading, selection and writing for *CCBC Choices* occurs during evenings and weekends throughout the year. In this respect, the three of us created *CCBC Choices 1998* as members of the Friends of the CCBC, Inc.

Kathleen T. Horning, Ginny Moore Kruse and Megan Schliesman

Introduction

Many perspectives on books for children and young adults are available to those associated with the Cooperative Children's Book Center (CCBC), a library of the School of Education at the University of Wisconsin–Madison. Additional information about the CCBC can be found near the end of this publication.

We created *CCBC Choices* within the environment of the Cooperative Children's Book Center. As a book examination center and research library, the CCBC receives review copies of almost all of the trade and alternative press books published in English in the United States for children and young adults during the year. Each week during 1998, we examined newly published books. We subsequently read many of them. We discussed hundreds formally or informally with other librarians and educators in Wisconsin and elsewhere in the nation, and many were discussed on *CCBC-Net*, the national electronic book discussion group moderated by the CCBC.

The CCBC receives daily requests for information about contemporary and historical books for children and young adults. We know firsthand from teachers and librarians, from university faculty, and from students who are studying to become teachers and librarians that they want to find books with accurate information on matters important to the young people in their classrooms, schools and libraries. The people we meet know that today's children and young adults have many questions and need information in order to better understand the society in which they live, the people they know and even themselves. Our colleagues are looking for books that are commended for these reasons.

Our criteria are uncomplicated: an excellent book is both interesting and accurate. The way in which these criteria are realized is as varied as the books themselves.

Book discussion is an important factor in our choosing books for *CCBC Choices*. We hold monthly discussions, open to any adult who would like to attend, to look critically at some of the new books we have received at the CCBC. Generally these books are so new they have not yet been reviewed in the professional journals. We strive through discussion to articulate our first critical responses to the books in question, using CCBC Book Discussion Guidelines (see Appendix III).

In addition to these monthly discussions, we host annual award discussions, using the criteria for eligiblity and excellence established by national book award committees. The award discussions provide an opportunity to look critically at some of the year's outstanding children's books. In late 1998 we held discussions of books eligible for the Batchelder Award, the Caldecott Medal, the Coretta Scott King Award, and the Newbery Award. We discussed books eligible for the Américas Award for Latino literature early in 1999, but this discussion was held too late for the outcome to be included in *CCBC Choices 1998*.

In *CCBC Choices*, we bring a wide range of books to our colleagues' attention. We hope everyone who uses this publication is aware that every book recommended here is not necessarily for every child or every classroom or every family. We are confident, however, that everyone using *CCBC Choices* will find a significant number of books that will delight, inform or stimulate the innate curiosity of many of the children and young teenagers for whom our colleagues have some level of professional, academic or career responsibility.

Results of the CCBC Award Discussions

CCBC Batchelder Award Discussion
(Translated book published in the United States)
Winner: *Thanks to My Mother* by Schoschana Rabinovici. Translated from the German by James Skofield. U.S. edition: Dial, 1998.

Honor Book: *Secret Letters from 0 to 10* by Susie Morgenstern. Translated from the French by Gill Rosner. U.S. edition: Viking, 1998.

CCBC Caldecott Award Discussion
(Distinguished illustration by a U.S. citizen or resident)
Winner: *Snow* illustrated and written by Uri Shulevitz. Farrar Straus Giroux, 1998.

Honor Books: *John Willy and Freddy McGee* illustrated and written by Holly Meade. Marshall Cavendish, 1998.
Lucy Dove illustrated by Leonid Gore. Written by Janice del Negro. DK Ink, 1998.
My Name Is Georgia: A Portrait illustrated and written by Jeanette Winter. Silver Whistle/Harcourt Brace, 1998.

CCBC Coretta Scott King Award Discussion: Author
(Distinguished writing by an African American author)
Winner: *The Skin I'm In* written by Sharon G. Flake. Jump at the Sun/Hyperion, 1998.

Honor Books: *Amistad: A Long Road to Freedom* written by Walter Dean Myers. Dutton, 1998.
Duke Ellington: The Piano Prince and His Orchestra written by Andrea Davis Pinkney. Illustrated by Brian Pinkney. Hyperion, 1998.
From Slave Ship to Freedom Road written by Julius Lester. Illustrated by Rod Brown. Dial, 1998.

CCBC Coretta Scott King Award Discussion: Illustrator
(Distinguished illustration by an African American artist)
Winner: *Duke Ellington: The Piano Prince and His Orchestra* illustrated by Brian Pinkney. Written by Andrea Davis Pinkney. Hyperion, 1998.

Honor Books: *Black Cowboy, Wild Horses: A True Story* illustrated by Jerry Pinkney. Written by Julius Lester. Dial, 1998.
From Slave Ship to Freedom Road illustrated by Rod Brown. Written by Julius Lester. Dial. 1998.

CCBC Newbery Award Discussion
(Distinguished writing for children by a U.S. citizen or resident)
Winner: *Holes* written by Louis Sachar. Frances Foster Books/Farrar Straus Giroux, 1998.

Honor Book: *Bat 6* written by Virginia Euwer Wolff. Scholastic, 1998.

The Charlotte Zolotow Award

The Charlotte Zolotow Award is given annually to the author of the best picture book text published in the United States in the preceding year. Established in 1997, the award is named to honor the work of Charlotte Zolotow, a distinguished children's book editor for 38 years with Harper Junior Books, and author of more than 65 picture books, including such classic works as *Mr. Rabbit and the Lovely Present* (Harper, 1962) and *William's Doll* (Harper, 1972). Ms. Zolotow attended the University of Wisconsin in Madison on a writing scholarship from 1933 to 1936, where she studied with Professor Helen C. White.

The award is administered by the Cooperative Children's Book Center, a children's literature library of the School of Education at the University of Wisconsin–Madison. Each year a committee of children's literature experts selects the winner from the books published in the preceding year. The winning author receives a cash prize and a bronze medal designed by UW–Madison Art professor Philip Hamilton, based on an original drawing by Harriett Barton of HarperCollins. The award is formally presented in October, prior to the annual Charlotte Zolotow Lecture on the UW–Madison campus.

Any picture book for young children (birth through age seven) that is first published in the United States and written by a U.S. citizen or resident is eligible for consideration for the Charlotte Zolotow Award. The book may fall into any genre of writing (fiction, nonfiction, poetry, or folklore) as long as it is presented in a picture book format and aimed at an audience of young children. The committee works with a shortlist of titles, selected by the CCBC professional staff. Committee members may suggest additional titles they think should be included on the shortlist; however, all titles are subject to the approval of the CCBC professional staff. Books written by Charlotte Zolotow are not eligible for the award.

In addition to choosing the award-winning title, the committee may select up to three Honor Books, and up to ten titles to be included on a Highly Commended list that will call attention to outstanding writing in picture books. Authors of these books will receive a certificate citing the honor.

The selection committee is comprised of members of the Friends of the CCBC, Inc. Members are appointed to a two-year term by the CCBC professional staff, based on an individual's knowledge of children's books; a demonstrated ability to evaluate children's books and discuss then critically; and/or direct experience working professionally with children from birth through age seven.

Members of the second annual Charlotte Zolotow Award Committee were: Margaret Jensen, chair (1st and 2nd grade teacher, Huegel Elementary School, Madison, Wisconsin); Patricia Bakula (children's librarian, retired, Glendale, Wisconsin); Geri Ceci Cupery (librarian, Madison Public Library, Madison, Wisconsin); Helen Julius (preschool teacher, Luther Memorial Church Child Development Center, Madison, Wisconsin); Megan Schliesman (librarian, Cooperative Children's Book Center, UW–Madison); Joan Thron (assistant professor, Department of Curriculum & Instruction, UW–Green Bay); Laureen Yoshino (librarian, Midvale Elementary School, Madison, Wisconsin); and Kathleen T. Horning, ex officio (librarian, Cooperative Children's Book Center, UW–Madison).

The 1999 Charlotte Zolotow Award

Winner: Uri Shulevitz for *Snow*. Farrar Straus Giroux, 1998.

Honor Books:

Holly Meade for *John Willy and Freddy McGee*.
Marshall Cavendish, 1998.

William Steig for *Pete's a Pizza*.
Michael di Capua Books/HarperCollins, 1998.

Highly Commended:

Denise Fleming for *Mama Cat Has Three Kittens*. Henry Holt, 1998.

Kevin Henkes for *Circle Dogs*. Illustrated by Dan Yaccarino.
Greenwillow, 1998.

Bill T. Jones and Susan Kuklin for *Dance*. Photographs by Susan Kuklin.
Hyperion, 1998.

Lynn Reiser for *Little Clam*. Greenwillow, 1998.

Stephanie Stuve-Bodeen for *Elizabeti's Doll*.
Illustrated by Christy Hale. Lee & Low, 1998.

Observations about Publishing in 1998

How Many Books Were Available for Sale During 1998?

The most recent edition of *Children's Books in Print* (R.R. Bowker, 1999) states that there are 138,850 books from 8,050 U.S. publishers currently available for purchase in the United States. This number represents an increase of 12,250 books and 550 publishers from one year ago. The 1990–91 edition of *Children's Books in Print* (R.R. Bowker, 1990) cited a total of 66,268 books in print, which means there are 72,582 more books available now than nine years ago.

Clearly there is an abundance of books written, edited and published especially for children and young teenagers available for the youth of this nation, and an abundance of choices for individuals seeking out books for the young, whether for personal or professional reasons.

How Many Books Were Published During 1998?

As we look back at the calendar year of 1998, we estimate that at least 4,500 to 5,000 new trade books were published in the United States for children and young adults, a number similar to the estimate we've made during each of the past five years.

The number of new books always varies from source to source, according to who is counting and which new books are included in the totals. CCBC estimates are typically conservative, in that we do not include reprints, paperback editions of titles published earlier, large print books, book club editions, novelty books and other categories often reflected in the numbers provided within the book industry, most or all of which are included in the 138,850 books currently available for purchase. Additionally, the CCBC number represents the work of 75 to 100 trade book and alternative press publishers, nowhere near the 8,050 publishers represented in the *Children's Books in Print* statistic. As a result, our estimate for the number of new books has remained steady in recent years.

Collections of children's and young adult literature at the CCBC generally do not include books published for adults, even though some books published for adults do appeal to (and occasionally are claimed by) teenagers.

How Many Books Are in *CCBC Choices 1998*?

There are 298 books listed in *CCBC Choices 1998*. Of these, 16 represent the first published works of 16 authors and 10 illustrators; 31 were originally published outside the United States or simultaneously in the United States and their country of origin, three of which are translations; 11 were published by four small, independently owned and operated publishers. To our knowledge, 179 of the books we recommend in *CCBC Choices 1998* did not appear on any of the other nationally distributed lists of the year's best books as of February 3, 1999.

Most of the books in *CCBC Choices 1998* are published for an audience ranging in age from infancy to fourteen years, the upper age in the definition of "children" used by the book awards committees of the Association for Library

Service to Children of the American Library Association (ALA). A few of the books in this edition of CCBC Choices are recommended for older ages as well. As we comment on some of the books published in 1998, please note that not every book we discuss has been selected as a 1998 CCBC Choice. Books that are not recommended in this edition of CCBC Choices are designated by the inclusion of publisher information after their titles.

Searching for Multicultural Literature

Currently there is no agreement in the children's literature community on a single definition for the word "multicultural," nor is a single definition necessary. At the CCBC we designate books by and about people of color as multicultural literature.

Multicultural literature continued to be highly visible in 1998 in terms of overall numbers. For the eighth consecutive year, many children's book publishers published new books by and about people of color and one publisher has started an imprint devoted to this type of publishing. However, the special flyers, catalogs and mailings so common earlier in the decade have almost vanished, and it is important to realize that these numbers still represent only a very small percentage of the total number of new books published for children and young adults each year. Still, we are hopeful that publishers recognize that the continued creation of high-quality multicultural literature is important for all children, and that the Coretta Scott King, Américas and Pura Belpré awards (and their honor books and commended lists) are formal acknowledgements of excellence in multicultural publishing that certainly matter to teachers, librarians and parents.

Most of the literature journals, book review magazines and other professional publications concerning education, librarianship, books for children and young adults, and/or reading featured reviews, interviews, bibliographies, and articles about multicultural literature, continuing a trend of the 1990s. We continue to worry, however, that the collective interest of American teachers, librarians, parents, publishers and booksellers who are outsiders to specific cultural and ethnic groups is moving away from multicultural literature. It is critical that multicultural literature be viewed as a substantial component of children's book publishing, rather than a passing fad or some kind of so-called "politically correct" type of book publishing, buying and reading. Only then will its past be honored and its future be guaranteed as an integral part of all children's and young adult literature.

If individuals and groups within the children's and young adult literature community begin to operate under the premise that they have all the multicultural books they need, the publishing of excellent new books will dwindle, new writers and artists will not be nurtured, and the perspectives on multicultural experience in our country will be lost in time. The continued—and increased—publication of a wide range of voices from a wide range of cultural perspectives will help ensure that all children and young teenagers will find validation in the books available to them to read, as well as a stronger understanding of what it means to be a citizen of their community, their nation and the world.

Books by and about Africans and African Americans

The number of books created by Black authors and illustrators in 1998 was only slightly higher than the number published during 1997. (The designation "Black" indicates that CCBC statistics include book creators from the Caribbean, England, and other countries whose works are published by U.S. publishers. Some books with themes and topics related to Caribbean countries are also designated as Latino.)

CCBC statistics also include books by Black book creators regardless of whether or not the theme or topic of a book contains cultural substance. Of the roughly 4,500 to 5,000 books published in the United States for young people in 1998, the CCBC documented 96 that were created by Black authors and/or illustrators. (The CCBC documented 88 in this category in 1997, 92 in 1996, 100 books in 1995, 82 in 1994, 74 in 1993, 94 in 1992, and 70 in 1991.) The 96 titles represent the published work of 85 individual authors and illustrators.

Approximately 188 books specifically about African and/or African American history, culture and/or peoples were documented at the CCBC during 1998, compared to 216 in 1997, 172 in 1996, 94 in 1995 and 166 in 1994.

Of the books by Black book creators published in this nation during 1998, 10 books were published by three small, independently owned publishing companies: Children's Book Press, Just Us Books, and Lee & Low.

Six new titles were published by Hyperion's exciting new imprint, Jump at the Sun, which is under the direction of editor Andrea Davis Pinkney and "celebrates the African-American experience." Four of the authors published on Jump at the Sun's inaugural list are new to the field of children's books. We applaud Hyperion's efforts to find and publish new voices in African American children's literature. One of these, Sharon Flake, won the CCBC's Coretta Scott King Author Award Discussion for her outstanding first novel, *The Skin I'm In*. Flake's skill at re-creating the ambiance of the junior high school social world through outstanding characterization and realistic dialogue makes her a promising newcomer in young adult literature. We hope to see many more books from her in the years to come.

We did not note many other new African American authors or illustrators entering the field in 1998, but we were happy to see two established writers expanding into genres beyond those for which they are best known. Angela Johnson, who has made a name for herself writing picture books and novels, published *The Other Side: Shorter Poems*, an outstanding collection of poems based on her growing-up years in a small-town African American community in Shorter, Alabama. Meanwhile, Nikki Grimes, best known as a poet, wrote a novel featuring a sensitive teenage girl who is frequently inspired to write poetry by the things she sees and experiences in her Harlem neighborhood. We were also glad to see author Virginia Hamilton, who has produced several wonderful collections of folklore in recent years, return to writing novel-writing with *Second Cousins*, a sequel to *Cousins* (Philomel, 1990).

Another longtime favorite, Pat Cummings, successfully tried her hand at a board book with the delightful *My Aunt Came Back*, a rollicking rhyme that's sure to please toddlers. Author/artist Ken Wilson-Max, who is originally from Zimbabwe and now lives in London, has pleased plenty of toddlers with his dynamic books about trucks, trains and planes. He will now catch the attention of their older siblings with an engaging book that introduces Zulu words in a story about a budding friendship. Closer to home, Gavin Curtis and E.B. Lewis's tender story of a father-son relationship, *The Bat Boy and His Violin*, is set during the waning days of Negro League baseball.

In general, African American fiction for any age level, whether in novel or picture book format, was hard to find in 1998, but we did choose many outstanding nonfiction books dealing with African American history. Among these, the McKissacks' absorbing biography of Lorraine Hansberry, *Young, Black and Determined*, introduces young readers to the life of this gifted playwright while the Pinkneys' jazzy picture book *Duke Ellington: The Piano Prince and His Orchestra* is likely to have young children dancing in their semicircles. Joyce Hansen uncovers history that's been obscured for centuries in *Breaking Ground, Breaking Silence: The Story of New York's African Burial Ground.* Perhaps the most daring and thought-provoking book of the year is *From Slave Ship to Freedom Road,* in which Julius Lester's text speaks directly to readers, encouraging them to look closely at Rod Brown's paintings of slavery times, and to confront their own racism. And in response to the continuing demand for more information about the *Amistad,* two outstanding histories for children were published in 1998: *Amistad: A Long Road to Freedom* by Walter Dean Myers and *Freedom's Sons: The True Story of the* Amistad *Mutiny* by Suzanne Jurmain. We have chosen both volumes for the 1998 edition of *CCBC Choices.*

Books by and about Latinos

At the CCBC, we try to keep track of all that is published for young people and to notice trends and changes, often a greater challenge for us than one might expect. Typically we have not been able to provide reliable documentation about the number of books by other racial or ethnic groups that is comparable to that which we can provide on Black book creators.

However, an increased number of books by Latinos and about Latino themes and topics since 1993 encouraged us, beginning in 1994, to make a concerted effort to document the number of such titles. In 1998, we counted 73 new titles by Latinos and/or about Latino themes in topics. In 1997 there were 88 titles, in 1996 there were 103, in 1995 there were 70, and in 1994 we counted 90 Latino titles.

It is discouraging to see this number decease significantly for the second year in a row, especially since fewer than half of the titles we counted in 1998 were produced by Latino authors and artists. Additionally, we would expect that the two awards established in the 1990s to draw attention to outstanding Latino books for children and young adults would be encouraging publishers to seek out works to add to this important body of literature. The Américas Award, with its mission to provide visibility for excellent books about Latin America and Latinos in the United States, was established in 1993 and is administered through the University of Wisconsin–Milwaukee's Center for Latin America. The Pura Belpré Award was established by REFORMA, a unit of the American Library Association, to formally acknowledge outstanding writing for youth by a Latino writer. This biannual award was first given out in 1996.

Of the small number of Latino books published in 1998, we were especially happy to see *La Mariposa,* a picture book written by Francisco Jiménez and illustrated Simón Silva. Jiménez came to the attention of the children's book community last year when his stunning collection of autobiographical short stories, *The Circuit* (University of New Mexico Press, 1997), won both the Américas Award and the Boston Globe-Horn Book Award, and was named an Honor Book in the Jane Addams Children's Book Award process. It is our hope that this marks the beginning of a long career in children's books for Francisco Jiménez.

Another newcomer, Amelia Lau Carling, fictionalizes her childhood experiences in the self-illustrated picture book *Mama and Papa Have a Store.* Written from the perspective of a child of Chinese immigrants living in Guatemala City, her story reminds readers that all of the Americas are comprised of nations of immigrants. We were also happy to note second and third books by Hector

Viveros Lee *(Get Set! Swim!)* and Leyla Torres (*Liliana's Grandmothers*), respectively. Both are promising new voices in Latino literature for the young.

Books by and about American Indians

The overall growth in the number and quality of new books about contemporary Native people since 1992 represents a welcome change. Unfortunately, the rate of that growth has been declining over the past several years. In 1998 we documented 55 books on American Indian themes and topics, down from the 64 we counted in 1997. In 1996 we counted 50 books, and in 1995 we found 83 that fell into this category.

The overall quality of the books that are published continues to improve, however. Source notes and specificity about a book's content is always an aid in the evaluation of books of information; they are especially valuable in books by American Indians and about American Indian themes and topics. An increasing number of books now designate the specific Indian nation from which a tale or subject comes or about which a story is told. More books are also recognizing the importance of nomenclature and are using the names by which specific American Indian peoples refer to themselves. We are optimistic that such specificity will continue to be seen in future books of fiction, information and folklore concerning American Indian themes and topics, and we are hopeful that the number of such books will increase again in future years.

Our records cite 24 specific Indian nations represented among the 55 books about American Indian themes and topics documented at the CCBC during 1998. Thirty-seven specific Indian nations were noted in the 64 books published in 1997, 22 were represented in the 50 books documented in 1996, and 32 were noted in the 83 books documented in 1995.

Of the books we documented in 1998, very few are written or illustrated by Native authors and artists. Of these, Joseph Bruchac continues to contribute the bulk of authentic Native literature. This year we were especially appreciative of *Heart of a Chief*, Bruchac's middle-grade novel that takes on timely issues such as Indian mascots and casino gambling, written from the point of view of a sixth-grade Pennacook boy growing up on a reservation. On a more whimsical note, Dogrib writer Richard Van Camp teams with Plains Cree artist George Littlechild to create a surprisingly funny and profoundly moving picture book about varied points of view in *What's the Most Beautiful Thing You Know about Horses?*

Books by and about Asians and Asian Americans

This year we counted 52 books published for children about Asian and Asian American themes and topics. In 1997 there were 66 books, in 1996 there were 49, in 1995 there were 91, and there were 65 in 1994. As in previous years, the majority of these books deal either with war or folklore and, were it not for the few photodocumentary books, and the few novels published each year by writers such as Laurence Yep, Lensey Namioka and Marie G. Lee, contemporary Asian and Asian American children and teenagers would be virtually invisible in the world of children's books. As it is, we are once again hard-pressed to find more than a handful of picture books featuring contemporary Asian children.

Among the books we especially recommend are two published by the small, independent press Lee & Low: *Cool Melons—Turn to Frogs!* by Matthew Gollub and Kazuko G. Stone, a marvelously creative introduction to the life and haiku poetry of Issa; and *Journey Home* by Lawrence McKay, Jr., a picture book about a child returning to her mother's birthplace in Vietnam to seach for family. Sherry

Garland's *My Father's Boat*, illustrated by Ted Rand, also involves a Vietnamese American child.

Books of International Interest

Forty-one books first published in the United States in English after having been translated from other languages were documented at the CCBC during 1998. Of these translated books only nine were of substantial length. Three translated books were selected for this edition of *CCBC Choices*. We especially enjoyed the humor (a rare commodity in translated books!) of Susie Morgenstern's novel *Secret Letters from 0 to 10*. Set in Paris, this delightful story is about a friendship between a boy and a girl who couldn't be more different from one another. Also from France, *And If the Moon Could Talk* is a gentle, understated bedtime book by Kate Banks and Georg Hallensleben, the same pair who created 1997's much-lauded *Baboon* (U.S. edition: Frances Foster/Farrar).

Participants in the CCBC's annual Batchelder Award Discussion selected *Thanks to My Mother* by Schoschana Rabinovici, translated from the German by James Skofield, as the outstanding translated book of the year. This memoir about a Jewish child's survival in a Nazi death camp provides a powerful tribute to the strength and courage of the mother who kept her alive.

This edition of *CCBC Choices* contains 28 books published elsewhere in English before being published in the United States or before becoming available here through distributors specifically promoting them in this nation. One of the books we especially appreciated in this category is Kerena Marchant's *Id-ul-Fitr*, which familiarizes readers with this joyful Muslim celebration marking the end of the holy month of Ramadan. Marchant's book was originally published in Britain. Another British book, the delightful fantasy novel *Harry Potter and the Sorcerer's Stone* by J.K. Rowling, is a runaway hit in that country and is already proving to be immensely popular here as well.

The Watertower, is an eerie, ominous picture book for older readers featuring the combined talents of Australian writer Gary Crew and illustrator Steven Woolman. Canadian writers show their mastery of the short story form in *What If...?*, a thought-provoking collection of short stories edited by Monica Hughes that is part fantasy, part science fiction, and all conjecture about the past, present and future of the human race. A version of a Persian folktale *The Stone: A Persian Legend of the Magi*, written by Dianne Hofmeyr with illustrations by Jude Daly, was first published in South Africa.

Outstanding Nonfiction

It was an exemplary year for books of information. From Barbara Lehn's singular *What Is a Scientist?*, which describes scientific discovery in terms young children can easily grasp, to Herman J. Viola's *Warrior Artists*, a book for middle and high schoolers that examines the 19th-century ledger art of two Plains Indians artists and discusses the U.S. government's forced removal of Plains Indians nations from their homelands, to the unusually high number of excellent biographies for children and young adults alike, there were outstanding nonfiction books for young people of almost every age. These fine books not only inform young readers but engage their hearts and minds.

Among the books we especially appreciated were two outstanding exposés on child labor, Susan Kuklin's *Iqbal Masih and the Crusaders against Child Slavery* and *Listen to Us: The World's Working Children* by Jane Springer. These volumes document the tragic, ongoing exploitation of children around the world as well as some of the efforts to end such exploitation.

Voices from the past recount harrowing experiences during the Holocaust in Milton Nieuwsma's *Kinderlager* and Michael Leapman's *Witness to War*, while young people today express hope for a brighter future in post-Apartheid South Africa in Tim McKee's uplifting collection of interviews, *No More Strangers Now*.

Artistic Profiles

It was the year of the artist with regard to biographies published for children and young adults, with many dynamic and inspiring portraits and self-portraits of individuals involved in the visual, literary, and performing arts. Elizabeth Partridge's unparalleled biography of photographer Dorothea Lange, *Restless Spirit*; Jan Greenberg and Sandra Jordan's fascinating profile of a distinctive contemporary painter in *Chuck Close Up Close*; Russell Freedman's flowing, energetic portrait *Martha Graham: A Dancer's Life*; Jeanette Winter's amazing picture book that captures the spirit and the essence of Georgia O'Keeffe's life and work, *My Name Is Georgia*; and Patricia and Fredrick McKissack's moving look at the life of playwright Lorraine Hansberry in *Young, Black and Determined* are among the finest examples of literature for the young, biographical or otherwise.

Mary E. Lyons has let the artist speak for herself in *Talking with Tebé: Clementine Hunter, Memory Artist*, in which Lyons compiled and edited oral and written interviews with the self-taught African American artist who never minced words, or images, when it came to portraying the hardships of life for poor Blacks in the southern United States. Lois Lowry also speaks for herself in *Looking Back*, a compilation of photographs, reminiscences and commentary that reveals how her storymaking evolves from events and experiences formed and reformed in her mind.

The Immigrant Experience

The experiences of those who leave their homelands are among the most dramatic and compelling to be found in literature for the young. When done well, such books challenge readers to understand more about the world, and to empathize with those whose experiences may be very different—or similar—to their own.

This year we especially appreciated Carol Bierman's *Journey to Ellis Island*, in which she tells the harrowing story of her own father and his family, who escaped from Russia during the Revolution and eventually made their way to America. Frances and Ginger Park's haunting tale based on their mother's escape from North Korea, *My Freedom Trip,* is also noteworthy.

An immigrant's journey is not over once he or she has reached the destination; the experiences of newcomers to a nation are an important part of the chronicle. Aliki details how a small girl who cannot speak English uses art to communicate her feelings in *Painted Word: Marianthe's Story*. Marianthe's gradual grasp of the English language eventually enables her to tell her classmates the story of her past in the companion story bound in the same book, *Spoken Memories*.

These and other nonfiction books included in this edition of *CCBC Choices* represent a high standard for nonfiction writing and publishing for children and young adults. We are appreciative of the efforts of the writers and artists, as well as publishers, who understand that high-quality books of information for young readers should not only be well-researched and well-documented but lively and compelling as well.

Picture Books for Children of All Ages

It was a great year for picture books! In fact, *CCBC Choices 1998* includes nearly 70 books in this category. In an attempt to make these selections a bit more accessible for users, we have for the first time divided picture books into two sections: those for younger children, which includes titles recommended for children up through age seven; and those for older children, age seven and older. We were glad to see many excellent original board books being published once again for babies and toddlers, thanks largely to Harper Growing Tree, a new series from HarperCollins. Exciting books in this new series include *Zoom City* by Thacher Hurd, *My Aunt Came Back* by Pat Cummings and *Do You Know New?* by Jean Marzollo. This year also marked the reissue of all eight of Rosemary Wells's original board books about Max and Ruby in newly illustrated, large-sized editions.

Many of the picture books we chose show children engaged in imaginary play. A resourceful child substitutes a good-sized, solid rock for a doll in the marvelously original *Elizabeti's Doll*, a first book by Stephanie Stuve-Bodeen. And a young boy actually *becomes* the object of his passion in *Fire Truck* by Peter Sís. In both *Cows Can't Fly* by David Milgrim and *Snow* by Uri Shulevitz, child characters find wonder in play, undaunted by adults who don't see what they see. But grown ups are not immune to play: even the parents get involved in the fun in books such as *Cowboy Baby* by Sue Heap, *Little Clam* by Lynn Reiser and *Pete's a Pizza* by William Steig. In Melrose Cooper's *Gettin' through Thursday*, it's Mama who sets the scene with her imagination so the family can have a party on the day before payday.

Humor was also easy to find in the year's outstanding picture books. The perilous journey of two guinea pigs through the long, dark tunnels of a pool table provides visual and verbal humor in *John Willy and Freddy McGee* by Holly Meade. In another household, a young boy has rodent problems of a different kind in Peggy Rathmann's *10 Minutes till Bedtime*, in which a group of enthusiastic hamster tourists shows up at an inopportune time. David Martin and Susan Meddaugh present an amusing context for the well-known baby's toe-wiggling rhyme in *Five Little Piggies*. For more (but not too much more) sophisticated tastes, Jon Scieszka and Lane Smith send up Aesop in *Squids Will Be Squids*, providing some very contemporary fables for children of our times. Squid, Mosquito and Piece of Toast notwithstanding, perhaps the most unusual set of characters to appear in a children's book in many years can be found in Laurie Keller's *The Scrambled States of America* starring—you guessed it!—the entire United States. Here the 50 states see what it would be like if they all changed places for a while, with hilarious results!

Fiction for Children and Teens

Fantasy, adventure, history, humor and contemporary realistic stories all were among the excellent fiction published for children and teens in 1998.

Included among our favorite flights of fancy are Dick King-Smith's *The Water Horse*, which gives the origins of a beloved contemporary legend an original and delightful twist. *Harry Potter and the Sorcerer's Stone* by J.K. Rowling creates a richly realized world of witchcraft and wizardry for children, while *The Dark Lord of Derkholm* by Diana Wynne Jones casts its own spell for young adults.

One of the most riveting adventure stories of the year is surely Iain Lawrence's *The Wreckers*, about a boy who is the sole survivor of a shipwreck off the coast of Cornwall. He washes ashore in a village where citizens earn their livelihood off of shipwrecks, but they cannot claim their bounty if anyone survives.

Outstanding historical fiction published in 1998 includes Virginia Euwer Wolff's *Bat 6*. This novel set in 1949 is skillfully told in more than 20 voices as the girls on two opposing softball teams tell of events that led to a Japanese American player on one team being attacked during a game by a player on the other team whose father died in the bombing of Pearl Harbor. Set during the Civil War, Gary Paulsen's *A Soldier's Story* gives teens an uncompromising look at the horror of war and its devastating after-effects on the life of a young soldier. A welcome, wholly engaging book of historical fiction for younger readers is Rosemary Wells's wonderful *Mary on Horseback*, three stories about Mary Breckenridge and the Frontier Nursing Service she started in Appalachia in the 1920s.

It is hard to find a book in 1998—funny or otherwise—that matches Louis Sachar's *Holes* for deft, intricate plotting. That this witty, outrageous story that is somewhere outside the bounds of reality also features highly memorable characters and emotional resonance makes it all the more amazing. Other truly funny books with warm hearts include Richard Peck's *Long Way to Chicago* and Susie Morgenstern's *Secret Letters from 0 to 10*. For young readers, *Marty Frye, Private Eye* is a wholly engaging addition to the newly independent reader scene and we hope to see more of this delightful poet detective who can't resist a good rhyme in the service of crime (detection that is).

Harry Mazer's *The Wild Kid* is an unusual portrait of a boy with Down syndrome—unusual because it is respectful and feels authentic. Other notable examples of realistic fiction for children published in 1998 include Theresa Nelson's *The Empress of Elsewhere*, with its intriguing characterizations, and the tension-driven *While No One Was Watching* by Jane Leslie Conly. Virginia Hamilton's powerful storytelling voice resonates in the lively and moving *Second Cousins*, in which Cammy Coleman, whom readers first met in the earlier *Cousins* (Philomel, 1991), discovers unsettling truths about her family, while Karen Hesse's quiet, graceful *Just Juice* tells of a young girl's struggle to learn to read.

Among the contemporary realistic fiction for teens is *Smack* by Melvin Burgess, a chilling portrait of heroin addiction. Sharon G. Flake addresses issues of self-esteem and skin color in her stunning debut novel, *The Skin I'm In*, while Jacqueline Woodson exposes societal racism and tender hearts in *If You Come Softly*.

Whether they are writing stories of hard-hitting, haunting realism, delightfully zany escapades, thrilling adventures or intriguing explorations of the past, the writers of these and other fine novels for young people in 1998 all have something in common: their books reflect the knowledge that children and young adults deserve the best that literature can offer.

Book Publishing and Book Buying: So Many Choices

The increase in the number of books published during the 1990s represents decisions made by U.S. publishers to invest in children's books. Such investments are made with the expectation that in all parts of the nation people are eager and ready to buy books for the young. Indeed, much evidence continues to indicate that the bookstore sales of children's books supports much of the children's and young adult book publishing industry, as well as book publishing for adults within several publishing houses, in the United States at this time.

The increase also represents an overwhelming number of choices. These choices begin with publishers, who decide which manuscripts to publish, which illustrators to employ, which books to advertise heavily, which authors to send on tour, and so on. Book industry representatives make decisions about paperback editions and reprints with specific consumers in mind. All of these decisions have an impact on the book-buying public: they determine what books we will ever see in print and, once books are published, which ones most book buyers are likely to hear about. At the same time, the book industry must expect that potential consumers will buy more than the best-sellers or the most heavily promoted, highly visible books or the most familiar authors or series; otherwise they would not invest in the hundreds and hundreds of other titles that they produce.

Commercial sales in bookstores are driven by parents and other adults, and by young people themselves in the case of some popular culture and series books that older children are often eager to obtain for their own recreational reading. The other significant group of children's book consumers is the so-called institutional market—the public librarians, school library media specialists, classroom teachers, child care providers and academic librarians responsible for collections of literature for the young. Individuals within these groups select and purchase books for use by more than one child, family or student. Institutional sales most often utilize public funding and are responsible for building collections that represent the diverse needs and interests of their users.

No matter who is buying what books for whom, consumers of books for the children and young adults have the luxury—and difficulty—of making choices because of the large number of titles available. Whether their decisions are spontaneous and unplanned or based upon complex judgments, total amount of money available for book buying, comparisons, special interests and unique needs, the fact that choices do exist cannot be overvalued among those who are committed to seeking out high-quality books for the young.

The Cooperative Children's Book Center offers an environment for discovery and learning, for making up one's own mind about the new books published each year and for making comparisons to books from other years and decades. We create *CCBC Choices* to identify the outstanding titles of the current publishing year in the hope that it will provide librarians, teachers, parents and others with assistance in navigating the wide and exciting array of choices available to them.

CCBC Choices is a guide, not a rule book. While we certainly have made an effort to find as many of the outstanding books of the year as possible, inevitably, in the course of the coming months and years, other books will come to our attention that we will have wished we'd included. Likewise, as mentioned earlier, not every book is for every child. The purpose of *CCBC Choices* is to offer a wide variety of books for a wide variety of individuals. We have attempted to compile a guide that provides something of high quality for everyone, not a core selection for all.

The
Choices

The Natural World

Arnosky, Jim. *All about Turkeys.* Scholastic Press, 1998. 28 pages. (0–590–48147–9) $15.95
Have you ever wondered what makes turkeys gobble or why they have wattles? You'll find the answers here. As he does in his other books in the "All About" series, Arnosky gives a basic introduction to the species, providing details concerning the wild turkey's physical and behavioral attributes. The text is concise and the detailed watercolor paintings include frequent references to scale, so that young readers can see exactly how big a turkey is in reality. (Ages 4–8)

Arnosky, Jim. *Watching Desert Wildlife.* National Geographic Society, 1998. 32 pages. (0–7922–7304–4) $15.95
Jim Arnosky turns his keen eye and talented artistry to painting and writing about desert wildlife of the southwestern United States. Arnosky tells readers in the short introduction that the desert, which is so different from the landscape of his northeastern United States home, has held a fascination for him for years. Only recently did he make his first trip, however, and here he captures with both words and watercolors some of the birds, animals and reptiles that survive on this arid land. Arnosky writes with his usual friendly style, sharing memories from his journey and facts about desert wildlife. The detailed paintings are colorful, large and dramatic, giving readers an up-close view of these creatures of the natural world. (Ages 7–10)

Bonners, Susan. *Why Does the Cat Do That?* Henry Holt, 1998. 32 pages. (0–8050–4377–2) $15.95
The basics of cat behavior are presented in a story about a man who takes care of his friends' cat while the family is away for the weekend. Bob's questions about Molly the cat—why she can sleep through the noise of a jackhammer on the street outside but awakens the minute Bob opens a packet of cookies—are answered in framed explanations concerning feline behavior in the wild, and how that translates into the way a domestic cat behaves. (Ages 4–8)

Branley, Franklyn M. *Day Light, Night Light.* Illustrated by Stacey Schuett. Newly illustrated edition. HarperCollins, 1998. 32 pages. (0–06–027294–5) $14.95
Branley makes a clear distinction between light from the sun and reflected light, and explains the meaning of light sources in an easy introduction to a topic of interest to many preschool and early elementary-school-aged children. Originally published in 1975, this edition has new illustrations by Stacey Schuett, who has created realistic full-color acrylic paintings that show children in everyday situations to demonstrate Branley's points: blowing out birthday candles, shining flashlights, and toasting marshmallows. (Ages 3–7)

Hooper, Meredith. *The Drop in My Drink.* Illustrated by Chris Coady. U.S. edition: Viking, 1998. 32 pages. (0–670–87618–6) $16.99
Beginning with a boy standing at a kitchen sink, filling up his water glass, the lyrical first-person text describes all the places a single drop of drinking water has been: inside ancient plants and dinosaurs, in underground caves and on

icebergs, in rainstorms and river currents. As the drop is traced through time, young readers will gain an understanding of the water cycle on our planet and will no doubt marvel at all the places an ordinary drop of water has been. Dramatic pastel paintings extend the narrative by zeroing in on specific details to illustrate the droplet's journey. (Ages 6–10)

Lasky, Kathryn. *Shadows in the Dawn.* Photographs by Christopher G. Knight. Gulliver Green/Harcourt Brace, 1998. 63 pages. (0–15–200258–8) $18.00; Pbk. (0–15–200281–2) $9.00

This compelling look at the lives of a troop of ringtailed lemurs on Madagascar follows a small group of researchers led by primatologist Allison Jolly as they track the lemurs' movements and interactions over a period of several days, watching both small and large dramas unfold. Lasky also writes about what has been conjectured about how this island became the only place in the world where lemurs, as well as certain plants, are found. A short profile of Jolly and how she became a primatologist is also included in this information-packed volume that ends with a warning about the pending ecological crisis on this island, where the lemurs' habitat is vanishing, and how Jolly's work will hopefully help the Malagasy government on Madagascar promote a sustainable environment for humans and lemurs alike. Christopher G. Knight's rich color photographs profile the lemurs, as well as Jolly and the researchers, in action. (Ages 8–11)

Powzyk, Joyce A. *In Search of Lemurs: My Days and Nights in a Madagascar Rain Forest.* National Geographic Society, 1998. 44 pages. (0–7922–7072-X) $17.95

No one knows exactly how lemurs got to Madagascar over 40 million years ago but today the world's fourth largest island is home to the greatest number of lemur species. Biologist Joyce Powzyk spent several months in the rain forest, observing different species of lemurs in the wild, and painting what she saw. To create this book for young readers, she combined descriptions of her day-to-day life in the wild with her exquisite watercolor paintings. Throughout, she provides us with a science context, information about each of the species she sees, a pronunciation guide, and a sense of what the life of a working scientist is like. (Ages 8–12)

Robbins, Ken. *Autumn Leaves.* Scholastic Press, 1998. 39 pages. (0–590–29879–8) $15.95

After a brief introduction in which the author guides young children through some of the things to look for when identifying species of leaves (shape, size, edges), he devotes a double-page spread to each of the following trees: smoke tree, birch, gingko, linden, sassafras, hickory, red oak, fern leaf beech, cherry, dogwood, yellow poplar, and maple. While the right-hand side of the page shows the entire tree in full autumn color, the left-hand side shows a life-size color photograph of its corresponding leaves, also as they appear in autumn. The stark white background of each page brilliantly sets off the fall foliage, so that the trees and leaves pictured here are as artistically beautiful as they are in real life. Each page also includes a few lines of text that give some additional information about the particular species of tree or leaf. We learn, for example, that the gingko tree was around in the time of dinosaurs and that the hickory tree has compound leaves, with five or more leaflets making up each leaf. All in all, a treat for young readers, be they budding artists, scientists, or both. (Ages 4–8)

Wright-Frierson, Virginia. *An Island Scrapbook: Dawn to Dusk on a Barrier Island.* Simon & Schuster, 1998. 32 pages. (0–689–81563–8) $16.00
On their last full day of vacation on the island, Amy and her artist mom rise before dawn so they can enjoy all the natural wonders it has to offer, as well as reminisce about their island experiences. Both mother and daughter keep a scrapbook of sketches and paintings they've made and their observations about nature. Their last day is filled with new experiences to add to their scrapbooks and, best of all, they are present when the baby sea turtles hatch and head for the ocean. An outstanding design combines watercolor paintings, adult and child sketches, and hand-written notes to give the book the appearance of a scrapbook. (Ages 7–11)

Zoehfeld, Kathleen Weidner. *What Is the World Made Of? All about Solids, Liquids, and Gases.* Illustrated by Paul Meisel. (Let's-Read-and-Find-Out-Science) HarperCollins, 1998. 32 pages. (0–06–027143–4) $15.95
An excellent easy science book clearly explains the three natural states of matter, and how water easily changes from one state to another, all in terms young children can easily understand. Zoehfeld's conversational style and frequent use of second person point of view will immediately engage the youngest readers. Her clear explanations use examples that are easily within the realm of early childhood, and she gives realistic suggestions of things children can do to see water in action: holding an ice cube in your hand, for example, or watching steam rise as water boils in a saucepan on the stove (with plenty of warnings about having an adult present). The book concludes with the step-by-step outlines for three easy science activities involving matter. (Ages 4–7)

See also: Anthology for the Earth; Circle of Days; Cool Melons—Turn to Frogs!; Counting on the Woods; Forest; Grand Canyon; Insectlopedia; Light Shining through the Mist; Little Clam; Morning on the Lake; Snowflake Bentley; Talking with Adventurers; Turtle Spring

Seasons and Celebrations

Arnold, Katya, reteller and illustrator. *The Adventures of Snowwoman.* Based on a story by V. Suteev. Holiday House, 1998. 32 pages. (0–8234–1390–X) $15.95
The children have decorated the neighborhood—all but a tree. No tree? Unthinkable. After writing a letter to Santa, they create Snowwoman using an abundance of the white stuff plus seven shiny apples (necklace), a carrot (long nose), and a stewpot (hat). Snowwoman is an unlikely emissary to carry their letter, but smiling benevolently she accepts the mission and sets off into the scary woods with Buddy the dog. During a blizzard they become "lost as lost could be." A quarreling Rabbit and Fox become part of the frigid ensemble's adventures. The intrepid little band is joined by Magpie and then by Bear, who leaves hibernation to help deliver the letter. According to Arnold's background note, her lively reworking of Vladimir Suteev's story "The Conifer" shifts the traditional Russian tree trimming from New Year's Eve to December 24. She writes that Snowwoman and other characters from the popular Snow family of Russian folklore appear in Russian stories and films and even in Rimsky-Korsakov's opera "The Snowmaiden." Suteev was a

successful Russian artist, writer and movie director who released the first of more than 30 animated films in 1931. Arnold is a Moscow-schooled artist now living in New Jersey whose affection for Suteev's story is evident in the broad strokes of her full-color images, her energetic child characters, her zany woodland cohort, and—most of all—her heroine. Snowwoman is an unforgettably cheerful, brave, bumbling, and likeable heroine who gets the job done with a little help from her many friends. (Ages 3–6)

Bauer, Marion Dane. *Christmas in the Forest.* **Illustrated by Diane Dawson Hearn. (Holiday House Reader) Holiday House, 1998. 48 pages. (0–8234–1371–3) $15.95**
The children have forgotten to put a gift under the tree for Cat. They've neglected to scratch and brush her and to feed Cat her flaked tuna. Cat decides she'll punish these Santa-happy children by depriving them of her company, but the children don't even notice when Cat runs away into the snowy woods. A miserable Cat meets little Mouse, who's never heard of Christmas and seems naive regarding the appetites of cats. Knowing that Cat won't talk and eat simultaneously, Squirrel, Bird and Rabbit appeal to her vanity by imploring her to tell about Christmas, about "special foods...shining trees... presents." Cat's report about "the baby" and the insight that "all babies are special" saves Cat from the threat of Bear. Hearn's full-color illustrations perfectly portray feline vanity. Bauer is a genius at creating real plots and genuine characterizations in stories for newly independent readers. In this six-chapter beginning reader, she's managed a minor miracle: a completely believable, secular, anthropomorphic story grounded in the mix of holiday excitement, cat behavior and maternal love. (Ages 3–7)

Bible. The Gospels of Matthew and Luke from the King James translation. *The Christmas Story.* **Illustrated by Gennady Spirin. James Bible. Henry Holt, 1998. 32 pages. (0–8050–5292–5) $19.95**
Thirteen exquisite tempera, watercolor and pencil illustrations of passages from the Gospels of Matthew and Luke comprise this extraordinary visual rendering of the traditional Christmas Story. Three glorious two-page spreads have no text: the Annunciation, the Heavenly Host, and the Adoration of the Magi. Additional paintings serve as borders for the textual excerpts from scriptures, for which each chapter and verse is noted within the page design. A two-page lay commentary opens the book serving to summarize the perspective of each Gospel. Spirin's note at the end mentions the dates on which Christmas observances are held today. Although Spirin now lives in New Jersey, his classical art training in Moscow and Orthodox heritage informed his meticulously developed paintings that are reproduced here in a handsomely designed 11 $^{1}/_{4}$ x 11 $^{1}/_{8}$" volume. (Age 5 and older)

Carney, Margaret. *At Grandpa's Sugar Bush.* **Illustrated by Janet Wilson. U.S. edition: Kids Can Press, 1998. 32 pages. (1–55074–341–4) $15.95**
The steps involved in harvesting maple syrup from more than one hundred trees in Grandpa's sugar bush are related by a young grandson with a February week of school vacation. First Grandpa drills holes on the southeast sides of the trees, and then the boy cleans out the wood shavings with a twig. They tap spikes into the holes, and before long the sap begins to drip into the buckets they've hung on each spike. That's only the beginning. Grandpa predicts that the sap will begin to run on the day they hear the first robin,

and it does. This is more than expository writing on the origin of maple syrup, it's a real story. The boy is a genuine help throughout the process, although adults will guess that Grandpa has his hands full in more than one way. This kind, knowing man most certainly realizes that the outcomes of their companionship and the satisfaction they share in creating something special by hand can be as sweet as the "tastiest syrup in the country." Carney is acquainted with the maple woods of her husband's family farm in Ontario, Canada. Wilson's beautiful oil paintings illustrate the two at work, the snowy vista, and some of the wildlife. (Ages 4–7)

Gelman, Rita Golden. *Queen Esther Saves Her People.* **Illustrated by Frané Lessac. Scholastic Press, 1998. 40 pages. (0–590–47025–6) $15.95**
According to an opening note, the scriptural story of Esther takes place more than 2,500 years ago in the ancient Persian Empire and is a "story of good and evil, of caring and callousness, and of the extraordinary courage of one young woman." The Jews living in Persia at that time spoke Persian and dressed like their Persian neighbors, even though they still practiced the Jewish religion in their homes. Without knowing Esther was Jewish, King Ahasuerus chose her to be his queen. All but one of the traditional elements of this Purim story from the scriptures is in place. Gelman included Mordecai's bravery and the treachery of the wicked Hamen (sic), but she omitted Queen Vashti's reason for refusing to appear at one of the king's parties. Lessac's unique, lovely visual suggestions of Persian cultural details were created using gouache. (Ages 5–9)

Gershator, Phillis. *When It Starts to Snow.* **Illustrated by Martin Matje. Henry Holt, 1998. 32 pages. (0–8050–5404–9) $15.95**
"What if it starts to snow? / What do you do? / Where do you go?" Brief rhymed responses within a pattern of repetition hint at what some creatures do: mouse, cat, black crow, sparrow, geese, beaver, fish, pig, cow, hen, rooster, worm, stoat, frog, deer, bear. At the end we see what a bat, snake, raccoon, squirrel, mole, rabbit, wolf and chipmunk do, too. What does a child want to do? Go out to play! Despite the large roster of creatures introduced in Gershator's short text, Matje's crisp lines and generous uses of white energize the simple idea. (Ages 2–4)

Hofmeyr, Dianne. *The Stone: A Persian Legend of the Magi.* **Illustrated by Jude Daly. U.S. edition: Farrar Straus Giroux, 1998. 32 pages. (0–374–37198–9) $16.00**
According to Marco Polo, in Saveh, Persia, he saw the three domed tombs of the Magi: Balthasar, Melchior, and Jasper. In this rendition of the story, three stargazers—magicians, possibly, or maybe healers or holy men—first noticed a bright star from a tower near Saveh. After searching through scrolls, they discovered an ancient legend about a baby whose birth would be announced by a star, an infant destined to become a king who would bring justice, healing, and peace to the world, and they set off on a journey to find him. When they do, the child presents them with the gift of a stone which miracuously bursts into flames, and the Magi realize that they must believe with a faith that is as strong as the stone for peace and healing to be brought to the world. According to Marco Polo's writings—which, to a certain extent, may also be legend—he was given this story of the Magi while his 13th century travels to the court of Kublai Khan. This particular version, richly

told and illustrated, was first published recently by a small press in South Africa. Hofmeyr's wonderfully written retelling is illustrated by Daly's dramatic, spare full-color artwork. Hofmeyr grew up in Gordon's Bay, South Africa, and now lives in London; Daly resides in Capetown, South Africa. (Ages 7–12)

Hoyt-Goldsmith, Diane. *Celebrating Chinese New Year.* Photographs by Lawrence Migdale. Holiday House, 1998. 32 pages. (0–8234–1393–4) $16.95
Elements of the traditional two-week observance of the Chinese New Year are interpreted and shown in a photo-essay featuring ten-year-old Ryan Leong and his family. General information about families with a Chinese heritage in San Francisco as well as details about Leong family preparations and activities are part of the mix. The Leong's shopping list and New Year's menu are pictured, there is a glimpse of the Chinatown Flower Festival, and readers can see a calligrapher at work painting a poetic saying for the Leong home. While reading how ancestors are honored during this time, readers also learn that Ryan's grandfather was the first Asian American to receive a Purple Heart for bravery during World War I. Ryan attends public school, and also Chinese school on a regular basis. The animals of the Chinese Zodiac are pictured with their dates and special qualities, and the Chinese calendar is briefly explained. There are photos of the Lion Dance and parade, and the role of the red envelopes of money is clarified. A glossary and index are helpful. *Gung hay fat choy* = May you prosper! (Ages 7–10)

Hughes, Langston. *Carol of the Brown King: Nativity Poems.* Illustrated by Ashley Bryan. A Jean Karl Book/Atheneum, 1998. 32 pages. (0–689–81877–7) $16.00
Five poems written by the famous African American poet Langston Hughes receive the gift of fresh visual interpretation by the artist and performer who so frequently introduces them to audiences in the United States and beyond. Along with the title poem, Bryan's paintings, rendered in tempera and gouache, are for "Shepherd's Song at Christmas," "On a Christmas Night," "On a Pallet of Straw," "The Christmas Story," and an anonymous verse translated from a Puerto Rican Christmas card. This handsome full-color volume has strong child appeal for all and a particular pleasure for the children of color who read and see "Three Wise Men, / One dark like me-/ Part of His / Nativity." Bryan has set the traditional story somewhere in the Middle East or Africa, while the final poem pictures a contemporary dark-skinned elder woman reading the Bible to a young girl and on another page, a similar setting with a man and boy. Thoughtful readers will realize that the Brown King can refer both to the Christ Child and one of the Magi. Observant viewers will notice Bryan's various uses of star images and discover other ideas, as well, about which to reflect and celebrate. (Ages 2–8)

Hurd, Thacher. *Santa Mouse and the Ratdeer.* HarperCollins, 1998. 32 pages. (0–06–027694–0) $14.95
Rosie Mouse helps trim the tree, and knocks it over while putting the star on top, but this is nothing compared to the problems Santa Mouse is having with his departure from the Mouse North Pole. Who would have thought he was such a procrastinator, or that his ratdeer were such grumblers, or that they would crash land in the middle of nowhere? Who but Rosie Mouse would have dreamed that the lost ratdeer would appear at her front door?

Who could imagine a Santa Mouse as oblivious to disaster as this guileless red-suited rodent? Thacher Hurd imagined this jolly trip from one crash landing to another, and from one of Rosie Mouse's angelic smiles to the next. There's scant need for the Mouse Prayer on the final page, nor for the "knock knock" joke at the very end, but unnecessary, inexplicable gifts are part of the season, too. "On Blunder! On Basher! On Lousy and Loopy and Bugsy and Twizzlebum!" Hot chocolate, anyone? (Ages 2–6)

Joseph, Lynn. *Jump Up Time: A Trinidad Carnival Story.* Illustrated by Linda Saport. Clarion, 1998. 32 pages. (0–395–65012–7) $16.00
"Is party time, is jump up time. / Oh yeah! Trinidad Carnival is here." Lily hears these lyrics on the radio while her older sister, Christine, stands on a chair so Mama can drape and pin shimmery red and green costume cloth around her. Christine insists on dressing as a hummingbird for her first Carnival, because Trinidad is the Land of the Hummingbird. Mama tells Lily, "When you start school next year, you can wear any costume you want...little Lil," and she rubs Lily's head. But it's hard to wait, to hear your baby name, and "to watch Christine dancing all over the house in her Carnival costume." After the family arrives at the Savannah and the last steps to array Christine in her hoop and feathers have been taken, she becomes nervous. Very nervous. Confusion and excitement reign. Someone is dressed as an Arawak Indian princess, and others are "giggling tadpoles, laughing poinsettias, and dancing mango trees." Lily suggests a way for Christine to overcome her stage fright. Christine responds to the situation and to Lily. Saport's warm pastels glow in picturing Joseph's affectionate family story replete with cultural details and a suggestion of regional speech. (Ages 5–9)

Little, Jean. *Emma's Magic Winter.* Illustrated by Jennifer Plecas. (An I Can Read Book) HarperCollins, 1998. 64 pages. (0–06–025389–4) $14.95
Reading out loud at school was out of the question. Emma was that shy. However, once Emma saw that Sally also had red boots, Emma became brave enough to venture into imaginative winter play with her friendly new neighbor. Before long Emma was reading to Sally's little brother. Due to the red boots, which the girls pretended were magic, their good times outdoors in the snow, and Sally's encouragement, Emma became brave enough to take the big step of reading aloud in class. Little offers a genuine story about shyness and the delight of imaginative play in only seven brief chapters. Plecas's colored pictures show Emma and her family to be light-skinned, while Sally and her family have dark skin. (Ages 4–6)

Luenn, Nancy. *A Gift for Abuelita: Celebrating the Day of the Dead = Un regalo para Abuelita: En celebración del Día de los Muertos.* Illustrated by Robert Chapman. Rising Moon/Northland, 1998. 32 pages. (0–87358–688–3) $15.95
Rosita loved being with her *abuelita* (grandmother) each day. She loved "the soap scent of Abuelita's everyday dress...and the strong warmth of her grandmother's arms." She loved what they did together, such as preparing *tortillas,* making up songs, and weeding the *chiles* in the garden. One day Abuelita taught Rosita how to braid a strong cord from three overlapping strands. After Abuelita's illness and death, Rosita became heartbroken. As the family prepared for the annual Day of the Dead observances by cooking, carving, weaving, and gardening, Rosita couldn't seem to think of an appropriate *ofrenda* (gift for the family altar) to create in Abuelita's memory. The harder

Rosita tried the more difficult it was for her to sense Abuelita's presence, until she remembered the cord Abuelita had taught her to braid. Chapman's muted mixed media illustrations on cast paper suggest three dimensions in an affectionate bilingual story about the endurance of family memory. (Ages 6–9)

Marchant, Kerena. *Id-ul-Fitr.* U.S. edition: Millbrook Press, 1998. 32 pages. (0–7613–0963–2) $20.90

The most joyous festival in the Muslim calendar is Id-ul-Fitr, which breaks the Ramadan fast. This celebrative time of new beginnings can involve serious and merry aspects: prayers at a mosque, family visits to the cemetery, *zakat* (welfare gifts on behalf of the general community), family gifts, parties, special songs and foods, Id cards featuring calligraphy, and—in some regions—polo and horse or camel races. Following the section about the month of Ramadan, there is a two-page spread interpreting how the new moon of Id is determined locally (by sighting) and officially (in Mecca). Helpful brief material includes information about other Muslim festivals, a bibliography, eight website addresses, a glossary, and an index. Marchant's valuable book bears a consistent global perspective and is replete with full-color photographs and facts rarely available to most American children, families and teachers, even though the United States has a Muslim population of considerable size. (Ages 8–12)

Moore, Clement. *The Night Before Christmas.* Illustrated by Jan Brett. Putnam's, 1998. 32 pages. (0–399–23190–0) $16.99

Moore's rhyming story about the "right jolly old elf" who delivered toys using a sleigh pulled by eight reindeer appeared in print for the first time with the title "A Visit from St. Nicholas" in 1823, in a newspaper in Troy, New York. Many editions have been published since then. Pleasing elements of this cheerful version include Brett's abundant uses of bright reds, blues, and greens, and her carefully developed images of the famous reindeer, here marvelously decked out in fancy blankets and bell-trimmed harnesses. Faux-Scandinavian-garbed St. Nicholas lands "with a bound" safely down the chimney, which is when observant preschoolers can begin noticing specifics about the gifts he delivers. They'll find the first names of dozens of boys and girls on gift tags scattered throughout Brett's border designs. They'll enjoy trying to identify the toys, and most will be ones about which their elder relatives can tell. "Merry Christmas to All, and to All a Good Night." (Ages 2–5)

Nerlove, Miriam. *Shabbat.* Albert Whitman, 1998. 24 pages. (0–8075–7324–8) $13.95

"I love Shabbat! It comes each week-/ a time to rest and play. / We like to be together on Shabbat, my favorite day!" These opening sentences signal an uncomplicated narrative for very young children in a picture book explaining the Jewish Sabbath, which begins every Friday at sundown. The book's strengths rest in Nerlove's pleasant full-color illustrations showing weekly Shabbat preparations: candles, *challah* (bread), blessings, and time at the synagogue. A reliable background note for adults appears at the end. Despite the text's somewhat forced rhymes and the omission of a Hebrew translation for the two Sabbath blessings traditionally offered in Hebrew, this easy picture book has a fresh, accessible, contemporary aura that both Jewish and non-Jewish families can appreciate. (Ages 2–5)

Podwal, Mark. *The Menorah Story.* Greenwillow, 1998. 28 pages. (0–688–15759–9) $15.00

"God tried many times to teach Moses how to make a menorah. But whenever Moses set about making one, he couldn't remember what it was supposed to look like. God even drew a picture of a menorah on Moses's palm and told him to copy it. Still Moses could not do it. ..." This intriguing legend opens a brief narrative. An unusual juxtaposition of background information and legend commends this appealingly laid-back yet fully serious picture book with an abundance of crisp white space and an overall pleasing design. The somewhat abstract brightly colored illustrations created with gouache and colored pencils will probably catch adult eyes more quickly than those of the young. A very short author's note and bibliography appear on an opening page. (Ages 5–9)

Santiago, Esmeralda and Joie Davidow, editors. *Las Christmas: Favorite Latino Authors Share Their Holiday Memories.* Illustrated by José Ortega. Knopf, 1998. 198 pages. (0–375–40151–2) $22.00

In 1996 the editors of *Sí* magazine invited prominent Latino fiction writers to submit brief pieces to the magazine for a Christmas issue that was meant to celebrate the different ways the December holidays are observed in the various Latin American countries and by Latino families in the United States. They were so overwhelmed by the number and tenor of the submissions that the editors decided to compile them into a book, and the result is this collection of 24 original short stories and essays, based on the authors' memories of childhood Christmas celebrations. Although the stories are intended for an adult audience, mature teenagers will appreciate the reminiscences, sometimes poignant and often humorous, that deal with the elevated sense of emotion and family strife holidays often bring. Many teenagers will recognize names familiar in young adult literature, such as Judith Ortiz Cofer, Victor Martinez and Gary Soto; others will be happy to discover authors such as Julia Alvarez, Denise Chávez, Sandra Cisneros, and Michael Nava. Recipes for favorite Christmas dishes and the lyrics to traditional songs, remembered from childhood, are interspersed throughout the book. (Age 14 and older)

Shulevitz, Uri. *Snow.* Farrar Straus Giroux, 1998. 32 pages. (0–374–37092–3) $16.00

"The skies are gray. The rooftops are gray. The whole city is gray. / Then... one snowflake." Using verbal understatement and perfect pacing, Shulevitz creates a sense of the season's first snowfall, beginning slowly and softly, and gradually leading up to a blizzard of words that expresses a child's delight with snow. Throughout the story, a small boy and his dog revel in the transformation of the gray city into a winter wonderland. He relies completely on his own observations, as his grandfather and the people he meets on the street insist that the snow is insignificant. Here the adults put their faith in news reports which dully predict "no snow." But the child knows better, as he sees with all his senses, as well as with his imagination. That the snow works its magic on ordinary city streets is further enhanced in the illustrations that show Mother Goose characters coming to life and emerging from a book shop window to dance through the snowy streets with the boy and his dog. *Winner, 1999 Charlotte Zolotow Award.* (Ages 3–7)

Siddals, Mary McKenna. *Millions of Snowflakes.* **Illustrated by Elizabeth Sayles. Clarion, 1998. 25 pages. (0–395–71531–8) $13.00**
A preschool girl with the suggestion of Asian facial features enjoys playing in new snow. "I laugh. / I jump. / I run. / I spin." She's wearing brightly colored winter clothes as she counts snowflakes: one, two, three, four and—oh yes— five snowflakes. Too many to count but not too many to enjoy. A brief rhyming text suits this cheerful, uncomplicated $7^{1}/4$ x 7" book for the youngest. (Ages 18 months–3 years)

Slate, Joseph. *The Secret Stars.* **Illustrated by Felipe Davalos. Miles Cavendish, 1998. 32 pages. (0–7614–5027–0) $15.95**
On the night of the Three Kings, Pepe and Sila are tucked under a warm star quilt, one on either side of their grandmother. There are no stars outside tonight because of the rain and then the ice. The children worry. How will the Kings be able to ride through such weather? Can they find the family's Baby Manger, hay box and figs? Will they bring toys, maybe just a little *piñata,* or leave something tucked in their shoes? Grandma's soothing voice transforms her into a large bird with the star quilt for wings. She guides the children to see stars everywhere. Together they look at the frost covered garden flowers, a spider's nest, a fish and frog under the ranch pond, the rooster Reyo and the hens in the chicken coop, a deer at the barn, and the mule Placído. The strong images and deep colors in Davalos's illustrations were created using acrylics to portray the loving Latino family of Slate's story set somewhere in New Mexico. (Ages 4–8)

Summers, Susan, reteller. *The Fourth Wise Man.* **Based on the story by Henry Van Dyke. Illustrated by Jackie Morris. U.S. edition: Dial, 1998. 32 pages. (0–8037–2312–1) $16.99**
"The Story of the Other Wise Man" by Henry Van Dyke was first published in 1895 and is one of the most enduring fictional accounts of a fourth wise man or woman who searched for the infant Jesus. According to Summers's adaptation, Artaban is a Persian "follower of the faith of Zoroaster" when he and three colleagues in astrology—Caspar, Melchior, and Balthazar— observed a new star one night. The men discerned that the star signified the birth of a great teacher who was to be born among the Jews. They decided to locate the baby, but by the time Artaban secured three precious jewels to present to the infant King of Kings, his companions had gone ahead. Traveling alone, Artaban spends years trying to find the child, giving one of the jewels to help a dying man and the second jewel to save a male infant from Herod's mass slaughter along the way. As years passed, Artaban continued his search for the teacher, all the while healing sick people, visiting those in prison, and feeding the starving. Thirty-three years later Artaban found himself outside of Jerusalem near the site of a crucifixion, and at that time he gave his last jewel to ransom a woman being sold into slavery. According to a note, this fictional good man practiced the teachings of Jesus, "dedicating himself to a life of service as he searched for the King of Kings and not discriminating against people belonging to different races or holding different belief systems from his own." Morris created powerful, compassionate full-color paintings to accompany Summers' effective, abbreviated version of Van Dyke's classic work. Her painted map on the end papers offers an aesthetically pleasing opening and closing for this lovely $9^{1}/4$

x 11" picture book. Summers lives in England where, as a teacher, she has used this story with her students for years. (Ages 6–10)

Willey, Margaret. *Thanksgiving with Me.* **Illustrated by Lloyd Bloom. A Laura Geringer Book/HarperCollins, 1998. 32 pages. (0–06–027113–2) $14.95**
"Sit down, Mother, and tell me again. / When are my uncles coming? When? / All of your uncles will be here soon; / they promised to be here by afternoon." An impatient fair-skinned girl and her mother are aproned for the visit of six adult uncles. There will be a "tower of biscuits, a bushel of peas, / a tub of potatoes, a wheel of cheese, / a dozen pies, a barrel of juice, / cranberries, plums, / and a Thanksgiving goose!" The child wants to be reminded about Cory and the time he "sang louder than the morning crows," and Fred, "who couldn't see past his nose," and Davey, Joe, Henry, and Will. She wants to hear the vigorous family tales about her rollicking, singing, dancing relatives. Bloom's always memorable elongated figures perfectly envision Mother's long-legged brothers when they were teenagers: Cory, the singing daydreamer, and Fred, with his nose in a book, and the other four. Mother reminds her daughter that they will "eat like wolves and lions and bears...Oh, the kitchen will quake, / the oven will roar, / the music will flow / from window and door!" Bloom's images painted with oils and reproduced in full color perfectly complement Willey's rhyming text to embrace the rural men who gathered for a reunion, the little girl who remembers them so affectionately, and her mother, who nurtures those memories. (Ages 3–6)

See also: *Autumn Leaves; Bear's Hiccups; Bunny Who Found Easter; Christmas Tree in the White House; Fiesta Fireworks; Outlaw Thanksgiving; Prairie Town; Snowflake Bentley; Turtle Spring*

Folklore, Mythology and Traditional Literature

Aylesworth, Jim, reteller. *The Gingerbread Man.* **Illustrated by Barbara McClintock. Scholastic Press, 1998. 32 pages. (0–590–97219–7) $15.95**
A roaring fire burns in the fireplace, teacups can be seen on end tables, a framed portrait hangs near the mantle where lovely flower arrangements and decorative plates are placed, and a cat plays with a ball of yarn from a knitting basket when a little old woman stopped reading and suggested making a gingerbread man. "Yes, let's do!" said a little old man whose reading has been interrupted by that sudden possibility. Wearing their aprons this genteel pair "shaped the little arms, and they shaped the little legs...with raisins they made the little eyes and the little nose...then with sugar glaze, they dressed him in a fancy suit of clothes." This is no ordinary retelling of a familiar cumulative tale but rather a handsomely designed, full-color version printed on heavy creamy paper with hand-lettered display type. It's not too fancy to catch the fancy of the preschoolers who will enjoy Aylesworth's spirited oral style. There's enormous child appeal in the cookie chase involving McClintock's wonderfully costumed butcher with a knife, a black-and-white cow, and a muddy old sow. All wind up staring "sadly at the fox. He hadn't left a single crumb for anyone." The artwork was rendered in watercolor, sepia ink, and gouache. (Ages 3–6)

Babbitt, Natalie. *Ouch!* **Illustrated by Fred Marcellino. Michael Di Capua Books/HarperCollins, 1998. 32 pages. (0–06–205066–4) $14.95**

When a fortune-teller foresees that the newborn child of a commoner will grow up to marry a princess, the king isn't happy. No royal daughter of his is going to marry "nobody special." The king's attempts to outwit fate are hilariously superseded in this snappily told story that is one of the lesser known tales from the Brothers Grimm. The lack of specific source information for this rendition of the tale is puzzling. But Natalie Babbitt's witty text and Fred Marcelino's amusing full-color illustrations that mock the king while casting the young here, Marco, in an aura of goodness are a winning combination. (Ages 7–10)

Del Negro, Janice. *Lucy Dove.* **Illustrated by Leonid Gore. A Melanie Kroupa Book/DK Ink, 1998. 32 pages. (0–7894–2514–9) $16.95**

Lucy Dove is both a sly and witty story about a woman who is no one's fool and an eerie, haunted tale that will set hairs rising. When a rich laird is told that a pair of trousers sewn by the full moonlight in the graveyard of St. Andrew's Church will bring him good fortune, he offers a sack of gold to anyone who will make them. But the graveyard is rumored to be haunted by a "fearsome thing," and only aging seamstress Lucy Dove takes him up on the offer. "Lucy Dove could use that sackful of gold, having recently been sacked from the laird's own household." On the night of the full moon, Lucy takes her sewing to the abandoned churchyard and sets to work. Soon an awful smell assaults her. "It was the smell of dampness and decay. It was the smell of graves and corruption. It was the smell of death, without the promise of eternity to redeem it." Janice Del Negro's imaginative and evocative prose paints a richly embroidered story of evil that is humorously outwitted by a quick-thinking, table-turning heroine in this riveting story featuring an original character in a setting based on traditional Celtic tales. Leonid Gore's superb acrylic paintings escalate the drama and tension of the fine prose. His textured, darkly luminous palette and chilling, haggard images haunt the pages of this delicious tale. *Honor Book, 1998 CCBC Caldecott Award Discussion.* (Ages 7–11)

Gershator, Phillis, reteller. *Zzzng! Zzzng! Zzzng! A Yoruba Tale.* **Illustrated by Theresa Smith. Orchard, 1998. 32 pages. (0–531–09523–1) $15.95**

A marvelous introduction opens this lively tale: "In the days when all things came together to make the world as it is, when root married trunk and trunk married branch, when sun married day and moon married night, so it was for the animals too. That is why Mosquito flew around looking for someone to marry." Buzzing sounds are featured in this retelling, as Mosquito visits Ear, Arm, Chest, Leg, and Hips—first to woo each and then to sting them. Mosquito's final words remind each body part that she's still nearby, buzzing and stinging. Smith's artwork features strong colors and bold shapes and was created in pastel and crayon. (Ages 3–6)

Harber, Frances. *The Brothers' Promise.* **Illustrated by Thor Wickstrom. Albert Whitman, 1998. 32 pages. (0–8075–0900–0) $15.95**

Chayim was a rich farmer, and he was a good one, too. "Rows of beet leaves, fat cabbages, potato plants, and sun-kissed wheat filled his fields." He was a wise person who taught his two sons that everything on earth has its own season. When Chayim was on his deathbed, he made his sons promise to divide the land and the work exactly in half and to always take care of each other. They promised. Keeping the promise became almost impossible for Yankel and Josef. They were that different from each other. When hard times came—and they did come—Yankel and Josef each figured out an anonymous way to help the other out. That made each brother's anger even greater. Their eventual reconciliation became an occasion for the angels to weep tears of joy, just as their father had said it could be. Wickstrom chose to set Harber's vigorous version of this moving story from the *Talmud* in Eastern Europe during the late 19th century. His powerful artwork was created in oil on board. (Ages 5–9)

Hausman, Gerald. *Doctor Bird: Three Lookin' Up Tales from Jamaica.* **Illustrated by Ashley Wolff. Philomel, 1998. 32 pages. (0–399–22744-X) $15.99**
According to the source note for these three unusual tales, the Doctor Bird is the national bird of Jamaica and is found only in that country. A stream-tailed hummingbird, it is held in great esteem by the Jamaicans and is believed by many to have the power to heal and the power to cast a spell. In these three entertaining tales, "How Doctor Bird Taught Mongoose a Lesson that Mongoose Never Remembered," "How Doctor Bird Taught Mouse to Look Up When He Was Feeling Down," and "How Doctor Bird Taught Brother Owl That It's Better to Be Who You Are Than Who You're Not," Doctor Bird also proves to be a funny, principled, compassionate, party-loving character who dispenses advice and punishment with equal charm as he flies among the members of Jamaica's bird and animal kingdom. Ashley Wolff's bright, bold illustrations done with black gesso and gouache are vivid accompaniments to these tales, which are told in standard English, and for which the author credits the principal storytellers from whom he originally heard them. (Ages 5–10)

Holden, Robert, reteller. *The Pied Piper of Hamelin.* **Illustrated by Drahos Zak. U.S. edition: Walter Lorraine Books/Houghton Mifflin, 1998. 32 pages. (0–395–89918-4) $15.00**
The Czech-born illustrator of an arresting retelling of an old tale of retribution and revenge has a style that's uniquely his own. The long slender volume (8 1/2 x 12 3/4") immediately gives readers a sense of the medieval village depicted within; its tall vertical shape is echoed both in the architecture and in the imposing figure of the stranger who comes to town, promising he can solve their rat problem. Zak makes the townspeople, rather than the piper, look crazed in this version, suggesting that perhaps the children who follow the piper will be better off. His detailed pen-and-ink illustrations are washed with bright touches of color in places he wants readers' eyes to fall; elsewhere they are left as black-and-white line drawings to provide background. The tight rhyming verses of Holden's retelling are similarly unadorned, providing a pared-down text that leaves space for the imagination. (Ages 7–10)

McCully, Emily. *Beautiful Warrior: The Legend of the Nun's Kung Fu.* **Arthur A. Levine Books/Scholastic, 1998. 40 pages. (0–590–37487-7) $16.95**
When Mingyi, a distressed peasant girl, approaches the great warrior nun Wu Mei, upset because her father has told her she must marry the bandit Soong Ling to save his business, Wu Mei decides she will try to teach the excitable

girl kung fu. "Tell Soong Ling...you will marry him if he can best you at kung fu," she directs Mingyi. Wu Mei then offers Mingyi a "crash course." "It will take a year," she tells her. During that year Wu Mei teaches Mingyi how to make her mind calm, how to be like the water and follow the path of least resistance, how to bend with suppleness and force like bamboo, and how to maintain balance like the stately crane. "Hadn't I better learn to fight?" asks a worried Mingyi? "You are learning," the serene Wu Mei replies. Emily Arnold McCully's original story is based on the legendary Chinese character Wu Mei. Her light-filled, graceful paintings illustrate the story, which is told in a relaxed style that incorporates contemporary English vernacular. An author's note for this story set in 17th century China provides background information on *kung fu*, which, the author notes, means "human effort" and is a discipline of lifelong study that goes far deeper than the martial arts image often conveyed in western popular culture. (Age 5–8)

MacDonald, Margaret Read. *Pickin' Peas*. Illustrated by Pat Cummings. HarperCollins, 1998. 32 pages. (0–06–027235-X) $14.95

Little Girl planted a garden of peas, but oh, my, were those peas in for trouble! "Come July, those peas got ripe and ready to eat. Little Girl went out in her garden. Started going down the row. Picking peas. Started singing..." She leaves the "little bitty" peas to grow some more, but that's only because she hasn't met up yet with Mr. Rabbit. Little Girl thinks she's finally gotten the best of that rabbit, but one of the last pages shows him busily "Pickin' peas...and landin' on his knees!" Little Girl is a contemporary kid dressed in boldly colored summer clothes with her hair in ribbons and sunglasses in place on her face. Cummings' wonderful large-size images of this determined brown-skinned gardener and her pesky adversary fairly leap from sun-filled illustrations. MacDonald combined Southern written sources dated 1897 and 1922 to create this enjoyable picture book version for which she offers her own tune and directions for retelling the story with movements or acting it out. (Ages 3–8)

McKissack, Patricia and Fredrick McKissack. *Let My People Go: Bible Stories Told by a Freeman of Color*. Illustrated by James E. Ransome. An Anne Schwartz Book/Atheneum, 1998. 134 pages. (0–689–80856-9) $20.00

In a beginning note important to understanding the whole book, the McKissacks write about a former Sunday school teacher, "a masterful storyteller, who mesmerized us with narrations about ancient biblical characters and African American historical figures simultaneously." They used this technique in retelling some of the *Bible* stories so important in their slave ancestors' lives. Another decision involved the time and setting, which is early 19th century Charleston, South Carolina, a city that "played a major role in the American slave trade *and* was home to a large community of free blacks." The McKissacks' 12 "Old Testament" favorites are retold in the "distinctive voice of a fictionalized free black abolitionist, Price Jeffries," a character loosely based upon the actual Denmark Vesey. The narrator of the overarching 19th century narrative is Price Jeffries'daughter, a character modeled after Frances Ellen Watkins Harper, an "outspoken 19th century abolitionist, feminist, and poet." The daughter's speech is that of a well-educated woman of her time, while conversations she recalls from childhood echo her parents' speech. The authors challenged themselves as writers, and so did the artist who illustrated this handsome $11^{1}/_{4}$ x 8 $^{5}/_{8}$ book. Ransome also provides an introductory note, pointing out that his oil paintings for the *Bible* stories feature brown-and-olive-skinned Semites and lush colors, while he limited his palette for artwork illustrating early 19th century happenings. This unique, compelling volume offers opportunities for pleasure, information, and insight all on more than one level and all because the authors and artist envisioned it so. (Age 7 and older)

Paterson, John and Katherine Paterson. *Images of God.* **Illustrated by Alexander Koshkin. Clarion, 1998. 112 pages. (0–395–70734-X) $20.00**
Interpretations of the "word pictures" of God from 23 passages from the *Bible* are explored here by two Patersons: Katherine, a former Christian missionary and internationally acclaimed writer for children, and her husband, John, an ordained Protestant clergyman. Using the New Revised Standard Version of the *Bible*, they developed historical-critical commentaries on these scriptures. The organization of their interpretations is innovative: (1) All Nature Sings—Images from the Created World (Light, Water, Wind, Fire, Rock, Cloud, Dove, Eagle and Hen, Man and Woman; (2) To Earth Come Down—Images from Ordinary Life (Mother, Father, Housewife, Visitor, Host, Wrestler, Bread; and (3) With a Mighty Hand—Images of Watchfulness and Creation (Landowner, Gardener, Potter, Shepherd, Judge, King, Architect). A listing of Biblical references and an index complete a volume illustrated with 35 paintings executed in watercolor, tempera, and gouache by Koshkin, a Russian-born artist. Earlier the Patersons collaborated on *Consider the Lilies: Plants of the Bible* (Crowell, 1986; Clarion, 1998); K. Paterson and Koshkin's other joint work is *The Angel and the Donkey* (Clarion, 1996). (Age 11 and older)

Paterson, Katherine. *Parzival: The Quest of the Grail Knight.* **Lodestar/Dutton, 1998. 127 pages. (0–525–67579-5) $15.99**
"In the ancient days, when Arthur was a king of Britain, there lived a boy who had never heard of the great son of Pendragon or of his bold knights. The only home the boy had ever known was a cottage in the wilderness of Soltane, and the only parent he had ever known was his mother. He was never called by his proper name; indeed, he didn't even know that he had one." So begins Paterson's briskly paced retelling of an 800-year-old legend about the Grail Knight who, as a lad innocent of his true station, set forth to find the symbol of hope and eternal life. An annotated cast of characters titled "The People" precedes the adaptation in this handsomely designed, 7 x 4 1/4" volume numbering only 127 pages. The Parzival legend is a perfect vehicle for Paterson, because she flawlessly incorporates powerful characterizations, cleverly developed humor, and snappy dialogue within her fiction and she understands how to incorporate a Christian subtext without imposing doctrine. This legend is not new to Paterson's published works — it's central to her contemporary novel, *Park's Quest* (HarperCollins, 1989), which is filled with references to it. In both *Park's Quest* and *Parzival*, Paterson's naive hero sets forth, bumbling past various obstacles and figuring out for himself how to name the answer that will end his pilgrimage. Because of Paterson's *Parzival*, fans of *Park's Quest* can return to that novel to discover other meanings. Young medievalists will enjoy this compressed version of a tale inspired by a 25,000-line epic poem, for which Paterson provides a brief background. Katherine Paterson is the 1998 recipient of the Hans Christian Andersen Award given by the International Board on Books for Young People

(IBBY). Parzival is a wonderful addition to the marvelous body of work for which this accomplished author has been formally acknowledged in many other ways, as well. (Ages 9–13)

Prose, Francine. *You Never Know: A Legend of the Lamed-vavniks.* **Illustrated by Mark Podwal. Greenwillow, 1998. 24 pages. (0–688–15807–2) $14.93**
"According to Jewish tradition, there are at every moment, in every generation, 36 righteous individuals living in secret throughout the world," but their presence is known only when there is some threat to the community. "If the generation is worthy, one of these thirty-six hidden saints will become the Messiah." The threatened disaster in Plotchnik explores that idea in picture book form. For 40 days and 40 nights no rain has fallen in Plotchnik. Even Schmuel the Shoemaker offers to pray for rain, but how can the prayers of such a forgetful villager, one who can't even read, be of help? Even though people remember that Schmuel once saved everyone from a fierce bear, no one really cares whether or not this man offers a prayer. Readers know Schmuel's prayer did matter, because it rains—for forty days and forty nights—and they also see that another of his prayers causes the rain to stop. It takes a dream for the rabbi to realize that Schmuel is one of the holy Lamed-vavniks, and to connect him to the 36 times a menorah is lighted. Schmuel vanished after he could no longer live in secret, but he's been seen in quite a few places since then. "And someone saw him in your town, fixing your shoes and forgetting to charge you." It's best to be kind to everyone, no matter how poor. "After all, you never know." According to an end-note "Lamed-vav" refers to the number "thirty-six" in Hebrew. Gouache and colored pencils were used for the pleasing full-color art illustrating this warm, appealing version of the legend. (Ages 4–8)

San Souci, Robert D. *Cendrillon: A Caribbean Cinderella.* **Illustrated by Brian Pinkney. Simon & Schuster, 1998. 40 pages. (0–689–80668–X) $16.00**
This tale loosely based on a French Creole version of Cinderella is set in the Caribbean among people of African descent and is uniquely told from the point of view of the fairy godmother, in this case a poor washerwoman who has inherited a wand of magic from her mother. "Three taps will change one thing into another....But only for a short time. And the magic must be used to help someone you love." Cendrillon is the washerwoman's goddaughter in this version of the tale, which is seasoned with Creole words and phrases that are defined in a short glossary. Brian Pinkney's brightly colored, swirling illustrations lend an added sense of richness to the story. (Ages 6–8)

Van Laan, Nancy. *The Magic Bean Tree: A Legend from Argentina.* **Illustrated by Beatriz Vidal. Houghton Mifflin, 1998. 32 pages. (0–395–82746–9) $15.00**
A tale from the Quechua-speaking peoples of South America tells a legend about a great drought suffered by the First People on earth. After a summer with no rain, brave Topec goes out in search of water and learns from the oldest carob tree that the Great Bird of the Underworld has perched in her branches, blocking the gods' view of earth. Topec returns to his people and together they manage to figure out a way to frighten the Great Bird away. Argentinean artist Beatriz Vidal's stylized gouache paintings use golden hues to illustrate the parched earth, a lush shades of green for the carob tree, and deep blues and purples to portray the Great Bird of the Underworld. (Ages 4–8)

Van Laan, Nancy. *So Say the Little Monkeys*. Illustrated by Yumi Heo. An Anne Schwartz Book/Atheneum, 1998. 32 pages. (0–689–81038–5) $16.00

A lilting, rap-like rhythm and witty, engaging art combine to retell an energetic folktale that comes originally from the Indians of Brazil in which a band of monkeys would much rather play all day than build a home to protect them from thorny tree perches and the rain that inevitably falls each night. Each time they huddle together in the rain trying to stay warm, the monkeys declare they will build a home, but as soon as the sun comes out, "They swing WHEEE over here. The swing WHEEE over there. They sing, 'Jibba jibba jabba,' as they jump and run....Tiny, tiny monkeys having fun!" This refrain grows increasingly long and more involved as it is repeated throughout the story, and children will not be able to resist a little jibba-jibba-jabbering and WHEEEING of their own as they listen to the delightful sounds of the story. Even the rain (PLINKA PLINKA) and wind (WOOYAWOOYA) are infused with the delight. Yumi Heo lends her singular and distinctive style to the book with artwork that shows the monkeys in all their exuberance and all their restraint, with paintings that depict monkeys swinging wildly and joyfully across one page and huddling pathetically in the rain on another. And if you can get children to hold still long enough to look closely at the illustrations, they will love noticing the baby monkey that appears over and over again throughout this joyfully noisy volume. (Ages 4–7)

See also: *Ashley Bryan's African Tales, Uh-Huh; Queen Esther Saves Her People; The Stone; To Every Thing There Is a Season; Women of the Bible*

Historical People, Places and Events

Bierman, Carol. *Journey to Ellis Island: How My Father Came to America*. Hyperion/Madison Press Books, 1998. 48 pages. (0–7868–0377–0) $17.95

When war came to Poruset, Russia, in 1916, Rachel Weinstein decided it was time to move her young children, Yehuda and Esther, to a new home in America. But their journey on foot across war-torn Russia was treacherous. Along the way they got caught in a crossfire and Yehuda's hand was badly wounded. Even after he fully recovered at a hospital in Kiev, the family worried they would be turned back at Ellis Island, in spite of the fact they had an older son waiting for them in New York City. This highly visual account of the experiences of one Jewish immigrant family is told from the point of view of 11-year-old Yehuda, the author's father. His realistic worry that his weakened arm will be a problem, along with his anticipation about meeting an older brother he has only heard about, add dramatic tension to an already compelling story. Family pictures, documentary photographs of Ellis Island immigrants and artifacts, and original bronze-colored drawings illustrate Yehuda's story. (Ages 7–12)

Borden, Louise. *Good-bye, Charles Lindbergh*. Illustrated by Thomas B. Allen. Margaret K. McElderry, 1998. 32 pages. (0–689–81536–0) $16.00

A widely recognized international hero by 1929, Charles Lindbergh was known to land his biplane in remote, out-of-the way places when he traveled in order to escape media attention. Even so, when Gil, a Mississippi farm boy, was out riding his white horse across a field near his home, he couldn't believe his eyes when he saw Lindbergh land his plane near Mr. Meade's big hay shed! After landing, Lindbergh happily chatted for awhile with the few onlookers who joined Gil in the field, but when Mr. Meade offered the hero a bed for the night, he politely declined, indicating that he preferred to pitch his tent and sleep outside, next to his plane. Although his family doesn't believe his story that night at dinner, Gil talks his sister into getting up early the next morning to see Mr. Lindbergh off. This fictionalized picture book, based on a true childhood story the author heard from 83-year-old Harold Rea Gilpin, is illustrated with soft colors and hazy lines that enhance the historical setting. (Ages 5–9)

Burleigh, Robert. *Home Run*. Illustrated by Mike Wimmer. Silver Whistle/Harcourt Brace, 1998. 32 pages. (0–15–200970–1) $16.00
"He always had this swing. This easy, upthrusting swing. This 'pretty' swing, not taught by any coach. One day the Babe just swung— and it was there. It was his." That is an example of one of Burleigh's two narrative styles interpreting the life and times of Babe Ruth, and on most pages it's printed in a large typeface placed within a large amount of white space. The other is printed in a very small typeface within a make-believe vintage baseball card, such as #251, "Babe on the Mound," relating facts about the Babe's pitching—yes, pitching— record between 1914 and 1933. Wimmer's illustration on the opposite side of the same page shows three early 20th century boys, all looking at the same unseen thing high and far away; one has just swung at a pitch, one is a catcher, and one is another player. Young George Herman Ruth apparently "had this swing" early on. Fourteen such double-page spreads are organized in this engaging way, making it possible to read what is almost two books in one. Children can find repeated ways to enjoy this exciting tribute to the "babe in the woods," which they'll read as the origin of the famous nickname. (Ages 7–11)

Carlson, Laurie. *Boss of the Plains: The Hat that Won the West*. Illustrated by Holly Meade. A Melanie Kroupa Book/DK Ink, 1998. 36 pages. (0–7894–2479–7) $16.95
The creation of the Stetson, the hat that took the west by storm, is the subject of this delightful picture book history. A hatmaker in the East, John Stetson headed toward the West he'd always longed to see when poor health forced him to quit his work. His health improved in the clear western air and he joined the quest for gold in the Colorado hills. The scorching sun convinced him that he needed a better hat than the one he'd brought with him—something that would keep the sun from his eyes and the rain off his back. Something "big and picturesque" he declared, perhaps thinking of the western landscape itself. When a cowboy later offered him a five dollar gold piece for his high-crowned, wide-brimmed creation, the iea was planted for what would eventually become the "Boss of the Plains," the most popular hat west of the Mississippi, and the inspiration for the John B. Stetson hat company, which has gone on to make hats in many styles. Colorful artwork spanning the two-page spreads, a photograph of Stetson with a brief historical note detailing the popularity of his hats and the rapid growth of his Missouri factory, and a bibliography citing the author's sources provide the crowning touches for this volume. (Ages 7–10)

Cornelissen, Cornelia. *Soft Rain: A Story of the Cherokee Trail of Tears.* Delacorte Press, 1998. 115 pages. (0–385–32253–4) $14.95

In May, 1838, countless Tsalagi people were forced by agents of the U.S. government to leave their land in what is now known as North Carolina and three other Southern states. Men, women and children of all ages and health situations were forced to be relocated to "lands set apart for them in the West" in what the U.S. government officially called "the Cherokee Removal." The journey lasted many months, including a severe winter season. That tragic history unfolds here in a third-person narrative. A plucky nine-year-old girl, Soft Rain, is the main character. She reads and writes English, as well as the language created by Sequoyah and written on "talking leaves." Other memorable characters also earmark this historical novel, including Soft Rain's younger brother Hawk Boy, and their parents, grandmother, and courageous Aunt Kee. The author incorporated much dialogue along with cultural details into her story, making her novel fairly easy for young children to read, despite the harsh history she recounts fictionally. The endnote about the Cherokee Nation provides a factual context for the novel. Cornelissen's great-grandfather was about ten when he endured the Trail of Tears. (Ages 9–12)

Deem, James M. *Bodies from the Bog.* Houghton Mifflin, 1998. 42 pages. (0–395–85784–8) $16.00

The nature of most peat bogs causes them to be a perfect preservative for bodies that were buried thousands of years earlier. Occasionally in recent times across Europe, such bodies have been found in peat bogs. Archeologists call this type of mummy a "bog body." One such body discovered in 1952 near Grauballe, Denmark, is known as the Grauballe Man. Experts surmise that he died about 55 BCE, no doubt as a human sacrifice of Iron Age people. Deem discusses the methods utilized by scientists to reconstruct when and how each individual might have lived and died. The book contains archival photographs of skulls and mummified bodies that will fascinate young readers, but Deem does not disrespectfully sensationalize an admittedly quite sensational subject. (Ages 9–14)

Fleming, Candace. *The Hatmaker's Sign: A Story by Benjamin Franklin.* Illustrated by Robert Andrew Parker. Orchard, 1998. 32 pages. (0–531–30075–7) $15.95

Thrilled with his completion of the Declaration of Independence, Thomas Jefferson can't wait to show it to the Continental Congress. "Every word rang. Every sentence sang. Every paragraph flowed with truth." But when the inevitable arguing begins among the delegates over deleting this word here, that sentence there, Jefferson is crushed, and so his good friend Benjamin Franklin tries to console him with a story. The story is about a hatmaker who drafts a sign for his shop and shows it to various family members and friends. Everyone has a suggestion to make about something to cut, and by the time the hatmaker has arrived at the signmaker's shop, his sign is blank. Candace Fleming first discovered this story by Franklin in *The Papers of Thomas Jefferson*, in which Jefferson wrote, "Dr. Franklin perceived I was not insensitive to Congress' mutilation of my document, and tried to reassure me by whispering a parable." She frames her retelling of the amusing parable with a fictionalized recreation of the Jefferson-Franklin encounter in this delightful picture book illustrated with Robert Andrew Parker's full-color paintings in watercolor and ink. (Ages 8–11)

Geisert, Bonnie. *Prairie Town.* **Illustrated by Arthur Geisert. Walter Lorraine Books/Houghton Mifflin, 1998. 32 pages. (0–395–85907–7) $16.00**

A grain elevator connected to the outside world by the sky and a pair of railroad tracks has homes, a few businesses, a school, a post office, a couple of churches, a cemetery surrounding it. This small town located somewhere in the Great Plains of North America during the mid–20th century has all that—and there's more, much more. Evidence of people's routines is everywhere. They do indoor and outdoor work, run their machines, handle errands, and raise seasonal crops. There are occasional changes: a house fire, painting of the water tower, and modifications to a tree house. Puppies are born. The water tower is repainted, a new tombstone appears, and the school playground gets improved. There's a weekly livestock sale, and—sometimes—a visiting carnival. The weather dominates just about everything that happens: winter can be particularly fierce, and the sunsets are sensational. Both Geiserts did the thinking and planning for this unusual glimpse of one community and some of its happenings. Bonnie did most of the writing. Arthur created detailed views of the town in 21 remarkable full-color etchings, ten of which are double-page spreads. Children can look at length to make comparisons and notice differences as the seasons roll past. This affectionate summary of life in a particular small town all year round is a tribute to that way of living for examination from several perspectives. Why did it develop? What has changed? Ask someone who grew up in a similar town, or lives in one now, to respond to this fascinating sequence of images about community. (Ages 5–9)

Gerstein, Mordicai. *Victor: A Novel Based on the Life of the Savage of Aveyron.* **Frances Foster Books/Farrar Straus Giroux, 1998. 258 pages. (0–374–38142–9) $17.00**

Mordicai Gerstein was inspired by François Truffaut's 1970 film *The Wild Child,* about the boy known as the Savage of Aveyron, to research the story of the child who was found living wild in the Aveyron district of France in 1800 and taken to the Institute for Deaf-Mutes in Paris before French physician Jean–Marc Itard took a special interest in him. Gerstein has now created two books for young readers, the young adult novel *Victor* and the picture book *The Wild Boy* (see next entry). In *Victor,* Gerstein writes a detailed and fascinating portrait of this boy and of the efforts of Itard and his housekeeper, Madame Guérin, to teach him how to behave like other human children. For Victor, who had no sense of his own humanness, for Dr. Itard, whose great patience sometimes snapped, and for Madame Guérin, who lavished the boy with love, there were moments of understanding and success, and moments of failure, especially with regard to teaching Victor how to speak. There were other difficulties as Victor grew, especially with regard to his burgeoning sexuality. Ultimately, Itard, whose work with Victor, the author explains in an afterword, is believed by many to have been the start of special education, admitted he had failed Victor. In focusing on trying to teach him how to talk, as he did with the deaf children he worked with at the Institute, he ignored the possibilities of sign language and denied Victor a form of communication that might have come, if not naturally, then much more easily than the speech that he never learned. Gerstein has interspersed his compassionate third-person narrative with brief sections immersed in Victor's point of view that brilliantly illuminate his emerging sense of self and sensitivity, which was always limited by his restricted understanding of the larger world. Victor lived with the loving and nurturing Madame Guérin until he died in 1828. (Age 14 and older)

Gerstein, Mordicai. *The Wild Boy.* Frances Foster Books/Farrar Straus Giroux, 1998. 39 pages. (0–374–38431–2) $16.00

A tender depiction for younger readers of the life of the child who was discovered living wild in the Aveyron district of France in 1800, *The Wild Boy* will also be of interest to those who encounter *Victor*, the book that Gerstein has written for older readers (see previous entry). *The Wild Boy* is a sensitive picture book about this feral child who could not speak and who did not know what it was to be human. What the child did know, as the story opens, is how to live in the woods and how to survive, he knew hunger but also joyful abandon in the falling snow and the feel of the wind. Gerstein has masterfully and movingly related this story and these feelings in both text and stirring art. This child who had never known a caressing touch until physician Jean–Marc Itard and his housekeeper, Madame Guérin, began to care for him came to adore Madame Guérin and to trust the doctor, but he would never learn all that Itard hoped he would and his mind and his memories would always remain a mystery. Gerstein's expressive artwork is so emotionally charged that his visual images alone powerfully convey the essential elements of this superbly written story. (Ages 7–10)

Hansen, Joyce and Gary McGowan. *Breaking Ground, Breaking Silence: The Story of New York's African Burial Ground.* Henry Holt, 1998. 130 pages. (0–8050–5012–4) $17.95

In 1991, while excavating beneath the streets of lower Manhattan, archaeologists unearthed the remains of a male of African descent. It turned out to be the start of a rich discovery of great historical, cultural and spiritual significance—the 18th century African burial ground used by Manhattan's earliest black residents to lay members of their community to rest. As the excavaction of this site unfolds in the pages of this moving and important volume, the authors trace the history of this community and examine the ways in which the discoveries in the burial ground can illuminate the lives of individuals, even when their names aren't known, giving voice to a lost past. Artifacts and burial practices become a means of connecting remains back to a specific African culture, or determining defiance in the continuation of burial practices forbidden by Dutch, and later English, governments of the region. The history of Africans and African Americans in the region and the social and political conditions under which they lived is traced chronologically as the narrative progresses, beginning with the first known arrivals early in the 17th century, who came as slaves of the Dutch, and continuing through the mid 1800s . Black-and-white photographs of burial remains and artifacts along with archival drawings illustrate this volume. An epilogue documents efforts to preserve and protect the burial ground and its remains and the overwhelming significance of this discovery to the African American community, and to us all. (Age 12 and older)

Haskins, James and Kathleen Benson. *African Beginnings.* Illustrated by Floyd Cooper. Lothrop, Lee & Shepard, 1998. 48 pages. (0–688–10256–5) $18.00

The golden tone of Floyd Cooper's lush illustrations convey the rich history of ancient cultures on the African continent, beginning with Nubia in 3800 BCE, which traded in gold, ebony, cattle, and ostrich feathers, and may have been the first culture to advance the idea of divine rulers, and ending with the Empire of the Kongo, which thrived from the 14th century to 1641, when its rulers were defeated by Portuguese armies. Arranged in chronological order according to the years each culture flourished, Haskins and Benson introduce young readers to these subjects, as well as Egypt, Kush and Meroë, Jenne-Jeno, the spread of Islam, Ghana, Mali, Songhay, Timbuktu, Benin, and Great Zimbabwe. Each subject is accorded a double-page spread that includes a brief text and a detailed landscape or city scene that gives a sense of time and place. (Ages 9–12)

Hermann, Spring. *Seeing Lessons: The Story of Abigail Carter and America's First School for Blind People.* Illustrated by Ib Ohlsson. Henry Holt, 1998. 163 pages. (0–8050–5706–4) $15.95
A blind child growing up in the United States could not get a formal education during the 1820s. A medical student from Boston found out about a school for blind pupils in Paris and then worked to develop such a school in New England. That person was John Fisher, the first teacher of his school was Dr. Samuel Howe, and its first pupils included Abby Carter and her sister Sophia. According to a note at the end of this fictionalized story, Abby Carter became one of the best students at what was later called the Perkins Institution for the Blind in Boston, and as an adult she and her sister Sophia traveled to advocate for the rights for all visually handicapped people at state legislatures. Abby became a teacher at Perkins, and later during her life she taught instrumental, vocal and choral music in her home town of Andover, Massachusetts. Hermann drew upon many records to create a story quite easy to read and featuring amazing actual individuals and a significant milestone in the history of education in the United States. (Ages 9–12)

Hines, Gary. *A Christmas Tree in the White House.* Illustrated by Alexandra Wallner. Henry Holt, 1998. 32 pages. (0–8050–5076–0) $15.95
A fictional story loosely based on actual events describes at time in the White House when President Teddy Roosevelt, ever the mindful conservationist, said no to having a Christmas tree. Determined not to miss out on a tree, his two youngest children conspire with their aunt, Anna Roosevelt. When Roosevelt discovers the boys are hiding a tree in their bedroom closet, he takes them to his friend Gifford Pinchot for a lesson in conservation. But it turns out the President has something to learn about conservation from the chief forester as well in this warm and amusing story. The details are not all true, the author points out in a note at the end in which she clarifies what is known fact in addition to providing information on Roosevelt and his family, but she has filled in the outline of a few actual events with the exuberant relationship that Roosevelt had with his children in a story that is illustrated with charming, folk-like, full-color art. (Ages 7–10)

Johnson, Dinah. *All Around Town: The Photographs of Richard Samuel Roberts.* Henry Holt, 1998. 32 pages. (0–8050–5456–1) $15.95
Richard Samuel Roberts, a self-trained studio photographer, was known around Columbia, South Carolina, for his distinguished photographs of the African-American citizenry in the 1920s and 1930s. In addition to weddings, graduations, and family portraits, he photographed baseball teams, magicians, school children, and musicians. Whatever the occasion, the people captured in these photos taken by Mr. Roberts look serious, hopeful and, above all, proud. Dinah Johnson has skillfully arranged the images so that young readers will see them not as a random assortment of old photos, but as one man's life work and legacy. Her brief accompanying text encourages

children to study these mostly anonymous faces and to wonder who they were and what their lives were like. Like an old family photo album, this is a book we want to return to again and again. (Ages 4–12)

Joosse, Barbara. *Lewis & Papa: Adventure on the Sante Fe Trail.* Illustrated by Jon Van Zyle. Chronicle Books, 1998. 32 pages. (0–8118–1959–0) $14.95

When an old traveler spends the night at Lewis's family's cabin near the Wisconsin River, he fills their heads with stories of adventure and the profits to be made in Santa Fe by selling goods from the East. After giving it some thought, Lewis's father decides to fill up his own wagon with goods such as nails and calico, and head west on the Santa Fe Trail to sell them. And, best of all, he decides Lewis is old enough to be of help. Much as he misses Mama and his Wisconsin home, Lewis loves the time he gets to spend with Papa and the other traders in their wagon train. Every other double-page spread includes a small map that shows their progress, as the wagon train face challenges such as heat, river crossings and a buffalo stampede. Through it all, Lewis and Papa grow closer in this story of a warm father-and-son relationship. While children's books about westward movement generally deal with settlers, Joosse's story is unusual for its focus on the trade route, and will be a welcome addition to elementary studies of American history. (Ages 5–9)

Jurmain, Suzanne. *Freedom's Sons: The True Story of the* Amistad *Mutiny.* Lothrop, Lee & Shepard, 1998. 128 pages. (0–688–11072-X) $15.00

In only 77 pages, Jurmain brings the famous *Amistad* mutiny and resulting series of imprisonments and court cases alive for young readers in a way unlike any other account of these events and the people involved. The final one-third of the volume contains information about what is known about what happened to each of the captured Mende men, women and children after they were "freed" to return to West Africa. Detailed source notes and an extensive bibliography of primary and secondary sources distinguishes this history. (Ages 11–16)

Lauber, Patricia. *Painters of the Caves.* National Geographic Society, 1998. 48 pages. (0–7922–7095–9) $17.95

In December, 1994, three people went searching for caves in the limestone hills near Avignon, in southeast France. Following an ancient mule path up a cliff, they noticed a passageway that they crawled into one at a time. At its end they discovered a cave. This was no ordinary cave. They had discovered one in which Stone Age paintings of animals had been preserved. More than 300 such paintings were later documented in what is now named Chauvet Cave after one of the explorers who discovered the long-hidden art created some 32,000 years ago in black, red, and yellow on those rock walls. Thought to be a hoax for a time after it was first discovered, Chauvet Cave is thought to be the oldest record of that type of human creativity found to date in Europe or elsewhere. Lauber writes about what is now known about Stone Age artists and cave art. She clarifies what is generally understood about the first early modern humans and compares them with what is known about the Neanderthals. The book contains full-color photographs of the extraordinary prehistoric animal images in Chauvet Cave. Other photos of artifacts, a helpful map, and information about carbon 14 dating make this subject accessible to young readers. (Ages 9–14)

Lester, Julius. *Black Cowboy, Wild Horses: A True Story.* Illustrated by Jerry Pinkney. Dial, 1998. 40 pages. (0–8037–1787–3) $16.99

Bob Lemmons was a former slave, known to history as a cowboy who was extremely skilled at herding wild horses. In this picture book based on his working life, we follow Bob and his horse, Warrior, as they track down a herd of mustangs, slowly gain their trust, and then lead them back to a corral on the ranch. Jerry Pinkney's dynamic watercolor paintings bring the horses to life with specific, accurate details showing the Great Plains in an earlier era. Julius Lester's exquisitely written text characterizes Bob as a wise and patient man with an instinct for horses. *Honor Book, CCBC Coretta Scott King Award Discussion: Illustrator.* (Ages 7–9)

Lester, Julius. *From Slave Ship to Freedom Road.* Illustrated by Rod Brown. Dial, 1998. 40 pages. (0–8037–1893–4) $17.99

Julius Lester was invited to write a narrative to accompany 21 of Rod Brown's disturbing paintings of scenes from African American history. He was a perfect choice, given his earlier writings about the "slave experience" for young people: *To Be a Slave* (1968), *Long Journey Home* (1972), and *This Strange New Feeling* (1982), all published by Dial. Lester himself made a perfect choice by creating multilayered narratives requiring responses from the viewer/reader. By shaping the book as he did, Lester assumed a basic amount of prior historical knowledge on the part of his readers, whoever they are. He wanted to challenge them to realize they bring their own perspective to the ideas and images in the book. Racism is real, and so is its legacy. Just because this is complicated doesn't imply that young people should not think about it. To encourage interaction with the book's content, Lester developed provocative "imagination excercises." Some are addressed to white people (it's their history, too), and others to African Americans. As readers of all backgrounds are confronted by the paintings, exercises, and other narratives, they react, because it's difficult, if not impossible, to maintain any emotional distance while handling this provocative volume. Lester writes, "Freedom. It's like a promise we are still learning how to keep." *From Slave Ship to Freedom Road* provides a challenging itinerary for one part of a supremely important journey. It's well worth the trip. *Honor Book, 1998 CCBC Coretta Scott King Award Discussion: Author; Honor Book, 1998 CCBC Coretta Scott King Award Discussion: Illustrator.* (Ages 11–15)

McCully, Emily Arnold. *An Outlaw Thanksgiving.* Dial, 1998. 40 pages. (0–8037–2197–8) $15.99

During 1896, Clara and her mother are traveling by train from New York State almost across the continent. Clara's mother worries about "germs, strangers, and train wrecks." During one of the stopovers Clara sees a poster offering a $4,000 reward to the person who turns in Butch Cassidy, an outlaw wanted for train robbery, cattle rustling, and bank robbery. She hears from a train newsboy that Butch Cassidy is "no worse than the robber barons who run these railways" and, furthermore, he's said to be "awfully good-hearted. Gives some of what he steals to needy folks…" Somewhere near the Utah border the train becomes snowbound. Nearby ranchers with sleighs rescue the stranded passengers, some of whom are taken to a small hotel where preparations have been made for Thanksgiving dinner. Clara recognizes one of the friendly cowhands hosting the surprisingly elegant dinner as the man whose picture she saw on the "wanted" poster. According to the author's note, a Thanksgiving dinner with those particular hosts was documented by a former Brown's Hole resident who attended it. McCully is particularly adept at writing an appealing story involving a young protagonist with a believable personality and in creating visual historical settings with carefully costumed characters and environments in which they interact with many others. Her lovely artwork for this splendid story was made using watercolor and tempera. (Ages 5–9)

Myers, Walter Dean. *Amistad: A Long Road to Freedom.* **Dutton, 1998. 99 pages.** (0–525–45970–7) $16.99

Much has been written about the people who were captured in West Africa and sent as part of the slave trade to Cuba, where a new ruling actually made this inhumane commerce illegal. That is why these Mende people were transferred to a ship called *Amistad* where their mutiny, subsequent imprisonment in the United States and ultimate court-won "freedom" was so important to American abolitionists in the early 1840s and later. Written accounts vary in their emphases and uses of documents about this complicated history, but all feature a young man, Sengbe Pieh, known to have been a rice farmer in the village of Mani in Mendeland before he lost his freedom. This man came to be known in America as Cinque, and it's Nathaniel Jocelyn's famous portrait of him on the front cover of this most Afrocentric *Amistad* account. Sengbe's history is documented, which is why he is well known today. The people of the *Amistad* are known because of the precedent-setting court cases ultimately involving former U.S. president John Quincy Adams and other prominent attorneys and politicians of that time, and because of the final Supreme Court decisions affecting the basic human rights. Myers' point of view is crucial and essential, and he writes with arresting style. There is much archival visual information, a list of further readings and an index. *Honor Book, CCBC Coretta Scott King Award Discussion: Author.* (Ages 11–16)

Park, Frances and Ginger Park. *My Freedom Trip: A Child's Escape from North Korea.* **Illustrated by Debra Reid Jenkins. Boyds Mills Press, 1998. 32 pages.** (1–56397–468–1) $15.95

A young girl describes her journey from North to South Korea in this haunting picture book that achingly reveals a small child's fear of leaving what is loved and familiar behind and of journeying into the unknown. Soo's friends have already been disappearing one by one from school, fleeing with their families in the night to the freedom of the south on the eve of the Korean War. When her father tells her that he, too, will be leaving, Soo begs him to stay but he promises her his guide, Mr. Han, will return for her soon, and then for her mother. One by one, he tells her, they will take their freedom trips. When the guide does return for Soo, she must go with this kind stranger into the night, leaving her mother behind and trusting that her father will be waiting at the end of her journey. The authors based the unforgettable story on their own mother's childhood. Their prose is as hushed and tense as a child in fear as Soo and Mr. Han move through the dangerous darkness, and Debra Reid Jenkins soft, somber-toned paintings underscore the emotional weight of the story. A key is provided to the Korean words used in the text and the Korean characters that appear as part of the design of each quiet, elegant two-page spread. (Ages 8–10)

Pferdehirt, Julia. *Freedom Train North: Stories of the Underground Railroad in Wisconsin.* **Illustrated by Jerry Butler.** Living History Press (7426 Elmwood Avenue, Middleton, WI 53562), 1998. 116 pages. Pbk. (0–9664925–0–1) $12.00 ($10.00 for schools and libraries)

A history of Wisconsin's involvement in the underground railroad perfect for fourth grade readers but of interest to many others as well draws on extensive research to present real-life stories of African Americans who sought refuge in Wisconsin during the time of slavery or who passed through the state on their way to freedom and individuals in the state, both black and white, who helped them. Pferdehirt emphasizes the intense desire for self-determination among African Americans that fueled the abolitionist movement and makes it clear that these were people intent on freeing themselves, although the assistance of white and black abolitionists became critical once an individual made the decision to run. Drawing an important distinction between what is known and what must be conjectured about the individual lives and events she describes, she explains in her introduction that "when a story includes spoken words, those words were actually said or written by these people many years ago. Thoughts and feelings described were also recorded by the people who experienced them. However, when personal accounts were not recorded you may be asked to imagine how people felt and thought." Underground Railroad activity in Wisconsin was not nearly as common as in states farther south and east, but Pferdehirt has retold events that happened across the eastern and central part of the state, from Beloit to Green Bay, Madison to Milwaukee, in towns both small and large. Specific communities mentioned in the stories are pictured on a map at the beginning of the book. Black-and-white reproductions of powerful paintings by Jerry Butler that depict scenes from a number of the stories, and black-and-white photographs of historical pictures and documents, bring added interest to each of the stories detailed. This singular volume also includes an extensive bibliography of sources and a chapter-by-chapter list of suggested books and web sites where readers can learn more about the specific events and the underground railroad in general. One copy of the book, which was funded by the Wisconsin Sesquicentennial Commission, has been distributed to each public and most private elementary and middle schools in Wisconsin, and to every Wisconsin public library. (Ages 9–14)

Pringle, Laurence. *One Room School.* **Illustrated by Barbara Garrison. Boyds Mills Press, 1998. 32 pages. (1–56397–583–1) $15.95**

In 1944 Miss Schackelton taught all subjects to all in the eight grades in School 14 somewhere in rural New York State. Some grades had as many as five pupils, and the third grade that year had only one. Basing this account on his boyhood experience in that one room school, Pringle writes, "She taught us all to read and write and multiply. She taught us the history of New York State, where we lived, and about the war that troubled the world at the time." Older children helped younger ones. Everyone had to concentrate while others were taught, and it could be interesting to listen, too. That fall Miss Schackelton read a long book aloud to the entire school. On days when the weather was too severe for recess, she conducted contests such as spelling bees. It wasn't unusual for a teacher to mete out individual punishment with a ruler in those years. A bookmobile, doctor, and dental hygienist made occasional visits to the school. There was always a Christmas pageant for which each pupil learned a poem or song. As an adult, Pringle writes books about nature for young people. He attributes "the roots of his concern about nature" to the chances he had to observe, enjoy and learn about the natural world in his former one room school. Today's young readers will point out ways in which their classrooms are like that one room school and also how they are different. Garrison's note explains how she created the full-color illustrations placed on each tan page to simulate pictures from a 1940s photo album; they are collagraphs (i.e., collage-graphics), a type of etching. (Ages 5–9)

Rubin, Susan Goldman. *Toilets, Toasters, and Telephones: The How and Why of Everyday Objects.* Illustrated by Elsa Warnick. Browndeer Press/Harcourt Brace, 1998. 132 pages. (0–15–201421–7) $20.00

How often do we think of a toilet or refrigerator or even a pen as a feat of engineering? How about as a work of art? As the author of this intriguing volume notes in her introduction, "Every day people use toilets, sinks, toothbrushes, clocks, telephones, TVs, refrigerators, ovens, toasters, trash cans, vacuum cleaners, hangers, paper clips, zippers, safety pins, pencils, and pens. These objects are so familiar we take them for granted. But how did these things come to look the way they do?" Susan Goldman Rubin's fascinating exploration of the history of many of these now common, everyday objects reveals that some of them have gone through enormous changes over decades, and sometimes centuries, to arrive at the way they look and function today. They are the product of what we now call industrial design, the marriage of form and function. Rubin's book is a delightful, eye-opening look at how industrial design has come to embrace not only ever-changing technological discoveries, but also shifting aesthetic sensibilities with regard to shape, color, line and other aspects of the decorative arts. Her colorful narrative documents some of the major changes in the development of various items in addition to chronicling how the way they are used has changed over time. Black-and-white photographs and drawings of the items illustrate each chapter, and while more of these would have been welcome, this is still a unique book with broad appeal that will be of special interest to students with an interest in art, engineering, or fact-collecting. (Ages 12–16)

Santiago, Chiori. *Home to Medicine Mountain.* Illustrated by Judith Lowry. Children's Book Press (246 First Street, Suite 101, San Francisco, CA 94105), 1998. 32 pages. (0–89239–155–3) $15.95

This picture book recounts one experience of the many endured by children who were made to attend a boarding school for Indian youth. This one took place during the 1930s in California. That was not the only place or time in which Indian children were separated from their families and made to attend U.S. government-operated schools hundreds of miles from their homes. The basis of this picture story rests in the actual life events of Lowry's father and uncle as boys, Stanley and Benny Len, who were completely cut off from their people, birth language, and value system. They were punished if they forgot to speak English, and the punishment was probably more harsh than the wooden ruler pictured here. When these boys learned that they had no way to get home for the summer and, instead, would have to stay at school and work, they used their ingenuity and courage to come up with a way to get home. A color photo of Lowry's father and uncle as men today concludes the story of how these two boys from the Mountain Maidu tribe actually did ride on the top of a railroad car all the way to Medicine Mountain in order to return home. The story for younger children only touches lightly on the surface of the Indian boarding school experience, an experience that inflicted deep pain and lifelong trauma on thousands and that is sometimes referred in other accounts as an attempt at genocide. (Ages 6–9)

Tarbescu, Edith. *Annushka's Voyage.* **Illustrated by Lydia Dabcovich. Clarion, 1998. 32 pages. (0–395–64366-X) $15.00**

Annushka and her little sister, Tanya, are traveling alone to America. Their father has sent them their tickets for passage and waits for them in New York. Excitement mingles with sadness as they say goodbye to their grandparents in Russia, and then it is up to Annushka to take care of them both as they make their way to Holland by train and then board the great steamer that will take them across the ocean. This story of two young Jewish sisters making the long journey to a new land is based on the experiences of the author's mother, who fled the persecution of Jews in Russia during the late 1800s when she was 13 years old. The full-color illustrations, rendered in pen-and-ink, acrylic and colored pencil, heighten the sense of what it might have felt like to be so small and alone among so many unknown people and in so many unfamiliar places on a journey that joyfully reunites them with their father but takes them far away from others whom they love. (Ages 7–10)

Viola, Herman J. *It Is a Good Day to Die: Indian Eyewitnesses Tell the Story of the Battle of the Little Bighorn.* **Crown, 1998. 100 pages. (0–517–70912–0) $18.00**

For more than 100 years, the Battle of Little Big Horn has been perplexing to white Americans who felt that their military power was far superior to that of Lakota and Cheyenne warriors. How could General George Custer and his troops have been so soundly defeated? To provide some answers and to recount the battle from a distinctively Native point of view, Herman J. Viola has compiled recorded first-person accounts from 13 Native warriors, and has arranged the 36 brief passages in chronological order, so that one gets a strong sense of the battle as a whole by reading the entire narrative. In addition to the reports of Lakota and Cheyenne witnesses, Viola has also included occasional accounts from Crow and Arikara scouts who served in Custer's cavalry unit to describe actions on the American side. He also includes a clear introduction and epilogue, black-and-white photographs of some of the people involved, short biographical passages for each of the narrators, a chronology of events, and note on his sources. (Age 11 and older)

See also: *Bat 6; Bat Boy and His Violin; Choosing Up Sides; Discovering the Inca Ice Maiden; Duke Ellington; Fire, Bed, & Bone; Gib Rides Home; i see the rhythm; Journey Home; Katarína; Kinderlager; Lacrosse; Let My People Go; Pioneer Girl; Shakespeare Stealer; Snowflake Bentley; Soldier's Heart; This Land Is Your Land; Warrior Artists; Witnesses to War; entries in section on Biography/Autobiography*

Biography / Autobiography

Anderson, William, compiler. *Laura's Album: A Remembrance Scrapbook of Laura Ingalls Wilder.* HarperCollins, 1998. 80 pages. (0–06–027842–0) $19.95
Arranged in chapters covering ten-year increments beginning with the decade when Laura Ingalls Wilder's parents first met and married in Wisconsin in the 1850s and ending with Laura's death in 1957, this scrapbook biography is a treasury that will please and fascinate Laura fans of any age. The easygoing, accessible biographical narrative is laid out on pages that are decorated with photographs of Laura and her family, greeting cards, letters, postcards and other memorabilia related to her life and the times in which she lived. Pa's fiddle, drawings he made for Laura and Mary, and the music box Laura received one Christmas are among the items pictured from the early years of her life along with family photographs. More photographs, newspaper clippings, marriage announcements, Laura's books, and fan letters she received are included as the narrative advances. Detailed captions describe the photographs and memorabilia, tying them to a specific incident or incidents in Laura's books when possible. A chronology of significant dates and events related to Laura's life is also included along with credits for each of the illustrations that will enable serious Laura Ingalls Wilder devotees to trace where the actual item can be viewed today. While the typface is fairly small, there is much to pour over and discover in this handsomely designed volume. (Age 9 and older)

Butler, Jerry. *A Drawing in the Sand: A Story of African American Art.* Zino Press, 1998. 62 pages. (1–55933–216–6) $24.95
Madison artist and teacher Jerry Butler chronicles his journey to becoming an artist and moments of social and political awakening throughout his life in this autobiographical volume that also draws attention to the realities of race in America in Butler's lifetime and explores the history of African American art. Butler writes about his childhood in Magnolia, Mississippi, where he first learned to draw with a stick in the red, sandy dirt, and where, early on, his grandmother called him an artist, affirming his talent and his ability, nurturing his belief in himself. Butler was nurtured in many ways other ways as he grew as well, enriched by the unity of his small black community. Leaving there to go to college at Jackson State, his world opened up by exposure to many black artists. He notes that it wasn't until he had graduated from college in 1968 that he really began to learn about racism, although he had learned in his childhood about the dangers of talking back to white people. As his education continued at UW–Madison, Butler began to integrate his growing social and political awareness into his art. Today, he notes, "My art now looks at how racism has affected all people in America." Brief biographical profiles of numerous African American artists and selections of their work are incorporated throughout this dynamic volume. It would have been helpful to have Butler's own artwork consistently labeled, and the all-capital-letter typeface will not be inviting to every reader, but this does not detract from the overall importance and appeal of this fine work. (Age 12 and older)

Dingle, Derek T. *First in the Field: Baseball Hero Jackie Robinson.* Hyperion, 1998. 48 pages. (0–7868–2289–9) $16.95
There have been several biographies written for young readers about Jackie Robinson in recent years but Derek T. Dingle offers a unique perspective

with this slender volume that combines appealing graphics and engaging prose. Every page includes at least one documentary photograph to give children a sense of the times in which Robinson lived, in addition to pictures of the subject himself, from infancy to retirement. Beginning with Robinson's two childhood heroes—Joe Louis and his own older brother, Mack Robinson, himself an Olympic Medal winner—we learn about the development of this gifted young athlete who excelled in football, basketball, baseball and track at UCLA; who demonstrated his leadership ability and commitment to social justice while serving as a lieutenant in the U.S. Army during World War II; and who learned a lot about baseball while playing for the Kansas City Monarchs after the War, competing against great players such as Cool Papa Bell, Josh Gibson and Satchel Paige. The text places Jackie Robinson in the context of social history, so that today's children can see the obstacles he faced in his life and his career. While the author obviously admires Jackie Robinson and his accomplishments a great deal, he avoids sentimentalizing or deifying him, allowing instead for the facts to speak for themselves. (Ages 7–12)

Duggleby, John. *Story Painter: The Life of Jacob Lawrence.* Chronicle, 1998. **55 pages. (0–8118–2082–3) $16.95**
When he was still a boy, Jacob Lawrence moved with his family from the South to Harlem, like countless African Americans looking for a better life early in the 20th century. He had begun to draw and paint at an early age, and folks always told him he had talent. In Harlem he found a community of like-minded artists who encouraged the talented teenager, in particular, sculptor Augusta Savage, who served as his mentor. Outside Harlem, however, he faced the sorts of obstacles familiar to many African-American men in his era who were trying to gain acceptance in a segregated nation. Through it all, he committed himself and his art to the subjects he knew and loved: his people's past and present. There is a reproduction of a Jacob Lawrence painting on every double-page spread of this attractively designed, accessible biography of the African-American painter. (Ages 9–14)

Freedman, Russell. *Martha Graham: A Dancer's Life.* Clarion, 1998. **175 pages. (0–395–74655–8) $18.00**
Martha Graham's life and work as a dancer, teacher, and choreographer helped shape and define American dance in the 20th century. In a way like no one before her had, Graham explored how dance could express the raw emotion, passion and delight of human experience, and she created works that were drawn deeply from the space where intellect and emotion combined. Russell Freedman's understanding of that space, and the unquestioned drive that compels an artist to create, defines this portrait of the dancer. The text moves easily from sketches of Graham's life off the stage to explanations of her dancing philosophy to descriptions of her groundbreaking, energizing performances. The result is a book giving young readers a sense of the ordinary and the extraordinary, the knowledge of Graham as an driven artist who also sewed her own costumes when there was no money for help, and whose heart could reach out–or break–just like anyone else's. Dramatic black-and-white photographs of Graham performing add to the artistry of the book as a whole while powerfully illustrating the intense emotional elements of Graham's work. Together, the text and photos provide a rich introduction to the deep layers of meaning in Graham's dances.

Additional photographs show Graham in aspects of her life off the stage and behind the scenes and include a remarkable picture of Helen Keller among the dancers in Graham's studio, her face a study in joy as she feels the rhythm and movement of dance. This well-researched , well-documented biography will speak to the artist, the visionary, the dreamer and the doer in many young adults. (Ages 12–16)

Greenberg, Jan and Sandra Jordan. *Chuck Close Up Close.* DK Ink, 1998. 48 pages. (0–7894–2486-X) $19.95

As a child, Chuck Close struggled in school. Learning disabilities that would not be diagnosed until he was an adult made academic work a difficult challenge. But he loved to draw and paint, and it was through art that he found solace and self-confidence. As an adult, Close's artwork has brought him him great critical acclaim, and in this fascinating profile of the artist Jan Greenberg and Sandra Jordan examine his development as an artist and as an individual, looking at the way his life and art relate to and inform one another. The authors approach the text as a means to understanding the artist's work and their highly appealing narrative is enhanced by Close's own insights into his artistic development. This open, airy volume will draw readers in visually as well. The text is surrounded by ample white space and illuminated by color reproductions of a number of Close's paintings, from his earlier, hyperrealistic work to his more recent portraits that emerge from intriguing compilations of color and shape. Photographs of Close at work bring a sense of scale to the artwork—he is a figure overwhelmed by the size of the art he creates. Observant readers will also discover in the photographs something that isn't revealed until quite late in the chronological narrative—today Close works from a wheelchair. In 1988 a rare illness left him almost completely paralyzed. Close eventually regained very limited use of is arms and legs and he now paints with a brush strapped to his arm, continuing to express his unique artistic vision. (Ages 10–14)

Hansen, Joyce. *Women of Hope: African Americans Who Made a Difference.* Scholastic Press, 1998. 32 pages. (0–590–93973–4) $16.95

Brief biographical essays of 12 African American women stress the challenges each one faced and the barriers she broke down in her lifetime. A one-page essay for each woman is accompanied by a stunning black-and-white photographic portrait; all were originally part of a series of posters printed and distributed by the Bread and Roses Cultural Project. The elegantly produced volume includes: Ida B. Wells-Barnett, the Delany Sisters, Septima Poinsette Clark, Ella Josephine Baker, Fannie Lou Hamer, Ruby Dee, Maya Angelou, Toni Morrison, Marian Wright Edelman, Alice Walker, Alexa Canady, and Mae C. Jemison. (Ages 8–14)

Leapman, Michael. *Witness to War: Eight True-Life Stories of Nazi Persecution.* U.S. edition: Viking, 1998. 128 pages. (0–670–87386–1) $16.99

The experiences of eight children who suffered at the hands of the Nazis are cogently related in a book that includes many documentary photographs and clear historical backgrounds for context. Seven of the eight lived to tell their stories; the eighth was Anne Frank. Each of the children represents a different kind of persecution and method of survival. Beate Siegel, the daughter of a prominent Jewish lawyer, was sent at age 14 to live with a family in England as part of the *Kindertransport.* Alexander Michelowksi was one of the thousands of Polish children snatched from their homes to be "Germanized" and adopted into German families. Barbara Richter was a Bohemian gypsy child who was sent to Auschwitz, where she was subjected to experiments conducted by Dr. Mengele. Joseph Steiner and his older sister, Ania, escaped the Warsaw ghetto just hours before it was obliterated by the Germans and lived by their wits for the next few years, sometimes serving as a messengers for the Polish Resistance. All of the stories are as gripping as they are heartbreaking, and most were gathered firsthand by the author. A recent photograph of each survivor is included at the end his or her story. (Age 11 and older)

Lobel, Anita. *No Pretty Pictures: A Child of War.* Greenwillow, 1998. 193 pages. (0–688–15935–4) $16.00

Caldecott-award-winning illustrator Anita Lobel writes about "a time from when I have very few pretty pictures to remember." Born in Krakow in 1934, Lobel was five when the German army invaded Poland in 1939 and began rounding up the city's Jewish population. Anita and her brother escaped the city with their beloved Catholic nanny, Niania, and spent much of the war moving from place to place with her, posing as her children. For Anita, who had dark, heavy features, the charade was devastating. "Every time I looked at myself in the mirror, all I could think was: Jew, Jew. Ugly, obvious Jew girl." Eventually captured, she was held first in Plaszów and then in Ravensbrück before being liberated in 1945. Seriously ill with tuberculosis, Anita was taken to Sweden to recuperate, and there she was reunited with her brother and parents, all of who had, miraculously, survived. This account of Anita's experiences during World War II and in the months and years immediately following is significant not only as an addition to the important body of literature that bears witnesses to the tragic events of the time but also as a profile of an artist who has gone on to create images that bring pleasure to children. (Age 12 and older)

Lowry, Lois. *Looking Back: A Book of Memories.* Walter Lorraine Books/Houghton Mifflin, 1998. 181 pages. (0–395–89543-X) $16.00

Lois Lowry offers an album filled with memories, feelings and fragments from her past in this singular autobiographical compilation of photographs and reminiscences. In the process, this acclaimed author for children uncovers the roots of some of her story ideas. Lowry's photographs and commentary are arranged in short thematic chapters, each of which begins with a quote from one of her novels. The connection between the quote and the photographs and personal stories that follow them are not always obvious, but here Lowry makes profound sense of it all nonetheless. After all, this is a book about ideas and the creative process as much as it is about her life, and stories rarely emerge fully developed out of a single event in a writer's experience. What emerges as the chapters progress is a sense of the writer's constant effort to make sense and story out what has happened in her life, to weave past and present into something new and original that is fiction, but with the heart of human experience at its core. There is a sense of sitting down one on one with the author as she shares these photographs, memories and musings in the casual tone of a narrative that speaks directly to the individual reader. The writing is intimate, with deep appreciation for the importance that human connections hold, including, or perhaps espeically, the one between the author and the individual readers of this book. (Age 10 and older)

Lyons, Mary E., editor. *Talking with Tebé: Clementine Hunter, Memory Artist.*
Houghton Mifflin, 1998. 48 pages. (0–395–72031–1) $16.00

Clementine Hunter was a sharp, dynamic, talented artist who lived to be 101. In all those years, Clementine, or Tebé (TEE-bay), as her family called her, never moved from the Cane River region of Louisiana where she was born. Indeed, she rarely even traveled out of the area. But her paintings are in collections across the country, praised for their honest, unsentimental depiction of African American life in the rural south, where, years after the Civil War, many blacks, Tebé included, labored long, hard days year-in and year-out on plantations for wages that would never let them know a life beyond poverty. It is Tebé's own distinctive voice, dancing with expression, that relates the story of her life and her art in this stunning book edited by Mary E. Lyons that includes numerous color reproductions of Tebé's vibrant folk-art paintings. Lyons gathered quotations from magazines, newspapers, and taped interviews to piece together these commentaries by the self-taught artist who had almost no formal schooling, could neither read nor write, but whose head was filled with images that would not leave her alone until she had turned them into pictures. Tebé depicted the harsh life of labor, picking cotton in the fields, cutting cane, gathering figs, and also the ways in which the African American community came together in celebration and mourning, or relaxed in their precious times of leisure. Her paintings were done at the end of long days of work as field laborer or house cook, and even after her fame begin to grow she did not make a living from her art and worried about keeping up payments on the small trailer she moved into after leaving the plantation. Lyons has done a masterful job piecing together Tebé's words in the various chapters, which are arranged around themes in her painting and events in her life, and she has skillfully and sensitively framed those words with an opening editor's note and chapter and a closing commentary in this richly satisfying volume. (Age 12 and older)

McKissack, Patricia C. and Fredrick L. McKissack. *Young, Black and Determined: A Biography of Lorraine Hansberry.* **Holiday House, 1998. 152 pages. (0–8234–1300–4) $18.95**

A compelling profile of the playwright and activist who died so young but left a legacy of art and ideas and a passion for life that speaks directly to young and old today. Born in 1930, Lorraine Hansberry lived in highly charged social and political times. Growing up in the black upper class on Chicago's south side where African Americans from all socio-economic classes lived together heightened her sensitivity to issues of race and class in our nation, and her understanding of both the pride and terrible hurt of generations of African Americans. She moved to Harlem at age 20 and joined a thriving African-American intellectual and artistic community that included W.E.B. DuBois, Langston Hughes, James Baldwin, Alice Childress, and others. The McKissacks' biography is a song of praise to the brilliant mind and compassionate heart of Hansberry, who is best known for her groundbreaking play *A Raisin in the Sun.* It is a song that finds the intricate notes of Hansberry's life and sounds them against the complex melody of the times in which she lived, a melody that Hansberry herself contributed to, and sometimes countered, in plays, articles, and commentaries she wrote, and in the ideas she sounded. Their thorough research includes interviews with individuals who knew Hansberry, who died of cancer at the age of 34 in 1965, and an analysis of the importance of her work, especially *A Raisin in the Sun,* that is presented as part of the text. This uplifting work takes its cue from Hansberry herself, whose drive and determination to live her own dream and speak the truth is inspirational. (Ages 11–15)

Martin, Jacqueline Briggs. *Snowflake Bentley.* **Illustrated by Mary Azarian. Houghton Mifflin, 1998. 32 pages. (0–395–86162–4) $16.00**

"In the days when farmers worked with ox and sled and cut the dark with lantern light, there lived a boy who loved snow more than anything else in the world." That boy was Willie Bentley, who lived in a part of Vermont where the annual snowfall is reported to be 120 inches. He was eager to learn, reading every volume of the family encyclopedias and keeping a record of the weather. He was especially fascinated by snowflakes. At 15, he began trying to capture the elusive snow crystals by looking at them under an old microscope and then drawing the beauty and individuality he observed. Bentley's passion about snowflakes was often misunderstood. "Neighbors laughed...'Snow in Vermont is as common as dirt,' they said. 'We don't need pictures.' Willie said the photographs would be his gift to the world." He felt called to photograph a leaf or spider web hung with dew. On the final page, Bentley's own words point out that although there were always others who would rise at dawn to milk dairy herds, his early morning work gave people something they otherwise would never have. Children may read either a story or a biography about this self-taught expert who developed his own technique of microphotography, because this book has two narratives. On the left and/or right side of most pages of the fiction, there is easy-to-read biographical information. Azarian's woodcuts, hand tinted with watercolors, serve as illustrations for everything in this intriguing picture book about a man who "loved the beauty of nature in all seasons." (Ages 6–9)

Matthews, Tom L. *Light Shining through the Mist: A Photobiography of Dian Fossey.* National Geographic Society, 1998. 64 pages. (0–7922–7300–1) $17.95

How far can a person's passion take them? For Dian Fossey, it carried her all the way from Kentucky to the Virunga Mountains in central Africa, to a job for which she had no formal training but for which she possessed a passionate interest. Tom L. Matthews captures Fossey's passion as well as her intelligence and integrity in this fine photobiography illustrated with numerous color photographs of Fossey at work among the African mountain gorillas. When she was chosen by Dr. Louis Leakey to study the gorillas, Fossey was already intensely intrigued by these animals. But she was not a scientist. She studied on her own and, once established in the isolated mountain region where the gorillas roam, she observed and documented their lives and relationships with painstaking patience and care. Eventually, she was trusted and accepted by the gorillas themselves, and she became a passionate advocate on their behalf, taking on poachers, herders, and the government of Rwanda as she sought to protect them from harm. Her position-protect the gorillas at all costs-was not a popular one, even among many of her colleagues, but it was born out of her respect for and devotion to the gentle gorillas. A sensitive, compassionate narrative touches briefly on Fossey's childhood and young adulthood before focusing on the life's work she began at age 34 and carried out until she was killed by an unknown attacker at her mountain camp in 1985. (Ages 11–14)

Meltzer, Milton. *Ten Queens: Portraits of Women of Power.* **Illustrated by Bethanne Andersen. Dutton, 1998. 134 pages. (0–525–45643–0) $24.99**

While we know that women from all walks of life and all economic classes have exhibited strength in myriad ways throughout history, it is the names and lives of noblewoman, leaders and rulers that tend to be known. Here, Milton Meltzer presents brief biographical portraits of ten such women, all of them queens who either "ruled in their own right" or, if they held the monarchy in conjunction with a spouse, "had as much or more to say about governing than their husbands." The ten queens are Esther, Cleopatra, Boudicca, Zenobia, Eleanor of Aquitaine, Isabel of Spain, Elizabeth I, Christina of Sweden, Maria Theresa and Catherine the Great. These monarchs, the author notes in his introduction, "like most people everywhere, at whatever time...were a mix of elements: complex, contradictory, unpredictable," sometimes working on behalf of the people they ruled, sometimes conspiring against them. In both his narrative about each woman and in his note on sources, Meltzer makes it clear that facts are sometimes scarce and history, including these histories, must sometimes resort to speculation and conjecture. A bibliography and index round out the information presented in this handsome volume graced with Bethanne Andersen's lilting artwork that includes a portrait of each queen and illustrations depicting aspects of the narrative. (Ages 11–14)

Nieuwsma, Milton J. *Kinderlager: An Oral History of Young Holocaust Survivors.* **Holiday House, 1998. 161 pages. (0–8234–1358–6) $18.95**

"Kinderlager" refers to a section of Auschwitz-Birkenau that was reserved for children. Few survived it. The three women whose personal stories comprise this volume were among the youngest Holocaust survivors; indeed, Tova Friedman was just six years old when the camp was liberated. Her memories of the Holocaust and its aftermath, as well as those of her family friends, Frieda Tenenbaum and Rachel Hyams, are recounted in detail in an extraordinary oral history, collected by journalist Milton Nieuwsma. The narrative is made even more powerful by the cumulation of details as each girl's first-person account mentions the other two, since their paths frequently crossed. Thus, we get to know them all as they see themselves and as others see them. Illustrated throughout with family pictures, past and present. (Age 13 and older)

Partridge, Elizabeth. *Restless Spirit: The Life and Work of Dorothea Lange.* **Viking, 1998. 122 pages. (0–670–87888-X) $19.99**

From the spirited, life-embracing black-and-white image of Dorothea Lange on the title page to the many striking reproductions of her powerful and socially relevant photographs to the illuminating text, this biography of the pioneering photographer is stimulating both visually and intellectually. As a child, author Elizabeth Partridge knew Dorothea Lange—both her grandfather and her father worked with Lange and the Partridges were part of Lange's close circle of friends and family. In researching this biography Elizabeth Partridge interviewed a number of those family members and friends in addition to drawing on a large body of published material to compose an insightful and inspiring portrait of Lange for young readers. Lange is seen as a sensitive, passionate child who realized from a young age that she saw and felt things more deeply than many other people. Determined to learn photography, as a financially struggling college student she walked into the studio of one of the best-known photographers in New York City and asked for a job. She learned how to take portraits, but it was with the onset of the Depression that she embarked on her life's work, taking pictures of everyday people, letting their dignity, their beauty, and sometimes their tragedy rise from the image, whether she was photographing destitute men in a bread line in California, a young black sharecropper in the South, or Japanese Americans who had been interned by the U.S. government. Especially in her earlier years but throughout her career, Lange struggled to maintain a balance between her personal and professional lives, sometimes sacrificing her art for the sake of her first husband's career and her children, and sometimes making the difficult choice to put her own needs first. Partridge astutely makes clear that every choice had its price to pay for all involved in this fine biography that lets the complex character and deep compassion of Dorothea Lange breathe freely on its pages. (Age 11 and older)

Pinkney, Andrea Davis. *Duke Ellington: The Piano Prince and His Orchestra.* **Illustrated by Brian Pinkney. Hyperion, 1998. 32 pages. (0–7868–2150–7) $16.49**

When he was a boy, Edward Kennedy Ellington's first love was baseball. At his parents' insistence, he took piano lessons and, by the time he was 19, music was his passion. He was able to earn his living by playing his own compositions — a type of music no one had ever heard before. This picture book biography focuses not so much on the events in Duke Ellington's life, but on his music, his orchestra, his skill with improvisation, and his impact in the world of jazz. Andrea Davis Pinkney's text grabs young listeners with its jazzy beat. Her playful use of language echoes the era in which Duke was king. Like the words they accompany, Brian Pinkney's spirited scratchboard illustrations swing with joyful vitality as they show the effect Ellington's music has had on listeners, past and present. *Winner, 1998 CCBC Coretta Scott King Award Discussion: Illustrator; Honor Book, 1998 CCBC Coretta Scott King Award Discussion: Author.* (Ages 7–11)

Rabinovici, Schoschana. *Thanks to My Mother.* **Translated from the German by James Skofield. U.S. edition: Dial, 1998. 246 pages. (0–8037–2235–4) $17.99**

"On June 22, 1941, I saw my father for the last time." These stark, striking words begin an amazing story of strength and survival in this Holocaust memoir. Soschana Rabinovici was born Susanne Weksler in 1932. In 1941, the Germans invaded her Lithuanian homeland. At first Susie and her mother and other relatives move into her grandparents house, where they hear frightening stories of Jews around the city being rounded up and taken away. But it's not long before they are forced into the Vilnius ghetto with thousands of other Jews, where the days are marked by mounting fear and growing horror despite the heroic efforts of the Jewish resistance. In 1943, the ghetto was liquidated, and Susie, her mother and her older sister are placed on a transport train heading to the camps. Over the next three years, Susie's mother saves her daughter over and over again through her ingenuity and fearlessness as they are moved from one cruel camp to another, and then forced on a brutal death march in the winter of 1945. In the end, Susie saves her mother, too, by infusing her with a will to live after they are liberated and her mother's sick body weary mind cannot go on. The vivid imagery of this memoir is intense and striking—there is such immediacy in the writing that one feels the panic of suffocation in the cattle cars, the hopeless resignation of those who no longer had the will to fight. Some of these individuals surrendered to certain death by the simple act of refusing to stand up or move, fully aware of what they were doing as the guards took aim. Susie's stepsister is one of those she witnesses committing this traumatic but understandable form of escape. Beneath it all there is aching pain, and the fierce determination of Susie's mother to keep her daughter alive. *Winner, 1998 CCBC Batchelder Discussion.* (Age 13 and older)

Sís, Peter. *Tibet: Through the Red Box.* **Frances Foster Books/Farrar Straus Giroux, 1998. 58 pages. (0–374–37552–6) $25.00**
When Peter Sís was a child in Prague, his father, Vladimir, traveled to Tibet as a documentary filmmaker and became stranded in that mysterious country. His family did not know what had happened to him, and for the boy Peter a sense of absence marked the time that followed. It is not clear how long it was until his father's return—was he gone for more than one Christmas, or did one Christmas without his presence make an indelible impression that shadows Sís's memories of other childhood holidays? In *Tibet: Through the Red Box,* Peter Sís weaves his own dreamlike memories into a book that also imagines the details of his father's experiences in Tibet during the time he was missing from young Peter's life. On a trek across Tibet in search of a means to return home, the father's journey as chronicled in a diary is no less dreamlike than the son's own memories as he experiences the extraordinary nature of that mystical place and travels toward the forbidden city of Lhasa ever more intent on warning the young Dalai Lama of the inevitable, tragic changes he senses the approaching Chinese will bring. The adult Peter Sís is both character in and creator of this unique artistic and literary journey that gracefully blurs the lines between fact and dream. Summoned by his father to his childhood home, Sís reads his father's diaries and is transported back to his own childhood and into his missing father's life, in the process finally filling the hole that the older man's absence had left during that time. The mystical quality of the narrative is echoed in the multilayered artwork, which is filled with details inspired by Tibetan culture and cast in deep, ever-changing hues. (Age 11 and older)

Stanley, Diane. *Joan of Arc.* **Morrow, 1998. 48 pages. (0–688–14330-X) $15.93**
This artfully illustrated biography of the French religious martyr pairs detailed text and artwork rendered in a glowing, almost luminous palette evocative of illuminated manuscripts from medieval times. Stanley begins with a brief history of the Hundred Years War to provide historical context for the story of Joan's life that follows. This history, along with additional explanations provided throughout the narrative, allows readers to enter the text more fully, understanding and accepting Joan's religious beliefs and her resulting actions rather than finding her visions, her passions and her devotion improbable. Each two-page spread features text bordered in gold and graced with a detail illustration on the left side and a full-page, gold-bordered illustration on the right. A pronunciation guide tells how to say the many names of French people and places that are mentioned throughout the book, while a bibliography and recommended reading list round out this elegant volume. (Ages 11–14)

Thomas, Jane Resh. *Behind the Mask: The Life of Queen Elizabeth I.* Clarion, 1998. 196 pages. (0–395–69120–6) $19.00

Elizabeth I ruled England for over 40 years, during a tumultuous period filled with danger for anyone in power, especially a woman who was called whore, bastard and heretic from the day she was born. But like her father, Henry VIII, Elizabeth was quick-witted, intelligent, and skeptical, characteristics that always put her a step or two ahead of her friends and her enemies. The princess's first-hand observation of the many power struggles that occurred during her childhood and adolescence helped her to grasp the importance of outward appearances: she consciously created a public persona and used it to her advantage throughout her reign. Based on documents written about Elizabeth and her times, both during her life and afterwards, Jane Resh Thomas has created an intriguing, accessible biography that strives to provide a portrait of the complex woman who is now regarded as one of England's greatest rulers. (Age 12 and older)

Warren, Andrea. *Pioneer Girl: Growing Up on the Prairie.* Morrow, 1998. 95 pages. (0–688–15438–7) $15.00

Grace McCance was only three years old in 1885, the year her father filed a homestead claim for 160 wide-open acres of Nebraska land. Years later, in the memoir she wrote as an adult, Grace could still recall her first glimpse of that prairie homestead: "Just two naked little soddies squatting on a bare, windswept ridge . . . Not another building in sight, not a tree, not an animal, nothing but grassy flats and hills." The story of Grace's childhood and young adulthood echoes that of many children whose famlies had the courage, determination, and desire to stake a claim for a place of their own in the breathtaking, unforgiving landscape of the Great Plains during the second half of the 19th century. Using Grace's life story as the centerpiece for her narrative and drawing on additional research, Andrea Warren chronicles what life was like for those early settlers, who faced isolation, endless hard work, and the ravages of nature as they struggled to build farms, raise families, and forge communities among distant neighbors spread out across the land. As Warren relates, the challenges were often overwhelming and there were many who eventually had to give up their dreams. For Grace McCance, these challenges were never too great to diminish her love for the land. This real-life story of a pioneer girl, which is illustrated with archival black-and-white photographs as well as pictures from Grace McCance's family, has great appeal as a book for children to read independently in addition to its obvious merit for classroom use. (Ages 10–14)

Winter, Jeanette. *My Name Is Georgia: A Portrait.* Silver Whistle/Harcourt Brace, 1998. 48 pages. (0–15–201649–X) $16.00

It's no easy task to make the life and art of Georgia O'Keeffe accessible to young readers but Jeanette Winter does it brilliantly in this picture-book portrait of the artist. As she did with muralist Diego Rivera in *Diego* by Jonah Winter (Knopf, 1994), Winter skillfully controls the scale of her own illustrations so that readers get a true sense of the largeness of the original art, an amazing feat in this 7 $^3/_4$ x 9 $^1/_4$" volume. She has subtly stylized her illustrations to suggest the inspiration O'Keeffe took from the surrounding landscapes of her life. The clouds in the sky, for example, are a direct reference to her "Sky above Clouds" series painted in the early 1960s. In a Manhattan skyline we see the edge of one of O'Keeffe's famous orange poppies peeking out from behind a skyscraper, accompanying a direct quote from the artist: "The distance has always been calling me." The spare first-person text that accompanies her artwork is also composed with skill and grace. Using occasional direct quotes from O'Keeffe's own writing (documented in notes), Winter gives us a sense of the artist's reclusive nature and commitment to her art. Her lyric simplicity not only makes the book accessible to begining readers, it also offers insight into O'Keeffe's character: "I painted a camellia. I painted it BIG, so people would notice. / I painted a jack-in-the-pulpit. I painted it BIG, so people would see." Taken together, the text and illustrations work in perfect harmony to bring this larger-than-life artist down to a child's eye view so they too will notice and see. *Honor Book, 1998 CCBC Caldecott Award Discussion.* (Ages 5–8)

Younger, Barbara. *Purple Mountain Majesties: The Story of Katharine Lee Bates and "America the Beautiful."* Illustrated by Stacey Schuett. Dutton, 1998. 32 pages. (0–525–45653–8) $15.99

It's not often we find primary research in a history book for children, much less in a picture-book biography. For this exemplary work, first-time author Barbara Younger went directly to the Wellesley College Archives, home of the diaries and letters of Katharine Lee Bates, and communicated with family members in order to research the subject of this lively historical account. Born in Massachusetts in 1868, Bates never considered herself a writer, although she kept a diary from age nine. In reconstructing Bates's life, Younger knows exactly what and how much to quote from these diaries in order to give young readers a sense of who Bates was and what the world was like when she lived. Always an adventurous free spirit, her cross-country trip in 1893 to attend the World's Columbian Exposition in Chicago and to accompany a group of fellow teachers to the top of Pikes Peak in Colorado provided the direct inspiration for her poem "America the Beautiful." When it was published two years later in the July 4th issue of *The Congregationalist*, it quickly became a national sensation. Originally it was sung to many different tunes; although a contest for original music yielded over 900 entries, a hymn composed by Samuel Ward continues to be the tune we use today. Younger's account is further enriched with intriguing details culled from Bates's life story, which will surely appeal to children: the fact that she used to read books about dogs to her dog, hold parties for parrots, was one of the first to ride a Ferris wheel, and saw a knight made entirely out of prunes at the Chicago Exposition, for example. Schuett's luminous paintings also bring the subject to life through her attention to historical detail and her skillful renderings of the majestic landscapes that inspired Katharine Lee Bates to heights of poetry more than 100 years ago. (Ages 5–9)

See also: *All Around Town; Black Cowboy, Wild Horses; Boshblobberbosh; Boss of the Plains; Cool Melons—Turn to Frogs!; Good-bye, Charles Lindbergh; Home Run; Iqbal Masih and the Crusaders against Child Slavery; Journey to Ellis Island; Katarína; Las Christmas; Mary on Horseback; My Freedom Trip; One Room School; Talking with Adventurers*

Contemporary People, Places and Events

Ancona, George. *Barrio: José's Neighborhood*. Harcourt Brace, 1998. 48 pages. (0–15–201049–1) $18.00; pbk. (0–15–201048–3) $9.00
Nine-year-old José Luís feels very much at home in *el barrio*, his neighborhood in San Francisco's Mission District. On his daily walks between his house and Cesar Chavez Elementary School, he passes brightly colored murals that tell the history of his people, both in his parent's native country, Mexico, and in José's country, the United States. In the neighborhood his culture is frequently celebrated with community *fiestas* and in school he learns not only about his own heritage, but about those of his African American and Asian American classmates. Over the course of several months, George Ancona documents José's life in *el barrio* with a concise text and with stunning color photographs that bring the neighborhood to life. Also available in a Spanish-language edition as *Barrio: El barrio de José* (pbk., 0-15-201808-5, $9.00). (Ages 5–10)

Ancona, George. *Fiesta Fireworks*. Lothrop, Lee & Shepard Books/Morrow, 1998. 32 pages. (0–688–14818–2) $16.00
Caren's father, grandfather, and uncles earn their living by making fireworks, as do many of the men in the small town of Tultepec, Mexico, which supplies most of the fireworks used in local festivals all over Mexico. The fireworks we see them making in the first half of this photo-essay, however, are special: they're being made for Tultepec's own fiesta, to celebrate the town's patron saint, San Juan de Dios, the protector of pirotecnicos, those who make fireworks. Through Caren's eyes and George Ancona's vibrant and lively color photographs, we see all the preparations leading up to the fiesta, including the construction of a castillo, a tower of fireworks that will be used in the fiesta finale. On the day of the fiesta, activities begin at dawn with a procession through town on an elaborately decorated path made of colored sawdust and culminate in a spectacular fireworks display as soon as the sun goes down. Ancona's photographs are filled with cultural detail specific to the Tultepec festival; in addition, they capture the universal thrill of a dazzling fireworks display. (Ages 5–10)

Bourgeois, Paulette. *Fire Fighters*. Illustrated by Kim LaFave. (In My Neighborhood) U.S. edition: Kids Can Press, 1998. 32 pages. (1–55074–438–0) $12.95

Bourgeois, Paulette. *Garbage Collectors*. Illustrated by Kim LaFave. (In My Neighborhood) U.S. edition: Kids Can Press, 1998. 32 pages. (1–55074–440–2) $12.95
The first two entries in the "In My Neighborhood" series made available in the United States deal with high-interest community helpers. *Fire Fighters* shows the team at Station Number 45 from the moment they get the dispatcher's call about a fire in on the top floor of an apartment building to the time they return to the station and clean up the equipment. Compelling information is accompanied by engaging watercolor and pen-and-ink illustrations that add a lot of character to the story. Additional details about how fires are fought in rural areas, on boats, and in forests are briefly noted,

as are some fire-safety tips. *Garbage Collectors* follows a similar pattern, showing us a typical day in the work life of Sam and Mabel, who work on the same garbage truck. As an added bonus, we get to accompany Mabel as she drives her full truck to the transfer station to dump the garbage, which is then pushed by a bulldozer into tractor-trailer that will take it to the landfill site. Author Paulette Bourgeois conducted in-person interviews with fire fighters and garbage collectors to find out exactly how they do their jobs. She has shaped this information into stories that will easily hold the interest of preschoolers in general. But the prime audience for both books will be those young children whose hearts skip a beat whenever they hear a fire truck's siren or the grinding blade of a garbage truck. (Ages 3–6)

Cooper, Elisha. *Ballpark.* **Greenwillow, 1998. 40 pages. (0–688–15755–6) $15.00**

Game day at a big league ballpark begins early in the morning with a lone groundskeeper mowing the field. Soon, delivery trucks start to arrive to unload boxes of peanuts, pretzels, hot dogs, and beverages while washing machines rumble in the laundry room as team uniforms are washed. Players arrive to suit up and start their pre-game routines and, before long, spectators begin to line up. Small details of a typical game day from beginning to end, on the field, in the dugout and stands, and behind the scenes, are shown in exquisite watercolor vignettes, accompanied by a wry text. (Ages 4–7)

Cummings, Pat and Linda Cummings, compilers and editors. *Talking with Adventurers: Conversations with Christina M. Allen, Robert Ballard, Michael L. Blakey, Ann Bowles, David Doubilet, Jane Goodall, Dereck & Beverly Joubert, Michael Novacek, Johan Reinhard, Rick C. West and Juris Zarins.* **National Geographic Society, 1998. 95 pages. (0–7922–7068–1) $19.95**

The adventurers here are 12 contemporary explorers—mostly scientists such as archaeologists, ethologists, and ecologists—whose work takes them to far-off lands. Similar to the author's previous *Talking with Artists* books (Bradbury, 1992; Simon & Schuster, 1995), each entry includes a childhood photo, color photographs of the subject at work, a brief autobiographical essay, and responses to a series of questions, such as: *what is a normal working day like for you?* and *what was the scariest thing that ever happened in your work?* Young readers often have romantic views of the lives of people like Robert Ballard and Jane Goodall (both of whom are featured here); these portraits offer a welcome dose of reality that describes the challenges of their work but will not discourage the aspirations of future explorers. (Ages 8–14)

Halperin, Wendy Anderson. *Once Upon a Company: A True Story.* **Orchard, 1998. 32 pages. (0–531–30089–7) $16.95**

Wendy Anderson Halperin's three children, Joel, Kale and Lane, were stuck inside the house on a cold November day when she first suggested they make Christmas wreaths and sell them to earn money for college. Joel was seven at the time, and Halperin writes in his first-person voice to describe how that suggestion blossomed into a thriving company. In the second year, the company expanded to include a summer food stand that serves cold lemonade and peanut butter and jelly sandwiches at local events ("Now we were chefs!") and, when wreath season came around, rented an empty store for four weeks, becoming part of their downtown business community ("Now we were merchants!"). By the sixth year, they had established a system for hiring employees, including college students, and earned over $16,000 for their own college funds. College is repeatedly emphasized as a place of wonderful discovery in this energetic, can-do narrative. The charmingly designed volume is illustrated with the author/artist's warm, folksy artwork detailing the large cast of characters and the many aspects of operating the business in their community, which appears in the illustrations to be predominantly white and middle class. The emphasis here is on fun and initiative as much as money, and the money, when mentioned, is always tied into college as the ultimate goal. (Ages 8–11)

Hoyt-Goldsmith, Diane. *Lacrosse: The National Game of the Iroquois.* Photographs by Lawrence Migdale. Holiday House, 1998. 32 pages. (0–8234–1360–8) $16.95

Thirteen-year-old Monte Lyons is an Onondaga Indian who has been playing lacrosse since he was small. In fact, lacrosse is a family tradition for Monte and his younger brother, Brook: both their father and grandfather have played lacrosse, professionally and internationally. Color photographs show the day-to-day life of Monte and his family, especially as their lives relate to lacrosse. Monte's grandfather, for example, is teaching him to make lacrosse sticks in the traditional way, quite simply because they've found wooden sticks superior to the metal and plastic sticks most people use today. The author includes details about the history of this ancient Iroquois game; the modern rules and equipment (with regional variations); and uses photographs of Monte and Brook in action to demonstrate the skills a good lacrosse player needs to master. (Ages 8–14)

Lehn, Barbara. *What Is a Scientist?* Photographs by Carol Krauss. Millbrook Press, 1998. 32 pages. (0–7613–1272–2) $19.90

A deceptively simple text explores scientific discovery in terms perfectly suited for young children. Each two-page spread pairs an easily understood statement about what scientists do on the left-hand page with a photograph on the right in which one or more children are pictured doing a child-centered experiment that reflects the concept. The children's activities are described in one or two sentences that accompany the photo. For example, the statement "A scientist notices details" is paired with a photograph of a young red-headed boy examining cut vegetables and determining that cucumbers have two sizes of seeds inside them. "A scientist draws what she sees" is paired with a photograph of a girl of Asian heritage mixing two different colored liquids and writing "The red drops beaded up inside the yellow liquid." The alternating use of female and male pronouns when referencing scientists, the inclusion of children from many different racial and ethnic backgrounds in the photographs, and the careful choice of activities that children can replicate themselves to understand accessible concepts make this a significant book that will be of interest to all who work with young children. (Ages 4–7)

McKay, Lawrence, Jr. *Journey Home.* Illustrated by Dom and Keunhee Lee. Lee & Low (95 Madison Avenue, New York, NY 10016), 1998. 28 pages. (1–880000–65–2) $15.95

Ten-year-old Mai accompanies her mother, Lin, on a journey to Vietnam. Her mother is trying to find the birth family she has never known. At the time Lin was left at an orphanage as a baby, her only possession was a kite.

Even after a day of fruitless searching through volumes at the People's Hall of Records in Saigon, Lin refuses to give up. She believes the hand-made kite might offer a clue as to her parentage. The details of how Lin uses this clue to solve the mystery of her identity will captivate young readers, while at the same time it will introduce them to one family's personal tragedy suffered during the Vietnam War. The Lees' colored pencil and oil paintings distinctively use darker shades of brown to show the scenes taking place in the past that Lin and Mai successfully uncover. (Ages 8–12)

McKee, Tim. *No More Strangers Now: Young Voices from a New South Africa.* Photographs by Anne Blackshaw. Foreword by Archbishop Desmond Tutu. A Melanie Kroupa Book/DK Ink, 1998. 107 pages. (0–7894–2524–6) $19.95

Tim McKee's interviews with 12 South African teenagers are presented here as lively first-person narratives, with each teen describing his or her life before and after the end of apartheid. Selected from 65 interviews the author conducted over a ten-month period in 1995–96, these 12 adolescent voices represent a range of personal histories and perspectives: Nithinia Martin, an 18-year-old Coloured woman, speaks candidly about race relations and her strong desire throughout childhood and adolescence to be like the white kids; 17-year-old Michael Njova was an abandoned child who survived by "stealing and stabbing" on the streets of Johannesburg until he was caught and sent to an orphanage at age 13; Vuyiswa Mbambisa, 16, grew up in exile with her mother in Angola and returned to Soweto as a young teenager to live with her grandmother, finding conditions much worse than she had expected; 16-year-old Mark Abrahamson had always taken his life of white privilege for granted until the breakdown of apartheid allowed him to see, close-up, how bad conditions were in the Black townships; and 15-year-old Pfano Takalani, living a traditional life in a remote rural area in Venda, comments that the biggest change in his life in the past few years occurred when his eldest brother was installed as chief in 1993. Eight of the 12 teens interviewed are Black and, with the exception of Pfano Takalani, each of them describes a childhood defined by poverty, brutality and oppression, and each one speaks with an amazing lack of bitterness. All 12 — Black, white, Coloured and Indian — have high hopes for a future where opportunity, freedom and equality will replace poverty, brutality and oppression. As 18-year-old Bandile Mashinini says: "We have a new constitution, and it's a great foundation, but it's still only ink on paper. I want to make sure we build well on top of it." This book gives us hope that he and his peers will be able to do just that. (Ages 12–18)

Reinhard, Johan. *Discovering the Inca Ice Maiden: My Adventures on Ampato.* National Geographic Society, 1998. 48 pages. (0–7922–7142–4) $17.95

Anthropologist Reinhard gives a first-person account of the 1995 discovery he made with his assistant, Miguel Zárate, while climbing an inactive volcano high in the Andes mountains. Amazingly, a frozen mummy bundle lay right out in the open near the summit! It had been dislodged a few days earlier from the rock in which it had been buried for over 500 years. The challenges Reinhard and Zárate faced just getting the mummy off the mountain before it was destroyed by exposure are described step-by-step, as are the details of the scientific exploration that followed. Crisp color photographs of the events as they unfolded make readers feel as though they are on-site at the excavation and subsequent laboratory study of a mummy that provided researchers with plenty of evidence about Incan life prior to European contact. John Reinhard is one of the scientists interviewed in Pat Cummings' *Talking with Adventurers* (see earlier entry in this section). (Ages 9–14)

See also: *Dance; Halala Means Welcome; Id-ul-Fitr; In Search of Lemurs; Iqbal Masih and the Crusaders against Child Slavery; Let's Dance!; Listen to Us; Seeing Things My Way; Sesame Street Unpaved; Shadows in the Dawn; Somewhere Today; Twins!*

Issues in Today's World

Allen, Judy, editor. *Anthology for the Earth.* **U.S. edition: Candlewick Press, 1998. 92 pages. (0–7636–0301–5) $21.99**
Most readers will find much with which to agree in this carefully selected and handsomely presented 9 $^{1}/_{2}$ x 10 $^{1}/_{4}$" assemblage expressing many values of and dangers to the Earth. The sum of Allen's many parts supplies energy rather than despair. The 92 anthology entries are placed within a highly visual and extremely varied design. The contents have a largely Western perspective, while a majority of the written and visual sources are connected to the United Kingdom. Thirty artists are represented by one or more works accompanying the writings, including Nicola Bayley, Quentin Blake, Reg Cartwright, Michael Foreman, John Lawrence, Flora McDonnell, Clare Melinsky, and Peter Sís. The 44 author biographies will be helpful despite their brevity. The authors represented by short writings include Douglas Adams, David Attenborough, Daisy Bates, John Bierhorst, Joseph Bruchac, Willa Cather, Anton Chekhov, Walter de la Mare, Gerald Durrell, Thomas Hardy, Rudyard Kipling, Aldo Leopold, Konrad Lorenz, John Muir, Alice Nannup, Ovid, Alan Paton, Albert Schweitzer, John Steinbeck, and Leo Tolstoy. The final excerpt attributed to Frances Bacon is illustrated by Bayley's tiny image of a weed growing between a bit of rubble one can see in any part of this planet: "Nature is often hidden, sometimes overcome, seldom extinguished." (Age 9 and older)

Kuklin, Susan. *Iqbal Masih and the Crusaders against Child Slavery.* **Henry Holt, 1998. 133 pages. (0–8050–5459–6) $16.95**
Susan Kuklin has written a consciousness-raiser and a call to action for young readers as she tells the story of, Iqbal Masih, a child laborer in Pakistan, and details the tragedy of bonded child labor in southern Asian. She writes of the horrors of child slavery and the dedication of those who have worked within these countries to free children from bondage. Iqbal was sold into bondage at age 4 and freed at age 10 by the actions of Pakistani activists calling for enforcement of laws to free children in bondage. At age 11, he received the Reebok Youth in Action Human Rights Award for his own efforts to educate others and free children still in bondage. When he was 12, he was shot and killed under circumstances that may or may not have been accidental. Drawing on interviews with and articles about Iqbal, conversations with those who knew him, and research into child slavery and activist movements, Kuklin has written a narrative both compelling and compassionate. She places child slavery in an economic context by chronicling the cycle of

poverty that leaves families dependent on the money that comes from "selling" their children into bondage, and in a global context by connecting products made by children in bondage—especially carpets— to consumers in the United States and other countries who purchase these lower-priced items. Kuklin also acknowledges the West's own exploitation of children as laborers during the industrial revolution in the late 19th and early 20th centuries. Above all, she honors young adults' strong sense of justice and compassion by empowering them to help make a difference if they want to get involved. She offers inspiration for activism and examples of what some children have already done to support the ongoing work of activists in Pakistan to free and educate child laborers. Included is a list of organizations and individuals to contact for more information or to get involved in supporting the work of anti-slavery activists. (Ages 11–14)

Lewis, Barbara A. *The Kid's Guide to Social Action.* Revised editon. Free Spirit Press (400 First Avenue North, Suite 616, Minneapolis, MN 55401), 1998. 211 pages. (1–57542–038–4) $16.95
This well-organized, accessible handbook intended for young people who want to make a change was written by a Salt Lake City elementary school teacher whose writing expresses implicit confidence in and respect for young people. The attractively designed, step-by-step guide moves logically from uncomplicated forms of action to more sophisticated approaches to social change and yet presents a realistic picture of the hard work necessary to effect such change. The manual is organized into five main parts: (1) Life beyond the Classroom (e.g. brainstorming, reflecting on what you have learned); (2) Power Skills (communication skills, responsible Internet use, petitions, fundraising); (3) Working with Government (e.g. changing a law, lobbying); (4) Resources (e.g. addresses for state capitals, federal government agencies, environmental groups); and (5) Tools (various forms). Each section contains "Kids in Action" articles illustrated with black-and-white photographs featuring actual recent episodes in which today's youth became effective change agents. The author has given persmission on specific pages to duplicate them for use. Readers will find a large number of website addresses throughout this substantial resource for individuals, school and community youth groups and their leaders, classrooms, and libraries. This is a welcome revision of the edition recommended in *CCBC Choices 1991.* (Age 9 and older)

Springer, Jane. *Listen to Us: The World's Working Children: A Book for Kids.* Groundwood/Douglas & McIntyre, 1997. 96 pages. (0–88899–307–2) $16.95
A nine-chapter presentation about child labor developed by a Canadian author and publisher spans the globe, beginning with definitions of childhood and child labor. Children who do household, farm or family business chores are typically not considered child laborers while children officially considered to be child workers are "paid to work in factories...hired out or even sold by their families to do farm work, domestic work, or to work as soldiers." The book addresses children who have been "thrown out of their homes by their parents, or who have run away and who will do any kind of work in order to survive." Major reasons why children work are covered, such as poverty, caste system, being female, and/or the globalization of many industries. Although employment in U.S. fast-food enterprises is briefly explored, that is not the largest workplace for child laborers; a chart cites

900,000 U.S. workers under the age of 16 in three other categories of labor: agriculture, garments, and sex work. The total estimated number of children "at work worldwide" is "at least the size of the U.S. population; these youth are "not just missing out on schooling and an opportunity for a better life, but cutting their lives perilously short." Moving accounts of specific child workers include several references to Iqbal Masih. Clearly reproduced black-and-white and full-color photographs on every page spread and a highly visual format for information within a global context earmark Springer's book. A list of goals to help child workers, and a list naming ways to help achieve those goals, offers hope. (Age 9 and older)

Thomas, Shelley Moore. *Somewhere Today: A Book of Peace.* **Photographs by Eric Futran. Albert Whitman, 1998. 24 pages. (0–8075-7545-3) $14.95**
An uncomplicated text about a complicated subject contains only 11 short sentences. Ten of them begin with the words, "Somewhere today someone is...." These ten sentences define ten distinct peace-making actions, such as "...being a friend, instead of fighting...planting a tree where one was cut down...learning to do things a different way." The words on the final page are "Maybe it is you." An assemblage of uncaptioned photographs reproduced in full color illustrates each of these actions, inviting readers to figure out or find out more about each example. The children and adults pictured suggest glimpses of racial, cultural, age and gender diversity. The author's selection of seemingly ordinary actions and her understanding of how young children might begin to think about the idea of peace are no doubt informed by her role as a teacher of first and second graders. (Ages 3–7)

Walter, Virginia. *Making Up Megaboy.* **Graphics by Katrina Roeckelein. A Richard Jackson Book/DK, 1998. 62 pages. (0–7894-2488-6) $16.95**
No one in the suburban community of Santa Rosita, California, knows why 13-year-old Robbie Jones walked into a liquor store and shot and killed Mr. Koh, the store owner. Everyone connected somehow to Robbie and the crime—witnesses, family, friends, schoolmates, authorities, and the local press — asks the same question: why? Robbie was such a quiet boy. He was so average. The only thing that seemed to stand out about him at all was his obsession with a superhero named Megaboy, Robbie's own invention. The story, told from multiple points of view, is built from bits and pieces, observations from people who thought they knew Robbie but who, in actuality, never did. They make him up, little by little, just as Robbie has created Megaboy. Their brief statements are accompanied by original graphics that provide additional clues in Robbie's perplexing story. As readers we become witnesses ourselves and, although we are never given any definitive answers — Robbie himself never speaks about the incident — we are given plenty to mull over and discuss, so that we can all make up our own Megaboy. (Ages 11–16)

See also: *Heart of a Chief; In Search of Lemurs; Little Factory; No More Strangers Now; Shadows in the Dawn; This Land Is Your Land; War and the Pity of War*

Understanding Oneself and Others

Aliki. *Painted Words: Marianthe's Story, One. Spoken Memories: Marianthe's Story, Two.* Greenwillow, 1998. 54 pages. (0–688–15662–2) $16.00

The side with the green cover of this 11 $^1/_4$" x 9 $^1/_4$" double story involves Mari's experiences as a new girl at school. Mari is an immigrant child who has not yet learned English. After her teacher, Mr. Petrie, discovers that Mari can draw at the easel, she is able to tell her classmates a bit about herself by herself. Mr. Petrie uses one of Mari's drawings about her feelings to talk with his pupils after one of them calls her "dummy." Mama tells Mari, "In life there will always be those who hurt and tease out of ignorance...look and listen so you will not be one of them." Mari makes progress learning English, and, at home, so does Mama. Readers must turn the book around and upside down to locate the orange-covered side relating Mari's life story in words and pictures. Aliki's full-color artwork created with colored pencils and crayons effectively shows Mari as a greatly cherished child in her family, glimpses of Mari's infancy and early years in her former village, and her new life. The artwork briefly becomes black and white to reflect Mari's account of an earlier war and famine. Aliki's two-part, double-sided picture story reflecting some of the school experiences and feelings of a transplanted child without a new language allows readers to guess Mari's age, grade, and birth country. According to book jacket information, Aliki herself began school in Philadelphia where she was born to Greek parents. (Ages 5–9)

Bunting, Eve. *Some Frog!* Illustrated by Scott Medlock. Harcourt Brace, 1998. 48 pages. (0–15–277082–8) $15.00

Billy's class at school is having a frog-jumping contest, and the winner will get two tickets to a Cubs game. Billy's dad has promised to take him to Miller's Pond to get a frog. Billy lives with Mom and Grandpa. Dad lives elsewhere, and even though he tells Billy he'll do things, he is unreliable. Readers will feel Billy's anguish on the school night before the contest while he waits for Dad to show up. He doesn't. He doesn't phone, either. Mom and Grandpa's healthy approach help Billy manage that reality. This contemporary family story also contains a considerable amount of cheerful action related to the frog-pond and the school frog-jumping meet! A book chronicling anticipation and disillusion has child appeal, a fine design, and strongly expressive illustrations created with oils and reproduced in full color. (Ages 4–9)

Carter, Alden R. *Seeing Things My Way.* Photographs by Carol S. Carter. Albert Whitman, 1998. 32 pages. (0–8075–7296–9) $13.95

On the opening page of this full-color photodocumentary about a child with a visual handicap, one notices a photograph of two little girls and reads, "I'm Amanda, and this is my friend Catherine. This is how she looks to you." On the opposite page, "And this is how she looks to me." Looking at the carefully created photographic image there, young readers have a chance to consider what Amanda's vision must be like. Ever since she lost much of her sight as a kindergarten-age child, Amanda has blind spots. Readers learn about the technical and personal adaptations making Amanda's life as close to normal as possible. There are brief references to several other children and adults— present and past—with differing vision impairments and adaptations. The important thrust of this account shows Amanda actively involved at home and school. (Ages 5–9)

Cole, Joanna. *The New Baby at Your House*. Photographs by Margaret Miller. Revied edition. Morrow, 1998. 48 pages. (0–688–13898–5) $16.00

The new and revised edition of a critically acclaimed book first published in 1985 makes a number of significant changes to the original. Superb color photographs by Margaret Miller have replaced the black-and-white photos by Hella Hammid in the first edition, giving the book a much updated look. Like Hammid, Miller uses several racially diverse families as her models; happily this feature that seemed so revolutionary in 1985 is taken for granted 13 years later. But here the photos have become more integral to the book as a whole, sometimes extending across a double-page spread to show us a baby who's nearly life-size. Cole has made many changes to the text, streamlining it to make it more accessible to the two and three year olds who are the book's main audience. Most welcome of all is her focus on Michael's dad, who seems to be the primary caretaker of Michael and his baby brother, Peter. In fact, throughout the book, fathers are seen engaged in all aspects of parenting from changing diapers to settling sibling disputes. In addition to Michael, we see how older siblings Molly, Julie, and Sara react and interact with the new babies in their households, while Cole provides basic information about infants and reassures their siblings that it's okay to have mixed emotions. The author's lengthy note to parents expands on the emotional impact of a new baby on a young child and offers helpful advice on how parents can make the transition easier. (Ages 2–5)

Heide, Florence Parry and Roxanne Heide Pierce. *Tío Armando.* **Illustrated by Ann Grifalconi. Lothrop, Lee & Shepard, 1998. 32 pages. (0–688–12108-X) $14.93**

Lucitita narrates this picture story about the year her grandmother's brother, Tío Armando, lived with her family—Mama and Papa, Eduardo and Julio, and baby Rosita.Tío Armando speaks mostly Spanish. In his new home and neighborhood he creates his own daily activities, including visits to hospital patients and the library. Grifalconi's watercolor brush and pencil illustrations show experiences Lucitita and her kind great-uncle enjoy together, during which Tío Armando shares wise insights about life and, occasionally, about loss. The 13 double-page spreads are each labeled with the name of a month beginning with May and ending the following May. Spanish language words and Latino cultural details are skillfully incorporated within this affectionate picture story about a contemporary extended U.S. family and its active elder who has a distinctive, memorable personality. (Ages 5–8)

Jukes, Mavis. *Growing Up: It's a Girl Thing: Straight Talk about First Bras, First Periods, and Your Changing Body.* **Alfred A. Knopf, 1998. 72 pages. (0–679–99027–5) $10.00**

Jukes writes in a warm adult voice to Everygirl, showing in each chapter that she respects each reader's personal questions and feelings about her body. On the opening page, she invites a reader to ask herself if she feels ready to read about her body and its connection to "how people grow up and make babies together." The author advises, "If you're not sure, ask a parent or teacher to help you decide if it's a good time to begin reading this book." Some girls have an adult caregiver who will provide reliable information and explicit directions about growing up, such as managing menstrual periods. This book can reinforce for them what they've already found out, and it will probably add overlooked details or options. For any number of reasons, many girls do not have such an adult female family member, especially one with Juke's comfort level. For these girls this 13-chapter book will approximate a reliable, informed woman friend. Jukes relates her own mother's skill at providing young Mavis with a comfortable way to ask personal questions; this offers one valuable model for a continuing dialogue. The six-page chapter "It's My Body" summarizes how to stay safe, a subject Jukes covers in her equally friendly, helpful book *It's a Girl Thing* (Knopf), recommended in *CCBC Choices 1996*. (Ages 9–14)

Lears, Laurie. *Ian's Walk: A Story about Autism.* **Illustrated by Karen Ritz. Albert Whitman, 1998. 32 pages. (0–8075–3480–3) $14.95**

A note about autism precedes a very short first-person picture story expressing a bit about how it feels to have an embarrassingly "different" sibling. The young narrator is Julie, who is probably in an upper elementary grade or the first year of middle school. Julie is able to take responsibility for Ian at her mother's request while they go to the park. Readers see Ian's responses to specific sounds, sights, smells, textures, and tastes during the outing. These brief scenes showing examples of sensory perception and emotional response are realistic. So is Julie's alarm while Ian momentarily vanishes, her affectionate relief when she locates him, and her greater tolerance for his publicly displayed idiosyncracies afterwards. (Ages 6–9)

Millman, Isaac. *Moses Goes to a Concert.* **Frances Foster Books/Farrar Straus Giroux, 1998. 40 pages. (0–374–35067–1) $16.00**

Mr. Samuel has planned a field trip to a young people's concert for his 11 pupils. Each of the children is deaf and communicates by using American Sign Language (ASL). Moses can be located on each page because of his red cap. After they ride in a school bus to the concert, Mr. Samuel has three surprises for his pupils, who appear to be kindergarten-age. He gives the children balloons to hold in their laps to help them feel the music. The children see that the featured soloist is a percussionist who is also deaf; she wears no shoes in order to follow the orchestra by feeling the vibrations of the music through her stocking feet. Mr. Samuel has arranged for the children to meet his percussionist friend after the concert. She answers their questions and invites them try out her instruments. That night Moses tells his parents about the concert in ASL, and some of his words are pictured in hand signs on the final pages, ending with "when you set your mind to it, you can become anything you want when you grow up." Moses tells about many choices, but right now he wants to become a percussionist. Sign-language diagrams with helpful arrows are located in small boxed areas on each page of this upbeat, unusual picture book written and illustrated in full color. (Ages 3–7)

Schwager, Tina and Michelle Schuerger. *The Right Moves: A Girl's Guide to Getting Fit and Feeling Good.* **Edited by Elizabeth Verdick. Free Spirit (400 First Avenue North, Suite 616, Minneapolis, MN 55401), 1998. 273 pages. Pbk. (1–57542–035–X) $14.95**

In 1995, the Center for Disease Control reported that only one in four U.S. girls eats more than one vegetable a day, not counting French fries, and that nine out of ten teen girls get insufficient amounts of calcium. Schwager, a certified athletic trainer, and Schuerger, a former competitive figure skater, have written a caring, down-to-earth book about self-esteem, food and fitness. Ninety pages about aspects of eating includes reasons to eat right and specific steps to take in order to do so, resources for vegetarians, understanding food labels, snacking while hanging out, eating at movies and the mall, making healthy choices when ordering fast-food, diet pills, reasons to say no to diets, eating disorders, and compulsive exercising. The final section on Fitness covers body types; cross-training; gear and shoes; injury prevention; stretching; and 25 workout options including walking, dance, racquet sports, strength training, team sports, yoga and snowboarding—and the pros and cons of each option. Website addresses, phone numbers of supportive organizations, and other essential information can be found throughout a book that takes girls and teenagers seriously by providing them with substantial, easy-to-understand information and many choices for serious life matters over which they can assume control. Occasional silly line drawings and equally irrelevant cover illustration do not represent the serious nature of this well-developed, helpful book. (Ages 9–16)

Scott, Elaine. *Twins!* **Photographs by Margaret Miller. Atheneum, 1998. 40 pages. (0–689–80347–8) $16.00**
Families with twins have dark skin and light skin, and twins have curly hair or straight hair. Miller shows this in her effective full-color photographs featuring a variety of sets of twins and family circumstances. Each page shows one of eight sets of twins in action, such as Malik and Aamir pictured with their individual birthday cake choices. Several questions are explored, such as, "Is it hard for you to share your favorite toy?" or "Would you want the same birthday present as your brother or sister, or a different one?" The format offers another kind of interaction. In the book the words italicized here are printed twice as large as others on the same page and in full color, rather than black. For example, "When twins arrive in a family there is *twice as much fun*, twice as much *work*, and twice as much *love* to go around." A young beginning reader or anyone new to reading English might choose to read only those words. The same visual device is used in the concluding six-page note for adults. The creation of twins at conception is not within the scope of Scott's narrative celebrating the individuality of any two individuals born as twins. (Ages 2–5)

Senisi, Ellen B. *For My Family, Love, Allie.* **Albert Whitman, 1998. 32 pages. (0–8075–2539–1) $14.95**
Allie wants to have something special to give to her relatives at an upcoming family reunion, and with her mom's help she comes up with a treat to eat that she can make all on her own in a photodocumentary significant for its welcome portrayal of a biracial family. Allie's dad is Black and her mom is white. The reunion brings together members of both sides of her family in a joyful gathering that features distinctive foods from their differing ethnic backgrounds, such as Jamaican jerk chicken and rice and Slovak sausage, along with universal favorites like fruit salad, corn on the cob, and, of course, Allie's own Peanut-Butter Treats. The vibrant photographs are wonderfully relaxed and unposed, letting the warm family feelings shared by the members of Allie's large extended family shine. (Ages 5–7)

See also: *Alfie and the Birthday Surprise; Cherish Me; Journey Home; Emma's Magic Winter; Gettin' through Thursday; Gift for Abuelita; I Love My Hair!; Joey Pigza Swallowed the Key; Just Juice; Liliana's Grandmothers; Mariposa; Pony Trouble; Rearranging and Other Stories; Smack; Space between Our Footseps; While No One Was Watching; Wild Kid*

The Arts

Ancona, George. *Let's Dance!* Morrow, 1998. 32 pages. (0–688–16211–8) $16.00

Ancona's splendid photographs show glimpses of people full of energy, people moving, people enjoying themselves. Sometimes the dancers are dressed in traditional clothes, and sometimes not. The entire volume is an invitation and an inspiration, along with providing brief information about many ways of dancing, old ways and new. "If you can speak, you can sing. If you can walk, you can dance. All you have to do is kick, step, turn, hop, jump, reach, leap, and wiggle. You can dance alone [the bacongo] or with a friend [Scottish country dancing] or with a whole bunch of people [circle folk dancing]." The full-color photographs mounted against white space on the first double-page spread show readers what each of those movements involved. The children making the movements are probably nine and older, and they look as if they're having fun doing it. They "look like America" in terms of ethnicity and casual attire. They invite readers to turn the page and maybe also to put down the book, and move! (Ages 5–9)

Armstrong, Carole. *Women of the Bible: With Paintings from the Great Art Museums of the World.* U.S. edition: Simon & Schuster, 1998. 45 pages. (0–689–81728–2) $18.00

Over the centuries many artists have been inspired to paint scenes and portraits of women in the scriptures. Seventeen such paintings are reproduced in full color in this collection of fine art, including images of Rebekah, Rachel and Leah, Abigail, Esther, Judith, Susanna, and Elisabeth. Each painting is accompanied by a passage from the King James translation of the *Bible* and Armstrong's one-page narrative retelling of the passage. The index contains small images of the same art, furnishing the artists' names and dates and indicating the world museums that own the originals. (Ages 9–13)

Aronson, Marc. *Art Attack: A Short Cultural History of the Avant-Garde.* Clarion, 1998. 192 pages. (0–395–79729–2) $20.00

Lively prose addressed directly to teenagers claims that it's young people who "take the most risks, who see the furthest, and who make the most challenging art." From the introductory summary to the final chapter-by-chapter listings of biographical dates and detailed source notes, Aronson brings insight and order to a subject that—according to the uninformed— often lacks both elements. Aronson's passion for both the avant-garde and for cultural history are a good match. He asserts that some avant-garde images have gradually made their way into the cultural mainstream, even though initially some were created at considerable risk, aesthetically and even politically. The book is illustrated with a wide variety of interestingly captioned artwork reproduced in black and white. All but one of the 14 chapters begin with an appealing suggestion of specific music to which one might listen while reading about avant-garde art. Few can remain neutral when confronted by avant-garde art (that's the idea, after all), or even while reading Aronson's blend of fact and opinion about this art. While one might be tempted to lift excerpts from this book, it is essential to see all the pieces in the context of their cultural history and consider this exciting, marvelously written volume as a whole. (Age 13 and older)

Borgenicht, David. *Sesame Street Unpaved: Scripts, Stories, Secrets, and Songs.*
Hyperion, 1998. 191 pages. (0–7868–6460–5) $24.95

This authorized history of the *Sesame Street* television program for preschoolers, occasioned by its 30th anniversary, can be opened on any page and read in any order. One page isn't enough, because each bit of background information is visually dynamic and full of engaging detail. The contents include "Can You Tell Me How We Got to Sesame Street?" (development of the concept); "I Can't Hear You—I've Got a Banana in My Ear" (classic moments); "Who Are the People in Your Neighborhood?" (The cast over the years); "Sing, Sing a Song" (music and poems of Sesame Street); and "Psst! Hey Buddy!" (behind the scenes). The page "Where were you the day Mr. Hooper died?" gives readers an inside perspective on the decision to tell young viewers about death. That anecdote reveals much about the program's commitment to honesty on behalf of its audience. Small details are also explained: the inside of Big Bird's Nest and why Gordon and Susan finally received a last name. It's a valuable inside view for older readers of an invaluable program they saw—if they were lucky—as preschoolers.
(Age 11 and older)

Dillon, Leo and Diane Dillon. *To Every Thing There Is a Season.* Blue Sky
Press/Scholastic, 1998. 40 pages. (0–590–47887–7) $15.95

A popularly quoted passage from Hebrew Wisdom literature celebrates "human existence—the mysterious ebb and flow of happiness and pain that is ultimately beyond our control." To illustrate these verses from *Ecclesiastes* (King James translation of the *Bible),* the Dillons developed personal visual tributes to art styles from various centuries, cultures, and nations: illuminated manuscripts (Ireland), tomb murals (Egypt), woodblock prints (Japan), screen-fold picture books (Mixtec), vase paintings (Greece), manuscript illustrations (India), woodcut art (medieval Europe), mural painting (Kuaua Pueblo), illustrated books (Ethiopia), shadow plays (Thailand), silk paintings (China), icon paintings (Russia), aboriginal bark paintings (Australia), stone-cut art (Inuit), and Persian miniatures (Iran). A final passage, "One generation passes away, and another generation comes: but the Earth abides forever," is illustrated by a painting of Earth as seen from space, suggesting a strong environmental interpretation. (Age 7 and older)

Guthrie, Woody. *This Land Is Your Land.* Illustrated by Kathy Jakobsen. With a
tribute by Pete Seeger. Little, Brown, 1998. 32 pages. (0–316–39215–4) $15.95

The most important fact about this full-color picture book edition of Guthrie's famous song is that it contains complete lyrics, including the verse about "No Trespassing" and the one about the hungry people. The scope of Guthrie's message is intact. So is the beauty of his idea. Jakobsen's glorious paintings show varied topography and people within "this land" in detailed scenes and individuals from Guthrie's life. According to a note, "the paintings were done in oil on canvas, and the painted borders were inspired by notch carvings found in traditional "tramp art"—boxes, picture frames and mirror frames crafted by tramps, hoboes, miners and lumberjacks in the early to mid–1900s." The final pages include quotes from Guthrie, such as "This whole world is your world and my world. Take it easy, but take it." Images from Guthrie's experiences are pictured, including two composite paintings of "all his friends" together—singing. Seemingly endless discoveries can be made when scrutinizing each illustration, depending on where readers have lived or traveled and what they know about Woody Guthrie's life and times. Pete Seeger's tribute and a biographical sketch are placed on the opposite side of a three page foldout of the nation and its people. The music for the song completes the book. (Age 5 and older)

Igus, Toyomi. *i see the rhythm.* Paintings by Michele Wood. Children's Book Press, 1998. (246 First Street, Suite 101, San Francisco, CA 94105) (0–89239–151–0) $15.95

Joyful paintings visualize the musical roots of centuries beginning with once forbidden drums of many African heritages to the beats of the 1990s. "Fathered by funk and nurtured by mother Africa, I see the rhythm of hip hop and the rhythm lives on in me," writes Toyomi Igus. Each page spread of this full-color history of black music can be enjoyed in multiple ways. A time line in a small typeface provdies selected historical background for each section: Origins, Slave Songs, Birth of the Blues, Ragtime, Jazz Beginnings, Swing Jazz, Jazz Women, Bebop, Coll Jazz, Gospel, Rhythm & Blues/Soul Music, Black Rock, Funk, Rap and Hip Hop. Igus previously collaborated with artist Michele Wood on the book *Going Back Home*, an autobiographical essay on the artist's personal roots. In this new venture, Wood has hidden a little girl in every scene. Sometimes this child is a baby on a mother's back, or she might be playing the piano. Although that is a small detail, it's one that can increase the visual pleasure of a singularly handsome volume, especially for children young enough to feel the power of Wood's words but not quite ready for the background information about history. (Ages 9–14)

Jones, Bill T. and Susan Kuklin. *Dance.* Photographs by Susan Kuklin. Hyperion, 1998. 32 pages. (0–7868–2307–0) $14.95

Kuklin's stunning photographs of dancer/choreographer Bill T. Jones float on the page with a genuine sense of air, space, and motion. Kuklin expresses a strong awareness of the human form, along with a way to communicate about the external and internal aspects of dance. Jones and Kuklin's supple, poetic text is breif but evocative of both the movement and the mystery of dance. "When I am dancing, I can fly high / and soar through the air. ...When I am dancing, I am everyone / and I am only one." From various perspectives readers see expressive hands, legs, feet, and arms. The crisp white pages and flowing typeface offset Kuklin's full-color photographs of Bill T. Jones' expressive movement. That movement is Dance! *Highly Commended, 1999 Charlotte Zolotow Award.* (Ages 3–9)

Kerr, M.E. *Blood on the Forehead: What I Know about Writing.* HarperCollins, 1998. 262 pages. (0–06–027996–6) $21.95

How can a famous novelist for young teenagers describe how she does what she does as a writer? It's easy, if you're Mary Jane Meeker, aka M.E. Kerr. Wrong. It isn't easy. On page one Kerr tells about the framed quote attributed to Gene Fowler hanging over her desk" "Writing is easy. All you do is sit staring at a blank sheet of paper until the drops of blood form on your forehead." Kerr describes some of the courtesies a writer should extend to each reader, such as remembering to include important facts, give characters interesting names, forgetting about using heavy slang or dialect, etc. She relates several real-life anecdotes and reprints a short story or chapter from her work for young adults to illustrate specific writing concepts. Kerr is down-to-earth, witty, and helpful. Her fans will enjoy these glimpses of Kerr at work, even if they don't think of themselves as writers. The book is dedicated to the "kids who hope someday to write...and to their teachers, very often first ones to recognize their talents and to cheer them on." (Ages 12–16)

Minor, Wendell. *Grand Canyon: Exploring a Natural Wonder.* Blue Sky Press/Schoastic, 1998. 32 pages. (0–590–47968–7) $16.95
With his paintbox and sketchbook, Minor visited the South Rim of the Grand Canyon for 12 days during 1997. He recorded some of what he saw on paper. One of his objectives had been to observe this "spectacular chasm" closely with "on-the-spot sketches," as did the artist Thomas Moran more than a century ago. Before color photography, Moran's watercolor field sketches of Yellowstone in 1872 had provided governmental authorities with information necessary to consider it for national park status. In 1919 Moran's art had been instrumental in doing the same for Grand Canyon. Minor recorded the date and time he created each watercolor, thus documenting the light and the season as well as natural features. In addition to more than a dozen full-page, full-color reproductions of Minor's field art, several tiny renderings of birds and wildlife are included in this unusual perspective of an artist at work. Minor's brief written remarks accompany the art, lending even more insight about this stark, magnificent—indeed—grand land form. (Ages 10–15)

Dr. Seuss and Jack Prelutsky. *Hooray for Diffendoofer Day!* Illustrated by Lane Smith. Alfred A. Knopf, 1998. 56 pages. (0–679–89008–4) $17.00
If the students of the wonderful Miss Bonkers at at the free-thinking Diffendoofer school do not do well on an upcoming test, they'll have to go to school in Flobbertown, where everyone does everything the same, where even the dogs are scared to bark. Miss Bonkers saves the day with a pep talk: "We've taught you that the earth is round, / That red and white make pink, / And something else that matters more-We've taught you how to think." Dr. Seuss's editor calls the book a "a story in celebration of individuality and creative thinking," something of which many earlier Seuss heroes are also guilty. Does the narrator of the newest madcap Seuss adventure sound like the ones children have enjoyed for more than five decades? Yes, remarkably so — remarkably because the late Theodor Seuss Geisel (known throughout the world as Dr. Seuss) did not complete this manuscript prior to his death in 1991. Janet Schulman, his editor for 11 years, called upon two of today's published humorists for children, poet Jack Prelutsky and artist Lane Smith, to try to work with Geisel's original ideas and sketches for a book about a teacher named Miss Bonkers. They more than met the challenge. There's even a bonus for observant Seuss readers: cameo appearances by some of the recognizable Seuss characters. The final 13 pages are Schulman's discussion of the story behind the story and contain reproductions of Geisel's notes, representing an unparalled view of Dr. Seuss's creative process. (Age 8 and older)

Shaik, Fatima. *The Jazz of Our Street.* Illustrated by E.B. Lewis. Dial, 1998. 28 pages. (0–8037–1885–3) $15.99
The big sound of a jazz band drum entices a sister and brother old enough to follow with their neighbors to a nearby street even though it isn't a holiday.

The young first-person narrator claims, "we have music the way other folks talk. So where some people might gather for speeches to remember the dead, honor births and great days in history...we follow a band to listen and dance in our own special way." The music reinforces a shared heritage and builds community whether it's "funny and lively, or reverent and sad." A buoyant first-person story about New Orleans jazz marching bands and their connection to the people sets its own pleasing pace. Her references to tradition, heritage, and the Tremé neighborhood people "both famous and not" are skillfully incorporated into a child-centered narrative. Full-color artwork created with watercolors by Lewis shows African American men, women, boys and girls moving and lifted by the spirited music. Shaik's note about New Orleans jazz marching bands, dance patterns, African musical tradition of "call and response" rhythms, and second lining offers important background information on the final page of this celebrative picture story. (Ages 5–9)

Viola, Herman J. *Warrior Artists: Historic Cheyenne and Kiowa Indian Ledger Art Drawn by Making Medicine and Zotom.* **With commentary by Joseph D. And George P. Horse Capture. National Geographic Society, 1998. 125 pages. (0–7922–7370–2) $35.00**
American Indian ledger art comprises a unique artistic and historical record of Plains Indians cultures and of the destruction of their traditional existence. Named for the ledger books that were often the earliest kinds of paper that the warrior artists had access to, this artwork speaks both to the traditional way of life that the warriors cherished and to the devastating changes that western expansion and policies of the U.S. government were bringing to their lives. Between 1875 and 1878, both Cheyenne warrior Making Medicine and Kiowa warrior Zotom were held as prisoners of the U.S. government at Fort Marion in St. Augustine, Florida. Along with several dozen others from Plains Indian nations, they were taken to Fort Marion because they refused to surrender and live on reservations. While prisoners at the fort, the two men created a prolific body of ledger art, much of which is presented in this important and compelling volume. The book begins with an introduction by Herbert J. Viola's that summarizes the fierce resistance among Plains Indians people to losing their freedom and their way of life, and the harsh and sometimes erratic responses of the U.S. government that led to the imprisonment at Fort Marion. The warriors' lives at Fort Marion are also detailed. The drawings themselves, rendered in pencil and pen-and-ink, comprise the majority of the book and are given fine treatment in reproductions that fill single pages or span double-page spreads. The style, and especially the subject, of each artist's work is distinct. The art by Making Medicine focuses on village life and customs, while Zotom's drawings emphasize conflict between his people and the U.S. government and life in prison camp. The artwork is illuminated by the commentary of Joseph D. Horse Capture and George P. Horse Capture that accompanies each drawing, explaining the significance of various elements in the scenes culturally and/or historically. (Ages 13 and older)

Weeks, Sarah. *Little Factory.* **Illustrated by Byron Barton. A Laura Geringer Book/HarperCollins, 1998. 36 pages. (0–06–027429–8) $19.95**
An original song by Sarah Weeks and Michael Abbott tells the story of a little factory that falls victim to its own success. Once it expands to such a point

that it turns into a giant factory, the workers no longer want to work there because of all the smoke. Luckily for everyone involved, the man who runs the factory comes up with a solution that brings all the workers back— he updates it to run on solar power in order to improve the working conditions. Byron Barton's boldly colored illustrations include enough heavy machinery to satisfy his diehard fans, even as they complement the sweet simplicity of Weeks's song. An accompanying CD-Rom includes both a fully animated version of the song, and an interactive game. (Ages 2–5)

Weitzman, Jacqueline Preiss. *You Can't Take a Balloon into the Metropolitan Museum.* **Illustrated by Robin Preiss Glasser. Dial, 1998. 35 pages. (0–8037–2301–6) $16.99**

A little girl with a yellow balloon goes with her grandmother to the museum for the afternoon. The balloon has to be left with a guard at the museum entrance. The balloon blows away while the two are inside viewing many exhibits, glimpses of which are shown to readers. The yellow sphere travels across Manhattan through Central Park, in and out of the Plaza Hotel, and to a Lincoln Center stage where the opera "Aida" is being performed. Hundreds of people of all ages and walks of life can be seen throughout these wordless scenarios. They look disarmingly like people in Manhattan on an ordinary afternoon. The guard chases the balloon. In a madcap dash an ever-growing line of balloon rescuers returns to the museum just as the child and her grandmother appear. The book's inside joke for observant children is the images on the paintings, sculptures, pottery, and period clothing seen on display by our grandma and granddaughter in the museum are similar to what can be seen on the streets of New York City. It's fun to discover the parallels, and it's also fun for older readers to identify the actual works of art to which some of the illustrations make reference. A list of the latter is at the end of this delightful 11 $^{1}/_{4}$" square, wordless book, which will serve in years to come as a chronicle of the late 1990s in the Big Apple. (Ages 3–8)

Wick, Walter. *Walter Wick's Optical Tricks.* **Scholastic, 1998. 43 pages. (0–590–22227–9) $13.95**

From the paper clip apparently fastening an edge of the endpaper to the last of the 13 formal optical illusions, readers are encouraged to see and think in new ways. In the opening two-page spread, "First Impressions," readers first see quite a few objects that have been impressed into white clay, but when they turn the page upside down, the impressions seem to pop out. One of the ingenious aspects of Wick's full-color photographic illusions of inanimate objects is that he doesn't repeat himself. Some of the illusions are easier to discern than others. However, what is easy for one reader might be difficult for the next one, and vice versa, because each individual brings a different perception to each illusion. Wick's helpful note at the back reminds everyone that even though experts aren't certain why such difference occur, it's important to realize that each reader can experience the book at his/her own pace. This is an art experience, not an intelligence test. Welcome to the mysteries of visual perception. (Ages 7–10)

Ziefert, Harriet, reteller. *When I First Came to This Land.* **Illustrated by Simms Taback. Putnam's, 1998. 24 pages. (0–399–23044–0) $15.99**

A cheerful man wearing a shirt, tie, patched suit and optimistic smile stands near a transatlantic ocean liner on the first of 13 two-page spreads unfolding the engaging lyrics and illustrations of this man's cumulative story song. On the same opening pages, a narrow lower-edge border includes a mixed media assemblage including portions of a ticket stub, postage stamp, deposit receipt, ads for long underwear and freckle/pimple lotion, and a newspaper headline proclaiming that immigrants are arriving. The eager man claims, "When I first came to this land, / I was not a wealthy man. / The land was sweet and good, / And I did what I could." Who else but he could name his wilderness acreage Muscle-in-my-arm, his plow Don't-know-how, his horse I'm-the-boss, or his shack Break-my-back. His wide-eyed coping soon becomes dissembling but contentment finally reigns as his wife Spice-of-my-life and son So-much-fun are added to the song about his new life in a new land. According to a note in the book, folklore scholar Alvin Schwartz reported that this folk poem story or song was first brought to Pennsylvania by a German immigrant. Taback's zany images will entertain all who read, recite or dramatize it; they'll need to look elsewhere to learn the melody. (Ages 3–8)

See also: *All around Town; And If the Moon Could Talk; Bat Boy & His Violin; Boshblobberbosh; Christmas Story; Chuck Close Up Close; Circle of Days; Drawing in the Sand; Duke Ellington; From Slave Ship to Freedom Road; Jazmin's Notebook; Looking Back; Martha Graham; My Name Is Georgia; Painters of the Caves; Prairie Town; Purple Mountain Majesties; Pickin' Peas; Restless Spirit; Shakespeare Stealer; Snowflake Bentley; Space between Our Footsteps; Story Painter; Talking with Tebé; Tibet; Toilets, Toasters, & Telephones; Young, Black and Determined*

Poetry

Alarcón, Francisco. *From the Bellybutton of the Moon and Other Summer Poems = Del Ombligo de la Luna y Otros Poemas de Verano.* Illustrated by Maya Christina Gonzalez. Children's Book Press (246 First Street, Suite 101, San Francisco, CA 94105), 1998. 32 pages. (0–89239–153–7) $15.95

Francisco Alarcón's second bilingual picture book collection of poems for children is brimming with summer sights, summer sounds, and summer memories. The shorter poems in the collection are startling for their clarity and sense of perfection as they describe a summer-related feeling, aspect of nature, or memory in as few as eight words. The slightly longer poems sing with the cadence of personal story as they chronicle experiences specific to a child of Mexican heritage, but they are no less accessible than the shorter poems to any child who has ever loved language, or who has attached meaning to specific people and places. This Spanish/English collection, like Alarcón's earlier *Laughing Tomatoes and Other Spring Poems* (Children's Book Press, 1997), is illustrated with Maya Christina Gonzalez's celebratory paintings that reflect a child's joy in nature and family. (Ages 7–10)

Bayley, Nicola. *The Necessary Cat.* Candlewick Press, 1998. 77 pages. (0–7636–0571–9) $17.99

"All my work is done in the company of cats," Nicola Bayley writes in her brief, explanatory introduction to this collection of poems interspersed with tidbits of factual information, sayings and lore about cats that she has collected over years. Here Bayley has compiled her "cat ephemera" and illustrated it so that each piece of artwork is stylistically suited to the poem or scrap of information with which it is paired. The book's overall appearance is reminiscent of Victoriana, but the illustrations are witty, charming and varied in style. Along with the poems, facts and lore, they will delight any child who, like the author, believes cats to be a "beautiful and necessary" part of her or his life. (Age 8 and older)

Carlson, Lori Marie, selector. *Sol a Sol: Bilingual Poems.* **Illustrated by Emily Lisker. Henry Holt, 1998. 32 pages. (0–8050–4373-X) $15.95**
There are 14 poems in this sparkling, lighthearted bilingual (Spanish/English) collection—eight by compiler Lori Carlson and one each by six Latino writers. Some of the poems were written originally in Spanish and others in English. Their presentation in both languages is arranged so that the version of the language of origin appears first on the two-page spread devoted to each poem. Almost all of the poems have specific Latino cultural content while their subjects and renderings infuse them with broad child appeal that is evident from the titles alone: "I Like to Ride My Bike," "The Wind Bragging," "Peeling Potatoes with Papi," "The Smell of Night." Playful, flavorful language and imaginative ideas further enrich a collection that is unified by the whimsical, vibrant acrylic paintings of Emily Lisker. (Ages 4–8)

Florian, Douglas. *Insectlopedia: Poems and Paintings.* **Harcourt Brace, 1998. 47 pages. (0–15–201306–7) $16.00**
After *Beast Feast* (Harcourt, 1994), *On the Wing* (Harcourt, 1996), and *In the Swim* (Harcourt, 1997), could a book by Douglas Florian about insects be far behind? Like his three earlier volumes of original poems and paintings about the natural world, *Insectlopedia* is a fanciful, imaginative compilation in which the author/artist creates synergistic pairings of poems and works of art. Each of the 21 humorous poems blend observations about an individual insect's appearance or behavior with whimsical leaps of logic. Sometimes the textual humor comes from form as well, as in several concrete poems in which the words create a visual image on the page. The poems can stand on their own, but the watercolor paintings that Florian has created to illustrate them are both graceful and teasing expansions of the humor of the text, so that words and visual images together are a fuller experience than either on its own. (Ages 8–14)

Gollub, Matthew. *Cool Melons—Turn to Frogs! The Life and Poems of Issa.* **Illustrated by Kazuko G. Stone. Lee & Low (95 Madison Avenue, New York, NY 10016), 1998. 40 pages. (1–880000–71–7) $16.95**
Like the haiku form of poetry itself, here is a book that is all grace and wonder. Writer/compiler Matthew Gollub has balanced biographical information about the Japanese haiku master Issa, who lived in the late 18th and early 19th century, with beautiful translations of Issa's haiku. Through the narrative story, readers meet Issa as a child and follow him through adulthood and old age. Gollub has skillfully chosen specific haiku poems by Issa to extend the reader's understanding of this sensitive, observant writer beyond the facts of his life to knowledge of his heart and mind as revealed in his poetry. This exquisite picture book is illustrated with Kazuko Stone's delicate watercolor and colored pencil paintings, and each two-page spread is bordered with the Japanese language characters for the haiku appearing on those pages. An author's note provides additional factual information on Issa,

the decisions that went into haiku chosen for inclusion in the text, and the research that Stone conducted for the artwork. Background notes for several of the haiku poems along with information on the translations and the haiku art form is also provided. (Ages 8–12)

Johnson, Angela. *The Other Side: Shorter Poems.* Orchard, 1998. 44 pages. (0–531–30114–1) $15.95

Shorter, Alabama, is the community of childhood and family for writer Angela Johnson. The place where she grew up, it is filled with memories that will soon be all that she has left of Shorter. Her Grandmama writes her, "They're pullin' Shorter down." And so the subtitle of this collection is a play on words that echoes with poignancy as readers move through a series of poems that are quiet reflections of childhood feelings and events seen through the eyes of an adult returning to the place of her past with appreciation for what was and sadness for what never will be again. Written without sentimentality or nostalgia but rippling with emotions rooted in childhood that continue to resonate, these poems also provide detailed, sensual observations of life and people in a small, southern African American community during the late 1960s and early 1970s. The book is illustrated with black-and-white photographs from the author's personal collection. (Ages 11–15)

Kuskin, Karla. *The Sky Is Always in the Sky.* Illustrated by Isabelle Dervaux. A Laura Geringer Book/HarperCollins, 1998. 48 pages. (0–06–027083–7) $14.95

A small, vibrant treasury of poems by Karla Kuskin offers 35 delightful poems from eight of the author's earlier collections. One new poem rounds out this lively gathering that is playful, quirky, and thoughtful all at once. Kuskin combines a keen understanding of humor that will appeal to children and a masterful skill with words to create poems that are both funny and richly satisfying, full of inventive ideas and language ("If I were a fish, / I would swim like a fish / silently finning / with nary a swish, ...) and distinctive, changing rhythms. Her poems exemplify how carefully chosen words create their own energy and set their own pace. Start reading a poem by Karla Kuskin and the beat becomes intuitive. But be careful! A Kuskin poem is as likely to change its pulse as it is to continue its steady heartbeat, and the rhyme schemes can be just as unpredictable. It is these surprises, along with fresh ideas and images and humor that affirms children as insiders to the joke, that distinguishes these poems. This collection, in which each poem is set against a brightly colored page featuring clean-lined, whimsical illustrations by Isabelle Dervaux, provides children new to Kuskin's poetry with an engaging introduction to her work. For Kuskin fans, it is an appealing invitation to revisit favorites. (Ages 5–10)

Lewis, J. Patrick. *Boshblobberbosh: Runcible Poems for Edward Lear.* Illustrated by Gary Kelley. Creative Editions/Harcourt Brace, 1998. 40 pages. (0–15–201949–9) $18.00

What better way to pay tribute to Edward Lear than with a collection of original nonsense poems about his life? The16 poems in this 13 $^1/_4$ x 9 $^1/_4$" volume, written in the spirit of Lear's own nonsense, are arranged in chronological order, beginning with "Born in a Crowd," a poem about his birth as the 20th child in a family of 21 children and ending with "Old Foss (The Cat) Recalls His Life with Mr. Lear," written in the voice of the beloved

16-year-old cat who died three months before Lear did. In between are poems about Lear's eccentricities, travels, and strange-but-true incidents in his life, each one further illuminated in notes at the end of the book. Gary Kelley's lush surreal paintings brilliantly capture the essence of Lear's bizarre internal and external worlds. (Age 12 and older)

Lindbergh, Reeve. *The Circle of Days.* **Illustrated by Cathie Felstead. Candlewick Press, 1998. 24 pages. (0–7636–0357–0) $15.99**
According to a note in this 11 x 10" illustrated version of "Canticle of the Sun," that 13th century assemblage of writings by the founder of the Franciscan order of monks has been adapted in poetry and song throughout the centuries. Lindbergh's reworking of the original ideas has pleasing appeal for today's young readers and families as a poem or a prayer of praise. She writes, "For all her children, fierce or mild, / For sister, brother, parent, child. / For creatures wild, and creatures tame, / For hunter, hunted, both the same. / For brother sleep, and sister death, / who tends the borders of our breath...For all your gifts, of every kind, / We offer praise with quiet mind..." Wonderfully designed double-page spreads usually contain one large illustration and several smaller images suggesting a global scope. The author and artist each discovered effective ways to interest children while honoring the wide diversity within earlier written presentations of this famous poem. Felstead's captivating images were done in watercolor, gouache, and collage. (Ages 3–7)

Myers, Walter Dean. *Angel to Angel: A Mother's Gift of Love.* **HarperCollins, 1998. 32 pages. (0–06–027721–1) $15.95**
A beautifully designed volume of poetry in which Myers again pairs selections from his collection of antique photographs of children, especially African American children, with his original poetry, here celebrating the bond between mother and child. Like the earlier *Brown Angels* (HarperCollins, 1993) and *Glorious Angels* (HarperCollins, 1995), *Angel to Angel* is an elegant book. Silver border designs frame elements on every page, and the shining faces on those pages look out from photographs that are also edged in silver. Not every photograph is necessarily of a mother and child. Some, Myers notes, may be of other adult women in the children's lives. Others are of children only. "It's the feelings of love that define a relationship," the author notes in the introduction, and certainly that feeling of love, of someone loving and treasuring the child that is pictured, can be filled in by the reader. Myers's poetry evokes a wide range of moods, from contemplative to deeply loving, sassy to silly, in another handsome book to be treasured by families. (Age 6 and older)

Nye, Naomi Shihab, selector. *The Space Between Our Footsteps: Poems and Paintings from the Middle East.* **Simon & Schuster, 1998. 144 pages. (0–689–81233–7) $19.95**
"It is quite possible that the Middle East is one of the most negatively stereotyped places on earth," Nye begins this anthology. "I can't stop believing that human beings everywhere hunger for deeper-than-headline news about one another. Poetry and art are some of the best ways this heartfelt 'news' may be exchanged." The work of 20th century poets and artists, women and men, from 19 Middle Eastern countries is compiled in a book that resonates with words and images at once both recognizable and

wholly distinct, as is the heart of every human being. Many of the poems are rich with details of places and customs unfamiliar to most U.S. readers, or familiar, as the introduction states, only through the news, which reports on guns and bombs but not hearts and souls. All of the poems hold the promise of discovery inherent in fine writing. The beautifully reproduced paintings are also points of entry into this too-often foreign part of the globe, and the visual images provide readers with the opportunity to make further connections between the paintings and the images expressed in poems placed nearby. Source notes, biographical information about the poets and translators, and indexes to the works are provided in this exquisite, important volume that brings diverse perspectives on life in the Middle East into focus through the human heart rather than the framework of political boundaries. (Age 12 and older)

Philip, Neil, editor. *War and the Pity of War.* Illustrated by Michael McCurdy. U.S. edition: Clarion, 1998. 96 pages. (0–395–84982–9) $20.00

"For most modern poets, war is about horror, not heroism," Philip notes in the introduction to this striking collection of poems that explores war's tragedy and human costs. The 72 poems included in the collection focus primarily on conflicts of the 20th century. The majority are European and American poems about World War I and World War II, such as Carl Sandburg's "Wars," William Butler Yeat's "An Irish Airman Foresees His Death," and Karen Gershon's "The Children's Exodus." But other nations and other times are also represented. There is Iraqi poet Sa'di Yusuf's "Guns," Zulu writer Mazisi Kunene's "For a Friend Who Was Killed in the War," and Ken Smith's "Essential Serbo-Croat." Martín Espada's "Manuel Is Quiet Sometimes" and "Hell No! I Ain't Gonna Go!" by Matthew Jones and Elaine Lavon are two of the selections about the Vietnam War, while early centuries are represented in poems about the American Civil War, the Napoleonic Wars; voices from China and ancient Greece; even a traditional Ojibwa war song. "I hope there is enough [here] from earlier days to set our century's story in the wider context of human history and human suffering." This singular collection is set in bold type and illustrated with stark black-and-white images that underscore the intensity of the experience of war. An index of poets that includes their dates and nation of origin, and an index of titles and first lines completes the volume. (Age 12 and older)

Rosenberg, Liz, editor. *Earth-Shattering Poems.* Holt, 1998. 126 pages. (0–8050–4821–9) $15.95

Rosenberg's dynamic compilation is prefaced with an outstanding introduction in which she describes collecting poems that "speak most powerfully to our most intense experiences and emotions." They are poems that she found "earth-shatteringly beautiful," or romantic, or scathing, or that "shattered [her] sense of time and place." The wide range of poetry in this collection includes a fragment by the Greek poet Sappho (620–550 BCE), a poem from 17th century Japanese haiku master Basho, and numerous selections from poets of the 19th and 20th century, including Emily Dickinson, William Blake, Langston Hughes, Pablo Neruda, Audre Lorde and many others. Rosenberg's introduction validates readers' own responses to these and other poems at the same time it acknowledges "it is all right to be partly confused by a poem; it's all right if you can only grab hold of a corner of it, because eventually that corner may be enough to pull you all the way through." Excellent biographical notes provide information on each poet's life and often suggest additional resources. A selected bibliography of other suggested reading rounds out this fine collection. (Age 12 and older)

Sandburg, Carl. *Grassroots*. Illustrated by Wendell Minor. Browndeer Press/Harcourt Brace, 1998. 40 pages. (0–15–200082–8) $18.00

An elegant picture book pairs evocative images of Midwest and country life written by Carl Sandburg with handsome watercolor paintings by Wendell Minor. The Sandburg poems, chosen from a number of his collections, are arranged to follow a course of the seasons, starting with spring and moving through summer and autumn to end with winter. They are brief, exquisite interludes and stolen moments suspended in time, preserving forever a rural sunrise ("Daybreak"), the sound of prairie grass in a gentle breeze ("Summer Grass"), or the impossible sight of a red rose against winter snow ("Red and White"). Each two-page spread features a single poem paired with or laid on top of Minor's corresponding image. The watercolors are richly hued and serve to extend the feelings that spring from the text of this exquisitely designed collection. (Ages 8–12)

Stevenson, Robert Louis. *Where Go the Boats? Play Poems*. Illustrated by Max Grover. Browndeer Press/Harcourt Brace, 1998. 32 pages. (0–15–201711–9) $16.00

Four of Robert Louis Stevenson's classic poems for children are given dazzling visual color treatment in this anything-but-quiet picture book. Max Grover's acrylic paintings illustrating Stevenson's "A Good Play," "Block City," "The Land of Counterpane," and "Where Go the Boats" surround the poems with color that pulses to the rhythm of the verses. No somber 19th century hues here, this is the palate of the late 20th century, in which diverse children play in a rooms with walls of vivid green, sunny yellow, or deep deep blue. Floors are a checkerboard of red and white; furniture and books and toys are dazzling in their purple, red, and seagreen hues. Four poems that already have great appeal in the listening are turned into a visual delight for today's young readers and listeners. (Ages 4–8)

Thomas, Joyce Carol. *Cherish Me*. Illustrated by Nneka Bennett. Joanna Cotler Books/HarperFestival, 1998. 20 pages. (0–694–01097–9) $9.95

A poem taken from Thomas's singular, inspiring collection *Brown Honey in Broomwheat Tea* (HarperCollins, 1993) is presented on its own as the text of this uplifting, joyous picture book about a brown-skinned child. Thomas celebrates the ways in which blackness is beautiful and unique: "clothed" in the colors of mother earth, skin "glazed" by father sun, "the pattern of night in my hair." "I am beautiful by design," the text affirms. And most certainly the joyful, dark-skinned little girl pictured in Nneka Bennett's warm illustrations is, as is every child with whom this book is shared. (Ages 2–5)

See also: *Carol of the Brown King; Counting on the Woods; Marty Frye, Private Eye; Night Before Christmas; What's the Most Beautiful Thing You Know About Horses?*

Concept Books

Adler, David A. *Shape Up! Fun with Triangles and Other Polygons.* Illustrated by Nancy Tobin. Holiday House, 1998. 32 pages. (0–8234–1346–2) $15.95

A clever introduction to geometry encourages readers to use some common household objects as props to define different kinds of triangles, quadrilaterals, and other polygons. All of the concepts are demonstrated using a toothpick, a slice of American cheese, pretzel sticks, a round sheet of paper, a piece of graph paper, and a pencil. Tobin's bightly colored illustrations and Adler's occasional bad puns ("Now that's what I call a square meal!") add touches of humor without overwhelming the sound information. (Ages 8–10)

Falwell, Cathryn. *Word Wizard.* Clarion, 1998. 32 pages. (0–395–85580–2) $15.00

Anna is a word wizard. With a little magic and a few scrambled words, she can do just about anything. When she meets Zack, who is lost and crying, she turns his **tears** into a **stream** (with the help of an added **m**). The stream flows into an **ocean**, which Anna turns into a **canoe**, and she and Zack climb in. When they reach the **shore**, she changes it into a **horse**, and so it goes in this playful anagram adventure. Bright, full-color illustrations accompany a picture book that will have children creating a little magic of their own as the secrets and pleasure of words are revealed. (Ages 5–7)

Godwin, Laura. *Little White Dog.* Illustrated by Dan Yaccarino. Hyperion, 1998. 24 pages. (0–7868–2256–2) $14.95

"Little white dog in the snow, snow's so white, where did you go? / Little blue bird in the sky, sky's so blue, where did you fly?" A green bug, brown horse, yellow chick, and black cat follow a similar pattern in which Yaccarino's illustrations show each animal camouflaged on the same colored background. Sharp-eyed preschoolers, however, will be able to find them by looking for telltale beaks, eyes, hooves and noses. (Ages 3–5)

Harris, Pamela. *Hot, Cold, Shy, Bold: Looking at Opposites.* U.S. edition: Kids Can Press (29 Birch Ave., Toronto, ON Canada M4V IE2), 1998. 32 pages. (1–55074–153–5) $10.95

Since most young children enjoy looking at photographs of their peers, Pamela Harris has found an appealing way to introduce opposites to toddlers. She uses photographs of children to demonstrate the concept and here the children's faces become the artist's canvas. With just a few words per page, a rhyming text points out the opposing features, beginning with "a hot face / a cold face / a shy face / a bold face." Engaging, remarkably unposed photographs show a wide range of children of various ages, along with a few adults who were needed to illustrate "an old face" and "a bearded face." The photographs are large and clear enough so that the book could be easily shared as a group read-aloud, although individual children will want to spend time pouring over the pictures, trying out some faces of their own. (Ages 1–3)

Hughes, Shirley. *Alfie's ABC.* U.S. edition: Lothrop, Lee and Shepard, 1998. 32 pages. (0–688–16126–X) $16.00

Most of the illustrations in this volume are reprinted from earlier stories about Alfie and his little sister, Annie Rose. Like the books from which they come, all depict a child's-eye view of the world, and the letters are represented by things familiar to young children: B is for bedtime and blanket, D is for door, M is for moon, P is for park and puddles, X is for xylophone, and Z is for zipper. Children who are familiar with Shirley Hughes's books about Alfie will delight in this introduction to the alphabet, and those who don't know him will still enjoy his child-centered ABC. (Ages 2–5)

Lyon, George Ella. *Counting on the Woods.* Photographs by Ann W. Olson. A Richard Jackson Book/DK Ink, 1998. 32 pages. (0–7894–2480–0) $15.95

"One path, a stick for a staff / Two birds, daybreak's words" begins this poetic counting book inspired by the observations of a young boy on a walk through the woods in Appalachian Kentucky. Ann Olson's distinctive photographs capture both the immense, lush greenness of the woods and the small details, such as delicate flowers and sturdy blades of grass, while George Ella Lyon's rhyming words often surprise us with their spare poetry. Together the text and pictures will help children focus on the sorts of natural wonders that are as common as those they may observe in their own backyards, as they count things such as nests, tracks, bugs, stones and flowers. (Ages 4–8)

Murphy, Stuart J. *A Fair Bear Share.* Illustrated by John Speirs. (MathStarts) HarperCollins, 1998. 33 pages. (0–06–127438–7) $14.95

Mama Bear promises to make her special Blue Ribbon Blueberry pie for her four cubs, provided they go out and gather enough nuts, berries and seeds. When each one brings the ingredients, Mama divides them into groups of ten and adds them up to see if she has enough. While the book is compelling enough to share as a read-aloud, the story does not detract from the introduction to the concept of tens and ones, and the appealing illustrations are designed to support and reinforce the concept. (Ages 5–8)

Root, Phyllis. *One Duck Stuck.* Illustrated by Jane Chapman. Candlewick Press, 1998. 32 pages. (0–7636–0334–1) $15.99

When one duck gets "stuck in the muck, down by the deep green marsh," she calls for help. First two fish come to her rescue, then three moose, four crickets, five frogs, and so on, until finally all the animals realize they must work together to help the duck. A strong verbal pattern that uses a rollicking rhyme and plenty of onomatopoeia makes this funny counting book a good choice for a group read-aloud story. (Ages 2–5)

See also: *Do You Know New?; Fire Truck; Halala Means Welcome!; Moses Goes to a Concert; Once Upon a Company; What Is a Scientist?*

Board Books

Cummings, Pat. *My Aunt Came Back.* (Harper Growing Tree) HarperFestival, 1998. 12 pages. (0–694–01059–6) $5.95
"My aunt came back from Timbuktu. She brought me back a wooden shoe. / My aunt came back from Bucharest. She brought me back a quilted vest." Each double-age spread introduces another faraway place and a gift a young girl's aunt brought from it. While the board-book set is not likely to know the pattern familiar to their older siblings, young children will nevertheless enjoy the lilting rhythms and exuberant illustrations that depict a warm relationship in an African American family. (Ages 2–4)

Hines-Stephens, Sara. *Bean.* Illustrated by Anna Grossnickle Hines. Red Wagon/Harcourt Brace, 1998. 16 pages. (0–15–201604–X) $4.95

Hines-Stephens, Sarah. *Bean's Games.* Illustrated by Anna Grossnickle Hines. Red Wagon/Harcourt Brace, 1998. 16 pages. (0–15–201606–6) $4.95

Hines-Stephens, Sarah. *Bean's Night.* Illustrated by Anna Grossnickle Hines. Red Wagon/Harcourt Brace, 1998. 16 pages. (0–15–201602–3) $4.95
Bean is a small black cat with green eyes who has a starring role in a new series of tiny (4 $^1/_2$ x 4 $^1/_2$") board books. In *Bean* we meet not only the cat but the baby she lives with. *Bean's Night* shows all her lively nocturnal activity—running through the house, climbing up onto the table, and pouncing on a toy mouse. *Bean's Games* shows her engaged in typical cat pursuits such as playing with string, playing in a paper bag, and lying on a human's lap while the accompanying text is composed of plays on words (string Bean, Bean bag, human Bean, etc.) that only the adult readers will understand, while children will be captivated by the illustrations. (Ages 1–3)

Hubbell, Patricia. *Wrapping Paper Romp.* Illustrated by Jennifer Plecas. (Harper Growing Tree) HarperFestival, 1998. 12 pages. (0–694–01098–7) $5.95
As she does in *Pots and Pans* (see entry in Picture Books for Younger Children), Patricia Hubbell once again offers a pleasing rhymed text based on true-to-life baby behavior. Here a baby and a feline companion have more fun with the wrapping paper and box a present comes in than they do with the three teddy bears enclosed as the gift. Each step of the unwrapping process inspires a baby game— waving the paper, wearing the paper as a hat, playing peek-a-boo, and, of course, tearing the paper, playful illustrated in a style reminiscent of Helen Oxenbury. (Ages 1–2)

Hurd, Thacher. *Zoom City.* (Harper Growing Tree) HarperFestival, 1998. 12 pages. (0–694–01057–X) $5.95
A whimsical board book with plenty of action for car-loving toddlers features dreamlike images of city streets at night. Neon-colored illustrations, composed of painted futuristic cars and collage assemblages using vintage cars, show animal drivers zooming down city streets until a fender bender requires a team of tow trucks to take them to the repair shop. The brief narrative is filled with playful rhymes and onomatopoeia, as well as the toddlers' mantra: green light, go! red light, stop! (Ages 1–3)

Marzollo, Jean. *Do You Know New?* Illustrated by Mari Takabayashi. (Harper Growing Tree) HarperFestival, 1998. 16 pages. (0–694–00870–2) $5.95

Each double-page spread poses and answers the question: "Do you know..." beginning with the title question, and then using a series of rhyming objects (blue, two, shoe, moo, boo, and you). Stylized illustrations help to interpret both the questions and the responses as they show children of different races involved in the rhyming game. The book ends with a mirror, so that the "you" referred to in the text will always be the child reading the book. (Ages 1–3)

Wells, Rosemary. *Max's Bath.* Dial, 1998. 10 pages. (0–8037–2266–4) $5.99

Wells, Rosemary. *Max's Bedtime.* Dial, 1998. 10 pages. (0–8037–2267–2) $5.99

Wells, Rosemary. *Max's Birthday.* Dial, 1998. 10 pages. (0–8037–2268–0) $5.99

Wells, Rosemary. *Max's Breakfast.* Dial, 1998. 10 pages. (0–8037–2273–7) $5.99

Wells, Rosemary. *Max's First Word.* Dial, 1998. 10 pages. (0–8037–2269–9) $5.99

Wells, Rosemary. *Max's New Suit.* Dial, 1998. 10 pages. (0–8037–2270–2) $5.99

Wells, Rosemary. *Max's Ride.* Dial, 1998. 10 pages. (0–8037–2272–9) $5.99

Wells, Rosemary. *Max's Toys.* Dial, 1998. 10 pages. (0–8037–2271–0) $5.99

These eight volumes, first published between 1979 and 1985, were among the first original board books produced especially with toddlers in mind. With just a few well-chosen words and brilliant strokes of the paintbrush, Wells managed to create a series of engaging stories centering on a stubborn little rabbit named Max and his bossy older sister, Ruby. All eight volumes have now been reissued in a larger size (7 x 7") with completely new illustrations that maintain the spirit of the originals. In addition, Wells has made minor changes to improve some of the texts, all in the interest of simplicity. But in the face of these changes, Max and Ruby's characters and their sibling struggles remain the same, and they will continue to delight a new generation of children. (Ages 1–3)

Picture Books for Younger Children

Banks, Kate. *And If the Moon Could Talk.* Illustrated by Georg Hallensleben. Translated from the French. U.S. edition: Frances Foster Books/Farrar Straus Giroux, 1998. 40 pages. (0–374–30299–5) $15.00

"Somewhere a pair of shoes lies under a chair. A window yawns open. Twilight blazes a trail across the wall. / And if the moon could talk, it would tell of evening stealing through the woods and a lizard scurrying home to supper." So begins the expertly paced pattern for a bedtime sequence, things a young child might see and hear at home, pictured on page spreads that alternate with those of distant landscapes-all illuminated by the same moon. Paintings executed in vibrant primary colors create a calm, secure, peaceful mood: stuffed animal resting in chair, music box sitting on shelf, mobile stirring in evening air, Papa reading story, Mama covering drowsy child. The extraordinary language and dependable rhythm of Banks' beautifully understated narrative express the gradual winding down of a little child's day. Banks' eloquent writing and Hallensleben's lush paintings, however, convey more than the reliable stuff of bedtime ritual. The globe on a dresser-top reiterates the subtle theme of a larger world. A painting hanging on the wall and a glimpse of a picture in the child's book subtly refer to the role of art in daily life in this book that invites quiet exploration. (Ages 3–6)

Blos, Joan. *Bedtime!* **Illustrated by Stephen Lambert. Simon & Schuster, 1998. 28 pages. (0–689–81031–8) $12.00**

At bedtime, a little boy claims he isn't the least bit sleepy, so his patient grandma helps set the mood by helping him tuck in his three stuffed animals, one by one. By the time all that work is done, the little boy realizes that he is really sleepy after all, especially when he sees how lonely his toys look without him. He's ready for his pajamas and a bedtime story. A gentle, patterned text, illustrated with soft pastels, shows a bedtime routine in which both the child and the adult ultimately get what they want. (Ages 2–4)

Crews, Donald. *Night at the Fair.* **Greenwillow, 1998. 24 pages. (0–688–11484–9) $15.00**

Once again, Donald Crews finds the drama in everyday life by beaming in on a subject that is innately exciting to young children. Just like a real trip to the fair, the story begins at the entrance and ends at the exit. In between, each double-page spread illustrates the highlights—the food stands, the games with prizes, and, of course, the rides, culminating with a ride on the Ferris wheel where you can see the entire fair, "where we've been and where we can still go." The illustrations' black backgrounds sharply contrast with golden-hued foregrounds to recreate the excitement and the ambience of a fair at night. (Ages 3–7)

Demarest, Chris L. *Honk!* **Boyds Mills Press, 1998. 14 pages. (1–56397–221–2) $9.95**

A lost gosling looks for its mother by asking all the animal passers-by the same question: "Honk?" Each animal, revealed when one lifts the flap, responds in its own tongue. Only the passing car seems to speak the gosling's language; luckily mother goose is not far behind! The charming story will invite two kinds of participation from young readers: they will be anxious to lift the flap, and to make the corresponding animal noise. (Ages 1–4)

Ehlert, Lois. *Top Cat.* **Harcourt Brace, 1998. 32 pages. (0–15–201739–9) $16.00**

The only cat in a household has trouble accepting a new kitten until he realizes that, as the dominant cat, he can entertain himself by teaching the newcomer everything he needs to know, like how to drink from the sink faucet, leave hair on the couch, chew the leaves on house plants, and, most important, how to run outside whenever the door opens! Humor is derived from the contrast between humans' view of good cat behavior vs. the feline perspective. Ehlert's cut-paper collages, though highly stylized, manage to capture the subtleties of cat posture, giving the artwork an amazingly realistic look. Her bold images and simple rhyming text will make this a good read-aloud choice for preschool story times. (Ages 3–7)

Feiffer, Jules. *I Lost My Bear.* **Morrow, 1998. 40 pages. (0–688–15148–5) $16.00**

A humorous, exaggerated story illustrated in Feiffer's distinctive cartoon style has at its core the psychological reality of a young child's obsession with finding a lost toy before bedtime. When her parents are unable to help her search for her bear, a little girl tries the solution offered by her older sister who suggests that she throw another toy, watch where it lands, and then see if her lost bear is anywhere nearby. Although this method doesn't help her find her bear, she does find many other things she's lost recently and each thing she finds distracts her—for awhile. A truly funny and original story about an age-old problem. (Ages 3–7)

Fleming, Denise. *Mama Cat Has Three Kittens.* Henry Holt, 1998. 32 pages. (0–8050–5745–5) $15.95

Of Mama Cat's three kittens, Fluffy and Skinny always do everything their mother does — washing their paws, sharpening their claws, chasing leaves, etc. — while the third kitten, Boris, naps. Denise Fleming uses rhythm, repetition, and predictability to great advantage here, making each turn of the page dramatic and satisfying for young listeners. As an illustrator, Fleming uses composition in much the same way, always placing the active cats prominently in the picture, while Boris sleeps curled up, away from the action, but his bright orange color always makes him clearly visible. The art is bold enough to be seen easily from a distance for children in a storyhour, while those seeing it close-up when being read to one-on-one will notice the details of a visual subplot involving a mouse who's building a nest for her own babies. There's an amusing childlike twist at the end when Mama Cat finally settles down for a nap herself, awakening Boris, who continues to march to the beat of his own drummer. *Highly Commended, 1999 Charlotte Zolotow Award.* (Ages 2–6)

Goldstone, Bruce. *The Beastly Feast.* Illustrated by Blair Lent. Henry Holt, 1998. 32 pages. (0–8050–3867–1) $15.95

"The beasts are having a feast! Animals from everywhere come with tasty food to share. . . . / Bears bring pears. Parrots bring carrots. / Antelope bring cantaloupe. Puffins bring muffins. / Mosquitoes bring burritos. Fishes bring knishes." As the fleas push their peas uphill, all seems to be going well at the beastly feast until the flies drop one of their pies and all the food and animals get mixed up. The only order remaining at the feast is in Goldstone rollicking rhyme which describes the mixed-up mess and brings the story to a satisfying conclusion (which involves some armadillos). Blair Lent's brightly colored prints capture the spirit of Goldstone's nonsensical verse— just how would a mosquito carry a burrito anyway? Lent has figured it all out! (Ages 3–7)

Heap, Sue. *Cowboy Baby.* U.S. edition: Candlewick, 1998. 24 pages. (0–7636–0437–2) $15.99

When Sheriff Pa says it's time for bed, Cowboy Baby must first rustle up his partners: Texas Ted, Denver Dog, and Hank the Horse. Even after he finds them, there's still time for a quick game of hide-and-seek with Sheriff Pa. The line between fantasy and reality is charmingly obscured in this large-sized (12 x 10") picture book about the power of imaginary play. Boldly colored illustrations skew and flatten perspectives to reinforce the notion that most of the action is taking place in Cowboy Baby's mind. And Sheriff Pa has obviously earned his badge for his willingness to play along with his creative little buckaroo. (Ages 2–5)

Henkes, Kevin. *Circle Dogs.* **Illustrated by Dan Yaccarino. Greenwillow, 1998. 32 pages. (0–688–15447–6) $15.00**
"In the big square house live two circle dogs. / See the dogs? See the circles? Shh. They're sleeping now." Soon enough the two curled-up dachshunds awaken and stretch, and we are treated to the sights and sounds of everyday life with two lively dogs, as seen from the perspective of a small child. Henkes is right on target with his wry observations, from the clinking of dog tags and clacking of toenails to the stomp, whoosh, grrrrowl of the midday mail. Yaccarino's flat, stylized illustrations are at once sophisticated and childlike as they combine abstraction with the familiar and comforting repetition of circles and squares. There's an old-fashioned feel to the book as a whole: Henkes's intimate child-centered text rivals the best writing of Margaret Wise Brown, while Yaccarino's style is reminiscent of Esphyr Slobodkina's illustrations for Brown's classic, *The Little Fireman* (William Scott, 1938). *Highly Commended, 1999 Charlotte Zolotow Award.* (Ages 2–4)

Hubbell, Patricia. *Pots and Pans.* **Illustrated by Diane de Groat. (Harper Growing Tree) HarperFestival, 1998. 20 pages. (0–694–01072–3) $9.95**
The one-year-old's perennial fascination with kitchen cupboards is joyfully acknowledged in a bouncy rhyming text. Under the feet of a busy parent in the kitchen, the baby opens cupboards and finds all sorts of makeshift toys— pots, pans, soup cans, and other kitchen implements. The dog and cat join the fun, which continues until the baby gets into the cupboard with boxes of cereal and cookies, at which time Dad puts an end to the baby's explorations. An everyday occurrence in any life with a baby is enhanced by Diane de Groat's realistic watercolor paintings drawn from a baby's perspective. (Ages 1–3)

Hughes, Shirley. *Alfie and the Birthday Surprise.* **U.S. edition: Lothrop, Lee & Shepard, 1998. 32 pages. (0–688–15187–6) $16.00**
Alfie helps with preparations for a surprise party for his neighbor, Mr. MacNally from across the street who's turning 52. It's a difficult time for the man, however, because his beloved cat just died of old age the previous week. Told from four-year-old Alfie's perspective, we see the interactions between the two families as they grieve for the cat and prepare for the birthday party. Alfie, his mom, and baby sister, Annie Rose, go shopping for presents, and Mrs. MacNally comes over to Alfie's house to bake the surprise birthday cake. There is a general air of excitement and anticipation for Alfie as everyone gets ready for the surprise party. But, best of all, Alfie is entrusted with caring for Maureen MacNally's surprise gift for her father — a tiny, rambunctious kitten who bats at the quilt on Alfie's bed and pounces on his feet throughout the night. "Alfie loved feeling him at the end of his bed," Hughes writes. "But he would not have wanted him there every night." As in her previous books about Alfie and his family, Shirley Hughes's vivid watercolor illustrations are at once charming and realistic, specific and universal. Her text ingeniously recreates the everyday drama in the life of a small child because she has chosen just the right details, screened through Alfie's point of view, to tell this child-centered, wholly satisfying story. (Ages 3–6)

McPhail, David. *Tinker and Tom and the Star Baby.* Little, Brown, 1998.
32 pages. (0–316–56349–8) $14.95
When a baby star falls from the sky, Tom and his bear companion, Tinker, work through the night to help the Star Baby get back to its home in the sky. While they work, Star Baby gets into things and causes some mischief, just as a human baby would do. A small child's imaginary play is presented as reality in an engaging picture book fantasy, illustrated with luminous watercolor paintings. (Ages 3–5)

Mahy, Margaret. *A Summery Saturday Morning.* Illustrated by Selina Young. U.S. edition: Viking, 1998. 24 pages. (0–670–87943–6) $15.99
A playful, repetitive rhyming text decribes the difficulties four children and one adult have when they take their two dogs along on a walk down to the beach. What might otherwise have been a peaceful venture turns boisterous when the dogs chase a cat and then a flock of geese (who chases them back!). It's all in good fun, however, as Mahy's delightful verses point out the humor in the situation. Selina Young's bright pen-and-ink and watercolor illustrations capture the spirit of the fun. (Ages 3–6)

Martin, David. *Five Little Piggies.* Illustrated by Susan Meddaugh. Candlewick Press, 1998. 32 pages. (1–56402–918–2) $16.99
Ever wonder about those five little piggies? Why the first one went to market and the second one stayed home? Why one had roast beef, while another seemed to go hungry? And what was up with all that wee-wee-wee-ing? David Martin had created a completely plausible context for it all in a hilarious story that casts all five little piggies as siblings with a wonderfully patient and understanding mother. Each of the five is given his or her own short chapter, delightfully illustrated by Susan Meddaugh, who is greatly skilled at drawing pigs that look remarkably like children we all know. (Ages 3–6)

Meade, Holly. *John Willy and Freddy McGee.* Marshall Cavendish, 1998. 32 pages. (0–7614–5033–5) $15.95
John Willy and Freddy McGee are guinea pigs, and they're bored by the same old routine. So when their cage is left open by mistake they're off and running. "Run, John Willy! Run, run, Freddy McGee!" encourages the energizing, urgent narrative voice of this marvelous picture book that bursts into an explosion of color and festival of language as soon as the guinea pigs make their escape. "Circling the hassock, scattering the marbles, squeezing beneath the table they scooted!" Holly Meade's scintillating text holds its own on dazzling pages of color showing the two small guinea pigs running through brilliantly decorated rooms that each have their own distinct and vibrant palette. A pool table is almost the animals' undoing, however—taking refuge in the comfort of its tunnels (guinea pigs know tunnels), they are unaware of the cat up above, who cannot resist batting the balls into the holes. Making their escape from this hilarious encounter at last, the guinea pigs trace their route back toward the safety of their cage, passing again through each of the rooms, where the author/artist has left clues for sharp eyes to discover that the human inhabitants of this house have come and gone since the animals last passed through. Spectacular design and masterful pacing round out this superb and delightful picture book. *Honor Book, 1999 Charlotte Zolotow Award*; *Honor Book, 1998 CCBC Caldecott Award Discussion.* (Ages 3–7)

Milgrim, David. *Cows Can't Fly.* Viking, 1998. 32 pages. (0–670–87475–2) $15.99

The young child narrator of this story is inspired by possibilities and undaunted by the lack of imagination and busy-ness of the adults around him. When he draws a picture of flying cows–each one round and bouyant as a balloon–his father scoffs. Then the wind catches hold of the picture and carries it away. It lands in a pasture full of cows, and the cows, too, are undaunted and inspired. "Hmmmm," they say, and to the child's delight, "Next thing I knew, to my surprise, a flock of cattle fluttered by!" His mother is too busy in her carpentry workshop to notice them, as is his grandmother on her mail route, and all the adults on the street are too busy looking down to look up. So the child enjoys the spectacle on his own. David Milgrim's delightful rhyming text and whimsical illustrations pays homage to the spirit of a child's imagination, inviting young readers and listeners to embark on fanciful flights of their own. (Ages 3–7)

Ormerod, Jan. *Who's Whose?* U.S. edition: Lothrop, Lee & Shepard/Morrow, 1998. 32 pages. (0–688–14679–1) $16.00

Throughout the week, the lives of three families continually intertwine as each one engages in day-to-day activities. Meals, after-school classes, caring for pets, grocery shopping and gardening all become communal events in this urban neighborhood, as friends and family members look out for each other and share their ups and downs. The story opens on the title page with framed portraits of the three families—that's the last time we see them as separate units. As the story progresses, we see children, parents, grandparents and pets in and out of each other's homes and lives. Ormerod's detailed pen-and-ink and watercolor illustrations depict the daily hubbub while her lively text describes the action and invites children to interpret what's going on by asking questions that begin with the word "who?" The delightful visual complexity will encourage repeated readings and observant readers may eventually have more than one answer for the question posed by the book's title. (Ages 3–8)

Paul, Ann Whitford. *Hello Toes! Hello Feet!* Illustrated by Nadine Bernard Westcott. A Melanie Kroupa Book/DK Ink, 1998. 32 pages. (0–7894–2481–9) $15.95

A day in the life of an extremely active young girl, as seen from the vantage point of her feet. From morning to night, her feet carry her through her daily routines, which include lots of spirited imaginary play. Bouncing verses are aptly illustrated with Westcott's lively cartoon drawings, which show the girl indoors and outdoors, wearing different kinds of shoes and, best of all, going barefoot. (Ages 3–6)

Reiser, Lynn. *Little Clam.* Greenwillow, 1998. 32 pages. (0–688–15909–5) $14.93

At bedtime, a mother and her small child engage in storytelling and imaginary play, providing a frame for this story-within-a-story about a little clam who must protect himself from the threat of predators. Reiser playfully combines the drama of the natural world with a strong narrative pattern to create conflict and build suspense. Young children will identify with the plight of the little clam who must figure out when to take care of himself and when to ask for help in order to survive. The book concludes with the steps for a Little Clam bedtime game that uses a pillow and bedcovers as props. *Highly Commended, 1999 Charlotte Zolotow Award.* (Ages 3–6)

Root, Phyllis. *What Baby Wants.* Illustrated by Jill Barton. Candlewick Press, 1998. 32 pages. (0–7636–0207–8) $15.99

Grandma, Grandpa, Aunt, Uncle, Big Sister and Little Brother all assure Mama they will take care of Baby so she can sleep. But when Baby begins to cry, each of the well-meaning elders proves to be equally inept at calming Baby down. Each one knows exactly what Baby wants but they each choose the wrong method (bringing in a sheep, for example, to keep Baby warm, and birds to sing him to sleep). Finally, Little Brother comes up with exactly the right thing: picking Baby up himself to cuddle and sing to him. Large, appealing illustrations and the use of repetition and onomatopoeia, along with the humor inherent in the relatives' outlandish solutions, will make this a good choice for a group read-aloud. (Ages 3–6)

Simmons, Jane. *Come Along, Daisy!* U.S. edition: Little, Brown, 1998. 32 pages. (0–316–79790–1) $12.95

Even after Mother Duck warns her to stay close, little Daisy still dawdles and finds all sorts of distractions in the pond. She doesn't even realize she's lost track of her mother until danger suddenly appears. Mother Duck returns to save the day, of course, and the close call was all Daisy needed in order to learn to do as her mother asked her. Slightly exaggerated illustrations lend a humorous tone to this gentle cautionary tale. (Ages 2–4)

Sís, Peter. *Fire Truck.* Greenwillow, 1998. 28 pages. (0–688–15878–1) $14.95

"Fire truck" are the first words Matt says when he gets up in the morning and the last words he says when he goes to bed at night. But it's still a surprise for readers to learn about the day Matt woke up and discovered he had turned into a fire truck himself! A deliciously detailed fold-out page shows children all the things with which Matt the Fire Truck is equipped—ladders, hoses, lights, wheels, etc—and encourages them to count each item. Only a pancake breakfast, it seems, has the power to turn Matt back into a boy. Sís's use of four colors (red, yellow, blue and black) gives the illustrations a retro look but his story of a young child's obsessive interest has a timeless appeal. Young fire truck enthusiasts will appreciate the details of the different toy fire trucks surrounding Matt the Boy and, of course, they will delight in the details on Matt the Fire Truck! (Ages 2–5)

Steig, William. *Pete's a Pizza.* Michael di Capua Books/HarperCollins, 1998. 32 pages. (0–06–205157–1) $13.95

The playful title and round smiling face on the jacket are the first hints of the fun that awaits readers between the pizza-box-shaped covers of Pete's a Pizza. When little Pete is in a miserable mood on a rainy day, his parents know exactly how to cheer him up: they pretend he's a pizza. After setting him on the kitchen table, they knead and stretch the dough (Pete), add then oil (water), flour (talcum powder), tomatoes (checkers) and cheese (paper), before carrying him to the oven (couch). Through it all, Pete plays the role to perfection (except for occasional bursts of the giggles) by lying perfectly still with his eyes closed. That is, until he hears it's time for the pizza to be sliced! Steig's droll narrative perfectly complements his amusing, low-key watercolor illustrations which show Pete's mom and dad enjoying the imaginary play as much as their son obviously does. *Honor Book, 1999 Charlotte Zolotow Award.* (Ages 3–7)

Stuve-Bodeen, Stephanie. *Elizabeti's Doll.* Illustrated by Christy Hale. Lee & Low (95 Madison Avenue, New York, NY 10016), 1998. 32 pages. (1–880000–70–9) $15.95

After her mother has a new baby, little Elizabeti wants a baby of her own to hold and cuddle. She has no doll but finds a rock that is just the right size and she names the rock Eva. As Elizabeti's mother cares for the baby, Elizabeti mimics her actions with Eva—feeding and burping her rock, changing its diapers, and tying it to her back with a *kanga* while she does her daily chores. When Eva the rock diappears one day, readers will be as surprised as Elizabeti to discover where she went, and they will find the resolution satisfying. Although the Tanzanian village setting will be unfamiliar to most children in the United States, they will recognize the warm family nurturing and Elizabeti's resourceful imagination. *Highly Commended, 1999 Charlotte Zolotow Award.* (Ages 3–7)

Zeifert, Harriet M. *Pushkin Meets the Bundle.* Illustrated by Donald Saaf. An Anne Schwartz Book/Atheneum, 1998. 32 pages. (0–689–81413–5) $16.00

Pushkin is a dignified white dog who wears a red jacket and acts pretty much like the human beings who keep him as a pet. As the sole object of his owners' affection for many years, he has difficulty adjusting to the new baby ('the bundle") his humans bring home one day. Older siblings who are trying to adjust to new babies themselves will no doubt identify with Pushkin's plight and they will do well to follow his example: try some tricks to make the baby laugh. Donald Saaf's gouache paintings invest both Pushkin and The Bundle with a great deal of personality. (Ages 3–6)

Zolotow, Charlotte. *Wake Up/Goodnight.* Illustrated by Pamela Paparone. HarperFestival, 1998. 20 pages. (0–694–01032–4) $9.95

There are two sides to this story about daily routines. *Wake Up* shows four anthropomorphized animals arising in the morning to get dressed, brush their teeth and sit down to breakfast, as the text calls out: "Wake up! The day's begun. / Wake up! Wake up! Wake up! The sun is out. The night is over." Flip the book over to read the about the end of the day. In *Goodnight* the mood is decidedly quieter as the same critters are tucked into bed: "The trees whisper. The birds are still. Goodnight. Goodnight. Goodnight. Sweet dreams are waiting. / Close your eyes. Close your eyes. Sleep." This newly illustrated edition of a book first published in 1971 has heavy-stock pages designed for rough handling from babies and toddlers. (Ages 1–3)

See also: *Alfie's ABC; Bunny Who Found Easter; Cherish Me; Gingerbread Man; Hot Cold Shy Bold; Little Factory; Little Scarecrow; Little White Dog; Millions of Snowflakes; New Baby; One Duck Stuck; Pickin' Peas; Snow; When It Starts to Snow; You Can't Take a Balloon...; You're Just What I Need; Zzzng! Zzzng! Zzzng!*

Picture Books for Older Children

Atkins, Jeannine. *Get Set! Swim!* Illustrated by Hector Viveros Lee. Lee & Low (95 Madison Avenue, New York, NY 10016), 1998. 32 pages. (1–880000–66–0) $15.95

Although Jessenia often tires of hearing her mother talk about her childhood in Puerto Rico, she finds that the stories give her unexpected strength and inspiration when she participates in a swimming competition at school, as she imagines her arms reaching all the way to her mother's island home as she swims each lap. Jessenia's *mami* and younger brother, Luis, are on hand to watch her triumph in the final race of her swim meet in this story that incorporates details of her bicultural heritage into an easy sports story for young readers. Hector Viveros Lee's pencil and watercolor illustrations aptly capture the blue hues of the swimming pool and of the blue skies of Puerto Rico that exist in Jessenia's imagination. (Ages 5–8)

Browne, Anthony. *Voices in the Park.* U.S. edition: DK Ink, 1998. 32 pages. (0–7894–2522-X) $15.95

The voices mentioned in the title belong to four people (ehr... gorillas and chimps) who cross paths in a city park. A well-heeled mother with her timid son and a down-and-out dad with his outgoing daughter seem to have little in common, other than a need to walk their dogs. Although the parents sit on the same park bench, they do not exchange a word; the children, however, play together on the seesaw, slide and climbing bars. What makes this distinctive is that the same event is recounted from four distinctive points of view and each brief chapter tells a completely different story about the same experience. For the mother, the trip to the park is fraught with worries, not the least of which is the scruffy-looking man who shares her bench. The dad thinks only of his own problems as he reads the want ads, looking for work. Although the children play together, they, too, give a different account. From the girls' perspective, her playmate is a wimp, although he does loosen up a bit as they play. He seems incredibly sad. The boy, however, immensely enjoys his free moments playing with the high-spirited girl, and hopes he'll see her again soon. In each chapter, the landscapes of Browne's surrealistic paintings subtly reflect the internal emotions of the character who's speaking; for example, the timid boy sees the shape of his mother's overbearing hat everywhere—on lamposts, in clouds and trees, and on a statue that casually holds a set of handcuffs. (Ages 7–10)

Carling, Amelia Lau. *Mama and Papa Have a Store.* Dial, 1998. 32 pages. (0–8037–2044–0) $15.99

This distinctive autobiographical picture book features a Chinese immigrant family living in Guatemala City. Told from the point of view of their youngest daughter, the story centers on all the activity in and around the family's busy store on a typical day. Aspects of the family's Chinese heritage are interwoven with cultural details relating to their new home in Guatemala; the brightly colored Chinese thread the family sells, for example, is popular with Mayan weavers, who take a bus from their village far away to shop in the Chinese store. Carling's detailed watercolor paintings give a good sense of life in on a bustling city street in Central America, as well as the specifics of little Amelia's family life. (Ages 4–8)

Cooper, Melrose. *Gettin' through Thursday*. Illustrated by Nneka Bennett. Lee & Low (95 Madison Avenue, New York, NY 10016), 1998. 32 pages. (1–880000–67–9) $15.95

> Money is tight in André's family and, because Mama's paycheck comes on Friday, Thursday is always a particularly tough day. They just have to make due, something that seems to come easily to André's upbeat and creative mom. In this African American family of four, education is a priority; Mama has made it clear that whenever any of her three kids makes the honor roll at school, they'll drop everything and have a party. But when André accomplishes this, there's a problem: his report card arrives on a Thursday. Mama's solution for throwing a great party, even on a Thursday, will please readers as much as it pleased André. Realistic paintings rendered in watercolor and colored pencil illustrate a heartwarming story of a family that pulls together in good times and bad. (Ages 6–8)

Curtis, Gavin. *The Bat Boy & His Violin*. Illustrated by E.B. Lewis. Simon & Schuster, 1998. 32 pages. (0–689–80099–1) $16.00

> Reginald is much more interested in playing his violin than he is in playing baseball but when his daddy needs a bat boy for the Dukes, the Negro League team he coaches, Reginald reluctantly agrees to go on the road, so long as he can take his violin along with him. Clumsy with the bats, he spends most of his time sitting in the dugout, playing his violin, much to his father's dismay. Surprisingly, the team starts a winning streak and they credit Reginald's music for their change of fortune. While the story is set in the past and includes details about life in the Negro Leagues, the real story here is about the relationship between a father and son who clearly value different things in life, a theme that will resonate with many young readers. E. B. Lewis's realistic watercolor paintings aptly portray the historical setting as well as bright summer days on the baseball field. (Ages 5–9)

Garland, Sherry. *My Father's Boat*. Illustrated by Ted Rand. Scholastic Press, 1998. 32 pages. (0–590–47867–2) $15.95

> Although there's a lot for a father and his young son to do working on their shrimp boat, since it's just the two of them out on the ocean alone for two days and one night, they find plenty of time to share stories about the father's past. He recalls when he was a young boy himself, working on *his* father's shrimp boat on the South China Sea. He explains why he had to leave and come to America when war came to his small Vietnamese village, and why his father had to stay. Together, they imagine the grandfather, still working on his shrimp boat on the South China Sea, and the father promises his son that some day he will take him to visit him. An understated, poignant portrait of a father/son relationship is illustrated with senstive watercolor paintings that show both the hard work of the fishermen and their dreams of past and future. (Ages 4–8)

Geeslin, Campbell. *On Ramón's Farm*. Illustrated by Petra Mathers. An Anne Schwartz Book/Atheneum, 1998. 40 pages. (0–689–81134–9) $16.00

> A wonderfully original picture book, set in Mexico, is organized into five short chapters, each one beginning with a glossary of five or six Spanish words that will be used in the upcoming text. Each chapter deals with little drama involving one specific species of animal on Ramón's farm. There's the goat who likes to climb up on the house or into a tree, the rooster that fights with his reflection in a bucket of water, and the burro that always takes one

step forward and two steps back. At the end of each chapter, Ramón makes up an amusing couplet that defines the animal's nature. Petra Mathers' bright watercolor, pen and colored pencil illustrations are perfect for Geeslin's droll humor. (Ages 4–8)

Keller, Laurie. *The Scrambled States of America.* Henry Holt, 1998. 32 pages. (0–8050–5802–8) $16.95

Uncle Sam himself tells the story of the day the 50 states, bored with their same old positions on the map, decided to trade places with each other. It all started when Nebraska and Kansas came up with the idea of having a potluck so that all the states could get to know each other. They hit it off so well that they launched a grand-scale exchange—Florida switched with Minnesota; Arizona with South Carolina; Alabama, New York, and Indiana with California. But soon the novelty wears off and the states begin to complain. From beginning to end, this highly original story is filled with visual and verbal humor, and each state is invested with a singular personality. (Ages 6–10)

Lee, Huy Voun. *In the Park.* Henry Holt, 1998. 24 pages. (0–8050–4128–1) $15.95

As Xiao Ming plays in the park on a bright spring day, his mother teaches him ten Chinese characters, based on some of the things they see or experience in the park: earth, insects, bird, chirping, tree, twig, etc. For each character, Xiao Ming's mother points out aspects that reflect the object in reality (strokes that resemble the feathers on a bird, for instance); this is further reinforced with stylized drawings beside the actual characters they resemble in the glossary that appears on the books' endpapers. As with her two previous books featuring Xiao Ming learning Chinese characters, *At the Beach* (Holt, 1994) and *In the Snow* (Holt, 1995), Lee uses colorful cut-paper collages to illustrate the story. (Ages 6–9)

Meddaugh, Susan. *Martha Walks the Dog.* Walter Lorraine Books/Houghton Mifflin, 1998. 32 pages. (0–395–90494–3) $15.00

Martha the talking dog is so competent and trustworthy that she walks herself every day. She knows all the neighborhood pets well—dogs, cats, and even a parrot who can also talk—but when a vicious new dog named Bob moves in down the street, Martha simply can't make friends with him. Surprisingly, the parrot offers a solution to curb Bob's bullying ways. As in the previous three volumes about Martha, the author/illustrator blends humor with a good storyline. And Martha, as always, is one snappy speaker. (Ages 4–8)

Polacco, Patricia. *Thank You, Mr. Falker.* Philomel, 1998. 40 pages. (0–399–23166–8) $16.99

Before she started school, Trisha looked forward to learning how to read more than anything else. But in first grade, when all her classmates are learning to read, she finds that she can't. Each year her problem gets worse and worse and, although she struggles to keep it a secret, she begins to think of herself as stupid and ugly. It isn't until Trisha is in fifth grade that she has a teacher who discovers her secret and helps her learn to read. An autobiographical story shows the frustration and determination of child who's different, and offers a tender portrait of the real-life teacher who made a difference in her life. (Ages 6–10)

Rathmann, Peggy. *10 Minutes till Bedtime.* Putnam's, 1998. 48 pages. (0–399–23103–X) $16.99

Strange things start to happen as soon as a father makes the bedtime announcement. His young son, who's been building a vehicle out of cardboard, paper clips and the wheel from his hamster's cage, suddenly notices the front door opening and 10 hamster tourists lining up for a tour of the boy's bedroom. As his father counts down and calls out the minutes, the hamsters take a whirlwind tour, engaging in typical tourist behavior: snapping photos, fishing, swimming, and relaxing under umbrellas. Children will delight in the ways in which ordinary things are viewed as novelties by rodent interlopers, and many of them will identify with the boy's procrastination as bedtime draws nearer. There's much to look at and laugh at in each uproariously funny double-page spread. Those who wish to continue the journey can call up www.hamstertours.com, a real-life web page, seen on a fictional computer screen in the book. (Ages 4–8)

Reiser, Lynn. *Cherry Pies and Lullabies.* Greenwillow, 1998. 40 pages. (0–688–13392–4) $16.00

Reiser, Lynn. *Tortillas and Lullabies/Tortillas y cancioncitas.* Coordinated and translated by Rebecca Hart. Illustrated by "Corazones Valientes." Greenwillow, 1998. 40 pages. (0–688–14629–5) $16.00

A pair of picture books celebrates how love is expressed through continuity and change in the families of two young girls, one Anglo (*Cherry Pies and Lullabies*) and one Latina (*Tortillas and Lullabies=Tortillas y cancioncitas*). Four brief vignettes in each book describe the way distinct traditions and activities are carried out from generation to generation in the child narrators' families, beginning with each girl's great grandmother interacting with her child—the girl's grandmother—and ending with the child herself, who continues the tradition in play activities with a favorite toy. *Cherry Pies and Lullabies* is illustrated by Reiser in bright watercolors and black pen and filled with elements of Americana, most notably the quilts, all of which are variations of the American quilt pattern "Cherry Basket." "Corazones Valientes," a Costa Rican collective of six women artists, created the lush, richly colored acrylic artwork set in South America for *Tortillas and Lullabies*. An author's note in Cherry Pies explains that the book was written for the Reiser's niece, to show her how much has changed over time, but also to affirm what has stayed true even in the midst of such change. After talking about that book with a friend from El Salvador, Reiser conceived *Tortillas and Lullabies*, realizing that families around the world are finding new ways to do old things, while the expressions of love at the heart of their actions remains constant. (Ages 4–8)

Roth, Roger. *Fishing for Methuselah.* HarperCollins, 1998. 32 pages. (0–06–027592–8) $14.95

Up in the North Country, lumberjacks Ivan and Olaf are always competing, trying to outdo one another. At the upcoming ice-fishing competition, the two men both brag that they are going to catch Moosehead Lake's humongous, legendary fish called Methuselah. As the competition between them escalates, the two men end up putting themselves in danger, and soon learn that the only chance they have for survival requires cooperation. An appealing tall tale with an unusual setting offers a good example of conflict resolution that satisfies everyone. (Ages 4–8)

Scieszka, Jon. *Squids Will Be Squids: Fresh Morals, Beastly Fables.* Illustrated by Lane Smith. Designed by Molly Leach. Viking, 1998. 48 pages. (0–670–88135-X) $17.99

Children will no doubt recognize many of their peers, and perhaps even themselves, in this original collection of side-splitting fables. And that's the point, as John Scieszka tells us: "If you can't say something nice about someone, change the guy's name to Donkey or Squid." Characters such as Elephant & Mosquito, Little Walrus, Straw & Matches, and Piece of Toast & Froot Loops are each engaged in contemporary childhood conflicts. When Straw and Matches play together, for example, bossy Matches always takes the upper hand and wants to do things his way. (The moral: Don't play with Matches.) Each double-page spread introduces a set of characters, a problem and a moral, illustrated with Lane Smith's comically sophisticated illustrations. (Ages 7–12)

Slepian, Jan. *Emily Just in Time.* Illustrated by Glo Coalson. Philomel, 1998. 32 pages. (0–399–23043–2) $15.99

Although Emily's been growing in competence and confidence, she's still too scared to spend an entire night at her grandma's house. Each time she tries, an unfamiliar noise wakes her up in the middle of the night and Grandma has to take her home so she can sleep in her own bed. On these occasions, her Grandma offers the comforting promise: "Someday you'll stay the night and not think anything of it." It takes several tries and plenty of time before Grandma's prediction turns out to be true. Jan Slepian's sensitive portrayal of a young child's realistic development has warm watercolor illustrations that show Emily's physical growth as well. (Ages 4–8)

Sorel, Edward. *Johnny on the Spot.* Margaret K. McElderry, 1998. 28 pages. (0–689–81293–0) $16.00

When the old, fading, static-ridden radio on which Johnny always listens to his favorite serial about heroic "Don Winslow of the Navy" gives up its last sound, Johnny turns to his mysterious neighbor Mr. Zaga for help. Johnny's parents can't afford another radio, but Johnny hopes Mr. Zaga can fix the broken one. Instead Mr. Zaga, an inventor who is working on a time travel machine, sends Johnny's radio one day into the future. The sound comes out perfectly now, but everything it plays is taking place tomorrow. When Mr. Zaga cautions Johnny that they can't do anything to change the future, even if it means preventing a bank robbery or fire, Johnny comes up with his own inventive ways to catch crooks and save lives from harm, earning him the nickname Johnny on the Spot from the hero-loving newspapers. At the same time, Mr. Zaga comes up with an inventive idea of his own. The full-color pen-and-ink and watercolor illustrations of this fantasy have a comic overtone and are rich with the look and feel of an earlier time. (Ages 7–10)

Soto, Gary. *Big Bushy Mustache.* Illustrated by Joe Cepeda. Knopf, 1998. 32 pages. (0–679–88030–5) $17.00

Ricky tires of hearing people tell him how much he looks like his mother. He'd much rather look like his father, a big, strong man with a big, bushy mustache. When his teacher, Mrs. Cortez, lets Ricky wear a false mustache to play the part of a soldier in the school's *Cinco de Mayo* play, Ricky is so thrilled that he secretly takes the mustache and wears it home from school and, unfortunately, loses it along the way. Ricky's parents help him come up with a solution in this warm, realistic story about a spirited Latino child. (Ages 4–8)

Stevenson, James. *Sam the Zamboni Man.* Illustrated by Harvey Stevenson. Greenwillow, 1998. 32 pages. (0–688–14484–5) $15.00

Growing up in the country, Matt has played plenty of hockey himself but when he visits his grandfather in the city, he goes to a real hockey game for the first time. In addition to all the usual excitement of being in the stadium, Matt has even more to look forward to: his own grandfather drives the big Zamboni, to clean the ice between periods. And Matt, of course, gets a special, up-close look at the Zamboni after the game. Grandpa's stories about the past, when he was a hockey player himself, bring grandfather and grandson even closer together as they share a mutual interest. Detailed watercolor paintings illustrate an unexpectedly poignant, intergenerational story. (Ages 4–8)

Tarpley, Natasha Anastasia. *I Love My Hair!* Illustrated by E.B. Lewis. Little, Brown and Company, 1998. 24 pages. (0–316–52275–9) $14.95

As Keyana's mother combs her hair, she tells her stories about all the ways it can be styled: in cornrows, as an afro, spun and woven into a puffy bun, or in braids with beads that make tap-tap clicky-clacky sounds when she walks. Her upbeat, positive portrayal of African American hair fills Keyana with pride. E.B. Lewis's realistic watercolor paintings extend the story with his imaginative interpretation of Keyana's thoughts as her mother combs her hair. (Ages 4–8)

Torres, Leyla. *Liliana's Grandmothers.* Farrar Straus Giroux, 1998. 32 pages. (0–374–35105–8) $16.00

Liliana, a Latina girl living in the United States, compares and contrasts her two grandmother, Mima and mama Gabina. Because Mima lives on the same street as Liliana, they see each other frequently. Mima sews, takes yoga lessons, is active in her church, and serves her granddaughter peanut butter and jelly sandwiches for lunch. Mama Gabina lives in another country and speaks only Spanish. When Liliana visits her, they enjoy talking to her pet bird, working in her garden, and dancing the *cumbia.* She always prepares a big lunch and takes a *siesta* afterwards. Colombian-born author/artist Leyla Torres provides a realistic portrait of a young child's growing awareness of her bicultural heritage. Also available in a Spanish-language edition as *Las Abuelas de Liliana* (0-374-34341-1) $16.00. (Ages 4–8)

Van Camp, Richard. *What's the Most Beautiful Thing You Know about Horses?* Illustrated by George Littlechild. Children's Book Press (246 First Street, Suite 101, San Francisco, CA 94105), 1998. 32 pages. (0–89239–154–5) $15.95

The thoughtful, engaging narrator of this richly poetic picture book is a young Dogrib Indian boy living in the Northwest Territories of Canada who is intrigued by horses. The boy wonders if horses have secrets, if they think that fireworks "are strange flowers blooming in the sky." And so on a frigidly cold day he asks members of his family and community, "What's the most beautiful thing you know about horses?" and their responses are both delightful and profound. Plains Cree artist George Littlechild lends his distinctive style to the artwork that accompany's Richard Van Camp's wonderful, deeply felt story. His boldly colored images are full of both whimsy and beauty, and imbued with a mystical quality as the spirits of horses seem to dance on many pages. "What's the most beautiful thing *you* know about horses?" the boy asks readers at the conclusion of this uplifting story. "And what's the most beautiful thing you know about you?" (Ages 5–10)

Waboose, Jan Bourdeau. *Morning on the Lake.* Illustrated by Karen Reczuch. U.S. edition: Kids Can Press, 1998. 32 pages. (1–55074–373–2) $15.95
    When an Ojibway boy spends a day in the company of *Mishomis* (grandfather), the two of them both claim morning, noon, and night as their favorite time of day. In the morning on the lake in a birchbark canoe, they see a family of loons; hiking up a cliff at noon, they see an eagle; and walking through the forest at night, they see a pack of wolves. The boy is initially frightened by each sight but he follows the example of his grandfather and stays perfectly quiet and still. After each animal has passed, *Mishomis* interprets cultural messages for the boy, thereby teaching him about his heritage. The subtle story of strong intergenerational relationship is illustrated with realistic watercolors that depict the beauty of the natural world. (Ages 5–8)

Wilson-Max, Ken. *Halala Means Welcome! A Book of Zulu Words.* Jump at the Sun/Hyperion, 1998. 28 pages. (0–7868–0414–9) $11.95
    A growing friendship between Chidi and Michael, two brown-skinned boys in contemporary South Africa offers a context for the introduction of 25 Zulu words that the two boys use in their every day play. More than a vocabulary lesson, however, Zimbabwean author/illustrator Ken Wilson-Max's gives us an appealing story about two friends who enjoy playing together after school. The 12 ³/₄ x 6 ³/₄" volume includes a glossary with a pronunciation guide. (Ages 4–9)

Zagwÿn, Deborah Turney. *Turtle Spring.* Tricycle Press, 1998. 32 pages. (1–883672–53–8) $15.95
    The birth of her brother at the start of summer has left Clee feeling "like a lost moon." Clee's uncle, Fishtank Hal, understands. When he comes to visit he brings her a turtle. " 'She ain't a gift for a baby,' he tells her. 'She's too big and would only pinch it.' Clee knew the feeling." As summer turns into fall, more changes take place in Clee's world. Her father leaves for a job far away from which he won't return for months; the relatives' visits to ooh and ahh over the baby subside; and the turtle, which spent early autumn sunning in the sandbox, begins burrowing under leaves for warmth. Clee's mother advises her to bring the turtle in at night, but Clee does not, and on a cold November day she finds the turtle in the compost pile, "stone still, stone cold." Heartbroken, she buries the turtle deep within the compost heap. But there is a happy surprise in store for Clee in this tender story that also depicts the funny, warm and subtly changing relationship between Clee and her baby brother. In illustrations that are as lyrical and inspired as the text, Clee, her family and the mystery taking place beneath the ground are set against a backdrop of boldly changing seasons in a book that is a quiet yet joyful. (Ages 4–8)

See also: *Adventures of Snowwoman; Annushka's Voyage; Ballpark; Beautiful Warrior; Black Cowboy, Wild Horses; Boss of the Plains; Brothers' Promise; Bunny Who Found Easter; Cendrillon; Cherish Me; Christmas Tree in the White House; Doctor Bird; A Fair Bear Share; Fourth Wise Man; Gift for Abuelita; Home to Medicine Mountain;*

Hooray for Diffendoofer Day!; Ian's Walk; Jazz of Our Street; Jump Up Time; Lewis and Papa; Lucy Dove; Magic Bean Tree; My Freedom Trip; Ouch!; Outlaw Thanksgiving; Pied Piper of Hamelin; Prairie Town; Secret Stars; Snowflake Bentley; So Say the Little Monkeys; Stone; Thanksgiving With Me; Tío Armando; You Can't Take a Balloon...; You Never Know; Zzzng! Zzzng! Zzzng!

Easy Fiction

Bauer, Marion Dane. *Bear's Hiccups.* Illustrated by Diane Dawson Hearn. (A Holiday House Reader) Holiday House, 1998. 48 pages. (0–8234–1339-X) $14.95

"This pond is mine. All mine," Bear tells the other creatures on the hottest day of summer in the forest. But Frog doesn't like being bullied, especially by Bear. Frog proclaims the pond is his, and bear roars "MINE!" with her jaws open wide. When she closes her mouth, Frog has disappeared. "Where is Frog?" ask Turtle, Minnow and others. Bear can only hiccup in reply. There is no need to worry, however. Marion Dane Bauer's book featuring many of the characters first introduced in *Turtle Dreams* resolves the mystery of Frog's disappearance happily in a story marked by gentle humor and spurred to its conclusion by the action of small, brave Turtle. Graceful language distinguishes this charming story for beginning readers. (Ages 6–8)

Gasque, Dale Blackwell. *Pony Trouble.* Illustrated by Stacey Schuett. (Hyperion Chapters) Hyperion, 1998. 56 pages. (0–7868–2267–8) $14.49

Although Amy always looks forward to visits from her city cousin, Rebecca, she often loses patience with her when Rebecca shows her superior attitude, especially when it comes to horses. As a country kid, Amy hasn't been given fancy riding lessons like Rebecca has, but she still feels she knows a lot more about horses, since she has her own pony and takes care of it herself. The rivalry between the two cousins almost leads to tragedy in a beginning chapter book that will appeal to many children, especially horse lovers. (Ages 7–9)

Godwin, Laura. *Forest.* Illustrated by Stacey Schuett. (An I Can Read Book) HarperCollins, 1998. 48 pages. (0–06–026664–3) $14.95

A realistic, appealing story for beginning readers about the relationship between humans and wild animals. When Jeannie and her parents find an abandoned fawn in the forest on the edge of their farm, she hopes they can take it home and keep it. Her parents are hesitant to intervene until it is clear the doe is not returning. Then they take the fawn home. "Just for tonight," Jeannie's mother makes clear as she prepares a bottle for the fawn. "Tomorrow we will take him to a place where they care for wild animals." But even knowing the fawn cannot stay, Jeannie still cannot resist curling up next to him in the middle of the night and giving him a name: Forest, "so you won't forget where you come from." A story admirable for its lack of sentimentality but still full of warmth. (Ages 4–7)

Kvasnosky, Laura McGee. *Zelda and Ivy.* Candlewick Press, 1998. 40 pages. (0–7636–0469–0) $15.99

Zelda and Ivy are foxes, but children will immediately recognize the emotions at the heart of their hilarious but loving sibling relationship in this collection of three short, fully illustrated chapters about a dynamic duo. Flamboyant, bossy Zelda is irrepressible, an older sister who never misses an opportunity to direct the activities she shares with younger sister Ivy. For her part, Ivy is almost always a bit worse off for her older sister's efforts ("Let's doozy up our tales like movie stars," Zelda suggests, and Ivy ends up with a tail dripping blue paint, glitter and tufts of fur, which Zelda trimmed into scallops, while Zelda's own full, swishy tale remains unscathed). But Ivy is irrepressible in her own, if more quiet, right as a younger sister who adores and appreciates her older sister's ultimately good intentions in this warm, funny depiction of childhood and family relationships. (Ages 6–8)

Tashjian, Janet. *Marty Frye, Private Eye.* Illustrated by Laurie Keller. (A Redfeather Chapter Book) Henry Holt, 1998. 78 pages. (0–8050–5888–5) $15.95

Marty Frye loves poetry and problem solving. Crime solving, that is. A self-proclaimed poet detective, he is hot on the trail of three disappearances in this witty book for young independent readers. First he must find his friend Emma's missing diary during recess. Then he is waylaid on the way home from school by news that a whole case of Action Chuck dolls—his favorite action hero!—has disappeared from Mr. Lipsky's toy store. Finally, he must discover what happened to his little sister Katie's flour—or is that flower? With a penchant for talking in rhymes while he's solving his crimes and following every lead to its conclusion, Marty Frye offers a fresh, funny, well-rounded character for new readers to enjoy. (Ages 6–8)

See also: *Christmas in the Forest; Emma's Magic Winter; Good-bye, Charles Lindbergh; Hatmaker's Sign; Home Run; Some Frog!; Wild Boy*

Fiction for Children

Bawden, Nina. *Off the Road.* Clarion, 1998. 187 pages. (0–395–91321–7) $16.00

Twelve-year-old Tom's grandfather, Gandy, has escaped from a controlled environment in which they live to the Outside. According to the small amount of history Tom had learned in school, his grandfather was named after "an Indian gentleman and famous cricketer." Gandy had insisted this was "rubbish," and claimed that way back in the last century, Gandhi had been a saint, a "revolutionary saint." Gandy leaves a literal and figurative door open for Tom to follow him. But Tom fears Outside; he has heard of the dangers there: "wild men...barbarians and bandits, outlaws and outcasts; great hunting dogs with slavering jaws; trolls from the mountains; dragons with hot glaring eyes." Eventually Tom does follow his grandfather, his own revolutionary saint, and on the Outside he meets their extended family, one with adults and children and more than enough secrets to go around. Tom discovers much about the only life he has ever known, but he also knows the way home. A not-so-distant future Outside and Inside are explored within an absorbing, relatively uncomplicated science fiction novel full of distinctive characters. (Ages 10–12)

Blackwood, Gary. *The Shakespeare Stealer.* **Dutton, 1998. 216 pages. (0–525–45863–8) $15.99**

Fourteen-year-old Widge is an orphan living in a small village in Elizabethan England. Theater owner Simon Bass has just purchased Widge from the minister to whom Widge was apprenticed, intent on having the boy steal Shakespeare's new play, *Hamlet.* Widge's job is to sit in the audience of the Globe Theater in London and copy the play down word for word as it is performed, using the special shorthand method that the minister had taught him. To make sure Widge follows through, Bass sends him to London in the company of the harsh and mysterious Falconer, a man who conjures images of the devil and Death in Widge's lively mind. Widge, who has never been out of rural England, is as awed by the drama of the theater as he is by the grand and dangerous city of London. Swept up in the action of the first performance of *Hamlet* that he attends, he fails to write most of it down. Fearful of Falconer's reaction, he returns to the theater intent on stealing the one written copy of the play. Instead, Widge slips out of Falconer's grasp and into the embrace of the company of actors at the Globe, where he is taken on as an errand boy and apprentice to a life on the stage. But the shadow of fear never leaves Widge—he knows Falconer is still in the city, watching for him, waiting for him to produce a copy of the play. Tension, drama, and period details heighten the reading experience of this highly original, fast-paced story with a colorful cast of characters. (Ages 10–13)

Branford, Henrietta. *Fire, Bed & Bone.* **Candlewick, 1998. 122 pages. (0–7636–0338–4) $15.99**

A point of view distinctive for two reasons distinguishes this singular and riveting short novel by Henrietta Branford that chronicles the lives of peasants under the harsh and unfair laws of England's ruling classes during the late 14th century. It is unusual to read a historical novel for children that so clearly addresses issues of economic and social justice. But this story of landlord cruelty and peasant unrest leaves no doubt as to where fairness and goodness do and do not lie. Even more unusual is the author's choice for narrator—a hunting dog who spends much of her time with Rufus and Comfort, two of the peasants whose lives are torn apart by their efforts to seek an end to their oppression. The dog is witness to the attempts of Rufus, Comfort, and others in their village to rebel against the landlords for whom they toil without benefit. These events become part of the drama of her life, along with puppies born and gone away, of sometimes running with the wild dogs and wolves. But this dog who knows what it means to run wild also knows loyalty and the touch of human kindness, and the hearth of Rufus and Comfort is where she will always return if she can. An unsentimental, wholly believable narrative voice propels this dramatic story. (Ages 10–12)

Bruchac, Joseph. *The Heart of a Chief.* **Dial, 1998. 153 pages. (0–8037–2276–1) $15.99**

"*The Heart of a Chief* is a novel, but it is based on the realities of contemporary Indian America and on the many years I've spent working with Indian kids," writes Joseph Bruchac in an author's note that precedes this story set on a fictional Penacook Indian reservation and in the neighboring community. Chris Nicola lives on the Penacook reservation with his grandparents and younger sister. Observant and thoughtful with a dry sense of humor, Chris has learned from both his father, who is currently seeking treatment for alcoholism, and his grandfather the importance of patience, of listening, of learning, but he doesn't know if this understanding will help him survive his first day of sixth grade, let alone the entire year. He is worried about starting at a new school off the reservation and worried about fitting in without making waves ("I think I can recognize the other sixth graders because we are the ones trying not to be noticed"). But Chris soon finds himself making waves regardless, both in town, where he leads the fight to get his school to stop using an Indian mascot, and at home, where a proposed casino supported by some of the tribal leaders threatens to develop land that Chris and his family hold sacred even as it promises economic opportunity for the impoverished people living on the reservation. Joseph Bruchac sheds light on these and many other challenges facing American Indian communities today in this issue-oriented novel that maintains its narrative tension without becoming too didactic thanks to Chris's heartfelt, convincing first-person voice. (Ages 10–13)

Butts, Nancy. *The Door in the Lake.* **Front Street, 1998. 159 pages. (1–886910–27–8) $15.95**
Was Joey Finney really kidnapped by aliens? At first he doesn't want to believe it, but he can't explain where he's been for the past two years. He disappeared while camping with his family and now he's back, with no memory of where he's been and looking, at age 14, exactly as he did when he was 12, right down to the clothes that he was wearing the last time anyone saw him. His "little" brother is bigger than he is now and all his old friends are academically and socially far ahead of him. It's a local college student who first suggests to Joey that he may have been kidnapped by aliens. Resistant at first to the idea, the more Joey learns and the more he remembers, the more he begins to believe it is true. But when he tells his former best friend, looking for a way to renew the bond they once shared, he is betrayed and the word gets around that Joey is crazy. His worried parents look to psychiatrists and medicine for the answer, but Joey needs someone to believe, someone to help him return to the door in the lake where he first disappeared. A riveting novel that could easily have become melodramatic or wholly unbelievable walks a fine line of tension instead as readers are swept up in the drama of Joey's circumstance. (Ages 9–12)

Cameron, Ann. *The Secret Life of Amanda K. Woods.* **Frances Foster Books/Farrar Straus Giroux, 1998. 201 pages. (0–374–36702–7) $16.00**
At 11, Amanda Woods feels plain, undistinguished, and uncertain. Perhaps because her mother thinks she is "average." But Amanda's feelings start to change the day her best friend, Lyle, moves away. Before he goes, Lyle and Amanda press their perfectly matched right hands together and Lyle shouts "Shazam!" And because Lyle "is a person who can do almost anything," Amanda can just about believe that they have traded hands; that his hand is now hers, and that some of his self-confidence is now hers, too. She draws upon that special knowledge often in the coming months. Amanda's older sister, whose future their overbearing, class-conscious mother has been shaping, is perfectly beautiful, perfectly smart, and perfectly well-behaved (at least in their mother's eyes). But she will be going away to college soon,

leaving their mother free to begin "improving" Amanda unless Amanda herself, with the help of her quiet father, can change things. Amanda's family owns a historic hotel in the small, northern Wisconsin community in which they live, and most of the other families do not possess the wealth necessary to meet the approval of Amanda's mother. But this novel set in the 1950s contrasts the hollowness of a life lived for appearances with the refreshing authenticity of Amanda herself, who is both funny and poignant, an 11-year-old with desires and loves and dreams and wishes that have nothing to do with wealth and class and everything to do with the need to make connections that are real. (Ages 10–13)

Conly, Jane Leslie. *While No One Was Watching.* Henry Holt, 1998. 233 pages. (0–8050–3934–1) $16.95

Five-year-old Frankie, his big brother, Earl, and his little sister, Angela, are staying with their unreliable aunt while their father finds work. It's a rough neighborhood, where sirens blare and Frankie once saw a man pull a gun in the middle of an argument. Across town, Maynard and his neighbor, Addie, live in a seemingly safe, secure part of town. The five children's lives become linked after Frankie and Earl accompany their bullying, violent older cousin, Wayne, into Maynard and Addie's upscale neighborhood. While Wayne and Earl steal two bikes, Frankie finds a rabbit in a cage. It's soft, and he wants it for his own. The rabbit is Addie's and she is heartbroken when she finds it missing. While Maynard and Addie begin a search for the rabbit that leads them closer and closer to the unknown dangers of the neighborhood where the other three children live, Earl finds himself trying to stop his and Frankie and Angela's lives from spinning out of control after their aunt disappears and Wayne becomes an ever-more-threatening presence. A harrowing novel in which events always seem to be teetering on the edge of disaster is skillfully told at various times from each one of the five resourceful children's point of view, clarifying their distinctive personalities and situations as it hurtles toward an ending that is, ultimately, a welcome sigh of relief. (Ages 10–13)

Creech, Sharon. *Bloomability.* Joanna Cotler Books/HarperCollins, 1998. 273 pages. (0–06–026993–6) $14.95

After problems develop at home with her older brother and sister, 13-year-old Dinnie is whisked away by her amiable aunt and uncle who are in charge of an international school in Lugano, Switzerland. Ironically, her new life in an unfamiliar place offers her a stability she has never known — she has grown up in a family that has moved from place to place as her father constantly seeks new opportunities. With her new-found sense of home, new friends for whom transience is a fact of life, and with distance from her old life, Dinnie is finally able to piece together who she is and how she fits into her family. She is even able to glimpse the opportunities (or "bloomabilities" as her Japanese friend Keisuke calls them) that await her in the world beyond her family. Once again, Sharon Creech offers her readers memorable characters and a gripping storyline, deftly combining humor with some of the serious issues that face young teenagers. Upon deeper examination, readers will find parallels between the people Dinnie knows in the United States and those she meets in Switzerland. This subtle mirroring allows Dinnie's growing empathy for her new friends to plant the seeds for understanding her family back home. (Ages 9–14)

Crew, Gary. *The Watertower.* Illustrated by Steven Woolman. U.S. edition: Crocodile Books, 1998. 32 pages. (1–56656–233–3) $14.95

Gary Crews's science fiction story is given chilling visual treatment in this tingling, page-turning picture book. The watertower has stood on Shooter's Hill in Preston for as long as anyone can remember, rusted and egg-shaped, casting its shadow over the town. But there is something ominous about that tower—something that artist Steven Woolman has turned into a masterpiece of visual imagery as the story of two boys who climb the tower for an afternoon swim unfolds. The tension and suggestion of evil in the narrative is played out deliciously in the art, in which it is clear that something's not quite right about most of the inhabitants in Preston, and that something has to do with the tower. The watertower's insignia, which looks like the partially open aperture of a camera or the pupil of an eye, is repeated over and over again in the illustrations, on hats that people wear, as tattoo-like images on their hands. The shape is repeated or suggested in other ways as well, both in the artwork and in the design and presentation of images and text on the page of a book that at one point literally turns around in the telling. They eyes of all the adults in Preston, with the exception of the two boys, are glazed and hard, almost inhuman, and by the end of the story one more person in Preston will have been transformed in this wonderfully eerie tale. (Ages 10–14)

Gantos, Jack. *Joey Pigza Swallowed the Key.* Farrar Straus Giroux, 1998. 154 pages. (0–374–33664–4) $16.00

Joey Pigza tries—he really *tries*—to behave. But in school and at home, his brain seems to be working against him. He's antsy. He can't focus. He blurts out answers without being called on and bounces up and down in his seat. And when his attention wanders, as it often does, it usually leads him into trouble he never intended. But Joey is a good kid—a very good kid. He is kind-hearted, funny, and brighter than his grades would allow. But when he tries to help out or do well, he often ends up making a mess of things. It's hard always being a disappointment, but Joey is finally getting help. Raised for several years by his grandmother, who has many of the same traits as Joey, his mother has come back into his life is determined to start turning things around. At the request of Joey's school, she takes him to the doctor, and that is when Joey is diagnosed with ADHD, or attention deficit hyperactivity disorder. The diagnosis is just the beginning, however. Over the course of a year there are disasters and successes both small and large as Joey and his mom learn together, with the help of doctors, therapists, his classroom and special education teachers and others, how to deal with ADHD so that Joey can succeed and feel good about himself. Readers will be instantly drawn into this sensitive, funny first-person narrative by Joey's energetic, insightful voice. He is a terrificly appealing child whose creativity and goodness shine. (Ages 9–12)

Garner, Alan. *The Well of the Wind.* Illustrated by Hervé Blondon. A Richard Jackson Book/DK Ink, 1998. 44 pages. (0–7894–2519–X) $14.95

An odd and strangely fascinating original fairy tale about a boy and a girl found floating in a crystal box begins, "Whether far or near, I can't say, but once there was a poor man living in a kingdom by the sea." The poor man is a fisherman who finds the box and rescues the boy and girl. They each have a star on their forehead, which the man covers with pieces from the red silk apron that the children were wrapped in. But the man dies soon after and as the children grow up alone they are plagued by a witch who tries to separate them. Twice she lures the boy away to dangerous places and twice he returns, having met a stranger each time who tells him how to overcome the danger. But the third time she lures him to the Well of the Wind, and when he doesn't return the girl goes in search of him. Told by a stranger how to reach the Well of the Wind by stepping into a mirror, the girl finds the boy turned to stone in that strange, dreamlike place, and in rescuing him unlocks the secret of their past. The courage and unfailing faith of both children is at the heart of this hypnotic tale illustrated with intriguing and unusual pastel images that cast their own spell on the story. (Ages 8–10)

Griffin, Adele. *The Other Shepards.* **Hyperion, 1998. 218 pages. (0–7868–2370–4) $14.95**

Years before Holland and Geneva Shepard were born, their parents had another family. Three children, John, Elizabeth, and Kevin, who were killed in a car accident as teenagers. That was almost 20 years ago, and now Holland, who is 13, and her younger sister, Geneva, live in a household where the memory of the brothers and sister they never met—the family they were never a part of—haunts their existence. Their mother and father are loving in an uptight, distant, undemonstrative way that starkly contrasts with the old photographs Holland and Geneva sometimes sneak a look at in which their parents and older siblings hug, embrace and laugh with ease. "I knew it," Geneva tells Holland. "The parents used up all the love on them." Geneva is prone to severe panic attacks and obsessive-compulsive behavior, and Holland is the one who often caretakes for her sister, with a maturity and understanding that defy her age although she also grows tired of the way Geneva manipulates their lives. But from the very moment Annie first enters their house, things begin to change. "It seems to me your mom and dad got a great second chance, right?...Lucky for them," Annie tells the sisters early on. "It is strange to think of the parents as blessed and lucky," Holland thinks as she considers people's reactions when they hear about the death of the other Shepards. "People almost never describe them that way." But who is this pale, ethereal young woman named Annie and where did she come from? As readers are drawn into this intricate novel that is grounded by Holland's perceptive, down-to-earth voice, they will be compelled by that very question as well as by the slowly changing landscape of Holland and Geneva's emotional lives. Is Annie real? Is she a ghost? Or is she imaginary, conjured in Holland and Geneva's minds to help their family heal? It's up to the individual reader to decide in this beautifully written, fascinating story. (Ages 11–14)

Hamilton, Virginia. *Second Cousins.* **Blue Sky/Scholastic, 1998. 168 pages. (0–590–47368–9) $14.95**

This follow-up to the earlier *Cousins* (Philomel, 1990) stands strongly on its own as the author continues to chronicle events in the life of Cammy Coleman. Now 12, Cammy is at the center of an intricate web of family relationships that unfold and are revealed in this lively, multilayered novel. It has been a year since Cammy's cousin Patty Ann drowned in the accident at the river and Cammy and her cousin Elodie have grown as close as sisters, bound by that event, of which they rarely speak, but also by the joys and adventures of childhood. As extended family members gather from around the country for a family reunion, Cammy and Elodie are thrown together with Gigi and Fractal, two of their cousins from New York City. This pairing of city cousins and country cousins leads to shifting relationships that leave Cammy a bit unsettled. First Gigi and Elodie hit if off, leaving Cammy somewhat hurt, and then Fractal (nicknamed for her love of the mathematical phenomenon), a smart, computer savvy teen, takes special interest in Cammy herself. Extensive discussions of current computer technology between Fractal and Cammy may date this novel in years to come, but they won't lessen its powerful emotional undertones. As the increasingly complex plot develops and moves toward the climactic family reunion, Cammy must deal with an unexpected, devastating revelation about her father and her relationship with Fractal at the same time she tries to prepare herself for the reunion itself. It will include a trip to the river, which she hasn't been to since Patty Ann died. It is Gram Tut, who helped Cammy through the trauma of Patty Ann's death, who leads the family to the river, where they enter the flow of memory and pain and healing and joy for all that has happened to generations past and for all who are to come. It is a transcendent experience—for Cammy and for readers of this novel distinguished by Virginia Hamilton's usual fine characterization and rich storytelling voice. (Ages 10–13)

Hesse, Karen. *Just Juice.* **Illustrated by Robert Andrew Parker. Scholastic Press, 1998. 138 pages. (0–590–03382–4) $14.95**
"I don't care much for school, and school, well it cares even less for me." That's how nine-year-old Juice feels about having been left behind the rest of her class. The truth is, Juice can't read. She is quick and talented with her hands but letters and numbers don't make much sense to her. It's a secret she's bent on keeping, especially from her little sister Lulu, who looks up to Juice in every way. So Juice stays home from school more often than not, and in doing so she can also spend time with Pa. He's been out of work for too long and Juice likes keeping him company so he doesn't get lonesome. Things are a struggle for Juice and her loving, close-knit rural family. Money is tight, Ma is expecting another baby, and they are at risk of losing their home because of unpaid taxes. But when Juice reluctantly returns to third grade after a visit from the truant officer, she begins to get special help from her new teacher, and slowly, with much hard work, the world of letters and words begins to unfold. Karen Hesse makes a strong statement about the importance of literacy in the context of this quiet, compelling novel about a young girl who is not only learning to read but also learning that she cannot solve all of her family's problems. Juice and her economically struggling family are portrayed with great dignity and grace. (Ages 8–11)

Jennings, Patrick. *Faith and the Rocket Cat.* **Scholastic Press, 1998. 232 pages. (0–590–11004–7) $15.95**
When Faith, her parents, and her electric dog, Eddie, return to San Francisco after a year or two in Mexico, they all have some adjustments to make, especially Eddie, who's never lived in the United States, and Faith who has to face her old adversary, Alex Wao, at Double Happiness Elementary School. Like its predecessor, *Faith and the Electric Dogs* (Scholastic, 1996), the story is told from the point of view of sly Eddie, the multilingual, literate dog, who seems to be just a little bit wiser than all the humans around him. His ability to understand several human languages, as well as Arf, Bowwow, and Mew,

makes him a true citizen of the world, a trait that comes in handy in the midst of a madcap plot involving a whippet, a lost cat, and a rocket Faith has built. (Ages 8–12)

Jiménez, Francisco. *La Mariposa.* Illustrated by Simón Silva. Houghton Mifflin, 1998. 40 pages. (0–395–81663–7) $16.00

First grade for Francisco beings with an overwhelming cascade of sounds—voices speaking in a language he doesn't understand. The child of migrant farm laborers, Francisco speaks only Spanish but at his school only English is allowed. The strain of trying to pay attention gives him headaches, and sometimes he escapes the chaos by focusing on the caterpillar kept in a jar near his desk and then imagining himself flying away to visit his father at work in the fields. He wonders how long it will take the cocoon that is now in the jar to open and for a butterfly to emerge. Francisco Jiménez's eloquent short story relates how a young boy's academic and social emergence at school is hindered by the denial of his native language, and how some barriers to communication and friendship are also overcome. The story is based on events in the author's own life and was told in a slightly different version in his outstanding novel for young readers, *The Circuit* (University of New Mexico, 1997). Here, it is presented as a fully illustrated picture book with strong-lined, full-color, glowing artwork by Simón Silva. (Ages 8–11)

King-Smith, Dick. *The Water Horse.* Illustrated by David Parkins. U.S. edition: Crown, 1998. 118 pages. (0–517–80027–6) $16.00

A charming and inventive fantasy about one of the best-known contemporary legends. On the west coast of Scotland in 1930, Kirstie is combing the beach after a storm with her little brother, Angus, when she comes upon a strange looking piece of tidal wash that soon hatches into a tiny sea monster. It's a Water Horse, her grandfather, Grumble, tells them with delight ("Grumble smiling!" Kirstie notes in amazement). Soon Kirstie and her family have christened the animal Crusoe, and over the coming months form a delightful bond with the affectionate beastie. But a rapidly growing sea monster is not easy to hide from the neighbors, let alone keep housed and fed. Eventually they move him to a large, secluded lake. The name of that lake isn't revealed in the story itself, but many readers will have already guessed it by the story's end, when an excerpt from a newspaper article dated 1933 confirms the first known sighting of the Loch Ness monster. Even readers who are not familiar with the Loch Ness monster will thoroughly enjoy this whimsical, lighthearted story with its appealing characters and captivating plot. (Ages 8–10)

Lawrence, Iain. *The Wreckers.* Delacorte Press, 1998. 196 pages. (0–385–32535–5) $15.95

Along the coast of Cornwall in the wild of a storm, the ship on which 14-year-old John Spencer is traveling is torn apart while trying to follow lights on the shore to safe harbor. John is the apparent sole survivor. He finds himself stranded in a village where people's only source of income is the cargo and contents of ships that have crashed on the coast. But no bounty can be taken if any of the sailors survive, and some of the village men are not above murder to claim whatever a wreck may hold. John is saved from these men by Simon Mawgan, a local landowner who seems intent on making sure the boy gets safely on the next boat away from Cornwall. But despite Mawgan's apparent efforts to help him, and the reassurances and insights of the landowner's spirited niece, John begins to suspect that Simon and others in the village are responsible for his shipwreck, and many others besides, by luring storm-tossed boats toward false harbors with lanterns from the shore. Iain Lawrence's riveting novel, set at the end of the 18th century, is a dramatic tale of adventure and mystery, full of the tensions that both human nature and the natural world provide. An author's note provides background information on the history of the wreckers who did indeed live along the Cornwall coast in centuries past. (Ages 10–14)

McDonnell, Christine. *It's a Deal, Dogboy.* **Illustrated by G. Brian Karas. Viking, 1998. 92 pages. (0–670–83264–2) $14.99**
The fifth book featuring Leo Nolan and his family and friends features five sweetly humorous chapter stories that begin with the last day of school, when Leo (aka Dogboy to his scathing older sister Eleanor) battles growing anxiety after Eleanor makes him doubt whether or not he will pass third grade. Each of the four successive vignettes describes one of soon-to-be-fourth-grader Leo's varied summer experiences: playing on a coed baseball team, getting a dog, babysitting his tag-along cousin, and making a dubious bargain with his sister in which she will trade her old tree house for the chance to practice her ear-piercing technique on Leo. Leo and Eleanor's sibling relationship is refreshingly realistic, a verbal battleground of taunting and teasing, complaining and deal-making that captures perfectly how it feels to see an older sibling change ("Last summer...she played croquet with him and did jigsaws with her mother on the porch table...Leo missed the old Eleanor. This summer it would be a waste of time to ask her to play croquet. She would say no"). Told in third-person from Leo's point of view, the stories are warm and funny and the characters lively and realistic and rooted in a nine-year-old's experiences. (Ages 8–10)

Mazer, Harry. *The Wild Kid.* **Simon & Schuster, 1998. 103 pages. (0–689–80751–1) $15.00**
A welcome, realistic portrayal of a child with Down Syndrome is at the center of a swift-paced novel in which 12-year-old Sammy develops a unlikely friendship with a tough runaway. Sammy is trying to track down his stolen bicycle when he wanders into the dense forest preserve near his home and gets lost. He literally stumbles upon Kevin, a runaway from reform school who has been hiding in the woods. At first their relationship is one of fear and confusion on Sammy's part and disgust on Kevin's. Sammy only wants to go home again and can't understand why Kevin has tied him up. For his part, Kevin can't believe how helpless Sammy seems but he's not willing to let Sammy go and risk having his own presence in the woods revealed. Eventually Kevin unties Sammy, but Sammy stays. He wants to go home and he trusts that Kevin will take him soon—he can't find his way on his own. And he likes that fact that Kevin never assumes he can't learn how to do things and patiently shows him new skills. At home, Sammy had felt babied but with Kevin his confidence begins to blossom. Sammy is a powerful influence on Kevin as well as his trusting nature and willingness to accept Kevin at face value give Kevin, who has built walls to protect himself, a new perspective on himself and on friendship. Mazer's third-person telling is centered on Sammy's point of view and his portrait of this child with Down syndrome as a singular individual with a fully developed personality not only

feels authentic, it gives the story a compelling and unique perspective that will engage its readers as much as the drama of Sammy and Kevin's relationship. (Ages 10–13)

Morgenstern, Susie. *Secret Letters from 0 to 10.* **Translated from the French by Gill Rosner. U.S. edition: Viking, 1998. 137 pages. (0–670–88007–8) $15.99**
Everything in ten-year-old Ernest Morlaisse's life is predictable, including Ernest himself. From the style of suit he wears to school each day to the marmalade on two pieces of toast that he always has for breakfast to the homework that he never fails to complete, Ernest never changes. In fact, he doesn't even think about change, or likes or dislikes. Like the grandmother who is raising him in her somber home, his life is pale and unfulfilled and he doesn't even know it. Then Victoria de Montardent blows into their lives. Victoria is the new girl in Ernest's class and absolutely nothing about her is predictable with the exception of her lively, dauntless, overwhelmingly forceful personality. Victoria is smitten with Ernest, the best student in their class. And, not surprisingly, Ernest, who has never had to learn the meaning of resistance, is absolutely bowled over by Victoria, who lives with her parents and 12 brothers in a house that is never quiet. Without even questioning what is happening, both Ernest and his grandmother begin to change under Victoria's influence. They get a telephone and a television. The actually go out to eat! And they discover that beneath the staid exterior of their dutiful relationship is a warm and loving bond. An absolutely delightful novel with unforgettable characters and a charming, quirky plot comes to U.S. readers from France, where it was originally published. *Honor Book, 1998 CCBC Batchelder Award Discussion.* (Ages 10–13)

Nelson, Theresa. *The Empress of Elsewhere.* **A Richard Jackson Book/DK Ink, 1998. 278 pages. (0–7894–2498–3) $17.95**
When 11-year-old Jim Harbert and his lively seven-year-old sister, Mary Al, are hired by their reclusive elderly neighbor to help care for a pet monkey, they aren't aware that Mrs. Monroe's disruptive, unfriendly granddaughter is part of the bargain. J.D. ("That stands for Juvenile Delinquent," the girl tells them) is cold not only to Jim and Mary Al, but to her grandmother as well. Only with the monkey does she show gentleness and compassion. But Jim and Mary Al begin to form a bond with J.D., at first around the little monkey, and then around the island, a heavily wooded piece of land in the middle of Lake Luly on Mrs. Monroe's property. It was a favorite place of J.D.'s father, who died in a car accident the previous year. It is the island of Elsewhere, J.D. tells Jim and Mary Al, recalling the stories her father once told her. But even the island is not enough to console J.D. When her grandmother won't let her go to Houston to see her mother, who is in the hospital after having a breakdown, J.D. is determined to go on her own, taking the monkey—now christened the Empress of Elsewhere—with her. Jim and Mary Al go along, unaware that J.D.'s stories about her mother expecting her aren't true; unaware of the depths of J.D.'s emotional hardship and sadness. Nelson's narrative, told in Jim's wonderful first-person voice, draws characters in vivid detail, and provides readers with many things to think about, from the contrast between Jim and Mary Al's economically struggling but openly loving family and the wealthy, reserved Mrs. Monroe's household, to the depiction of mental illness, briefly but senstively presented in the portrayal of J.D.'s mother, to the significance of the title. Who *is* the Empress of Elsewhere really? Distinctive characters, complex relationships, an intriguing setting and a compelling narrative voice distinguish this novel of families and friendship. (Ages 10– 13)

Peck, Richard. *A Long Way from Chicago.* **Dial, 1998. 148 pages. (0–8037–2290–7) $15.99**

Over seven consecutive summers, Joey and his sister, Mary Alice, spend a week every August with their Grandma Dowdel in a small Illinois town. Each of those eventful visits is detailed in the seven witty short stories that comprise this funny, warm-hearted novel. Joey and Mary Alice didn't know Grandma very well when they made their first visit in 1929. Joey was nine then, and Mary Alice was seven. "As the years went by... Mary Alice and I grew up, and though Grandma never changed, we'd seem to see a different woman every summer." Grandma Dowdel is one of the richest characters over the age of 50 to be found in literature for the young. She is principled and stern but not without humor or compassion. Indeed, Grandma has a lot to teach her two grandchildren about both those qualities as the years pass. When the hobos and tramps following the rails in the midst of the Depression are to be run out of town by the sheriff, it is Grandma who prepares a meal for them and serves it just inches over the town boundary, much to the sheriff's consternation. Even better (or worse), she used the sheriff's own boat to catch the catfish she is serving. Grandma is an enigma to Joey and Mary Alice, but over the years, as the children mature, more and more of the mysteries about her are revealed in this wonderful, distinctive portrait in which all of the characters are intriguing and a delight. Peck's masterful storytelling here extends to time and place as well. Small-town midwest life in the midst of the Depression is artfully, entertainingly captured in this fine novel that is an excellent choice for a read-aloud. (Ages 10–14)

Pullman, Philip. *Clockwork.* **U.S. edition: Arthur A. Levine Books/Scholastic Press, 1998. 112 pages. (0–590–12999–6) $14.95**

A taut and eerie original tale from Philip Pullman is set in a small German village "once upon a time." Everyone in the village is looking forward to the next day's unveiling of the latest addition to the grand clock of Glockenheim, a figure carved by the clockmaker's apprentice, Karl. But Karl has not carved a figure for the clock, and on the eve of the ceremony he is bitter and worried. As Karl broods in the tavern, his friend Fritz, a writer, begins telling his latest story to the others that are gathered there. It is about the dark and brilliant Dr. Kalmenius, a physician and master clockmaker who mysteriously saved the life of a young prince, Florian. Fritz has not actually finished writing the tale he is telling, however. "He was just going to wind up the story, set it going, and make up the end when he got there." But at a pause in his narrative the tavern door slowly opens. Dr. Kalmenius himself is standing there, with "eyes that looked like burning coals in caverns of darkness." As Fritz flees in terror and the townspeople make hasty retreats for their homes, only Gretl, the innkeeper's kind-hearted young daughter, and Karl are left behind. The powerful, magnetic man strikes a deal with Karl to provide him with a figure for the clock, beginning a series of tense and chilling events that unwind, nonetheless, to a satisfying and inevitable conclusion: happily ever after, of course! Pullman's masterful storytelling weaves an unusual and fascinating tale. (Ages 10–14)

Reeve, Kirk. *Lolo & Red-Legs.* **Rising Moon/Northland, 1998. 111 pages. (0–87358–683–2) $12.95**

When Lolo finds a tarantula near the fort that he and his two best friends have built in their East Los Angeles neighborhood, his grandfather helps him catch it. His mother won't let him keep it at home, but with the help of a nearby pet store owner, Lolo makes a suitable den in an oversized pickle jar and keeps the spider at the fort. Lolo is quiet, but he enjoys the interest that others take in Red-Legs, and in him by association, from his sixth-grade classmate Lisa to the pet store owner, Mr. Verdugo, who asks if he can take Red-Legs to the county fair and invites Lolo to go along—an invitation that will mean Lolo's first trip out of the neighborhood in which he has spent his entire life. But when some older boys whom Lolo and his friends taunted destroy the fort, Red-Legs disappears. Lolo doesn't know if she was stolen or if she is dead, only that his heart is broken. A novel set in the Latino neighborhood of East Los Angeles known as *Las Lomitas* is distinguished by its appealing characters and strong sense of place. Spanish langauge words and phrases used in the region are woven into the simple but captivating storyline; many can be defined in context, but a glossary is also provided. (Ages 9–12)

Ritter, John H. *Choosing Up Sides.* **Philomel, 1998. 166 pages. (0–399–23185–4) $15.99**

Luke Bledsoe has been fighting his left-handedness his entire life. Like his passionate minister father, 14-year-old Luke knows that the left hand is the hand of the Devil, and so he struggles to use his right hand only. In 1921, Luke and his family move to a new parish along the Ohio River and one of the biggest things in town is baseball. This means nothing to Luke until the day he absentmindedly tosses a stray ball back to players in a game. He uses his left hand, and the speed and strength of his throw amaze everyone who sees it. Pressured to join the team, Luke refuses. Not only is left-handedness forbidden by his father, but sports are too. Still, Luke can't help but start to wonder. If left-handedness is so bad, why would God make it so easy for him to do things with his left hand and so difficult for him to do things with his right? John H. Ritter has done an exemplary job creating three-dimensional main characters in this finely nuanced first novel. Luke's father, a fire-and-brimstone preacher in the pulpit, clearly loves his son and cares about his well-being and their relationship. He regrets his rage, when it flares up brutal and harsh, not only because it goes against the teachings of Jesus but also because it has hurt his child. Luke's transformation from follower to questioner to one who will honor his own inner truth rather than the teachings of his father's religion occurs slowly, subtly, and with the intense pain that comes with the realization that your parent, and all that you have been taught to believe, can be wrong. (Ages 11–14)

Rowling, J.K. *Harry Potter and the Sorcerer's Stone.* **Illustrated by Mary Grandpré. U.S. edition: Arthur A. Levine Books/Scholastic Press, 1998. 309 pages. (0–590–35340–3) $16.95**

J.K. Rowling's literary debut will not disappoint fantasy fans, but even those who've never felt much attraction to the genre might find themselves riveted by this fanciful, funny, not-too-scary British novel in which a 12-year-old boy's life is turned around by the discovery that he is a wizard. Harry Potter is a skinny, spectacled, orphaned child living with a comically hard-hearted aunt and uncle and obnoxious, bullying cousin when he learns he has been accepted at Hogwart's School of Witchcraft and Wizardry. The news might have been less shocking to Harry if he'd had even an inkling that he possessed the power of magic, but Harry did not know that witches and wizards existed, let alone that he himself was a candidate for study at a boarding school where magic is taught. The mysterious world of spells and potions, trolls and dragons, flying broomsticks and magic wands unfolds simultaneously for both Harry and readers of this highly imaginative, satisfying novel. Boarding schools, even ones for witches and wizards, are not without their share of snobs and bullies, but despite this, Hogwart's is a friendly, welcoming place to Harry, and it quickly begins to feel like his true home. Harry's initiation into Hogwart's social and academic life, along with the other first-year boys and girls at Hogwart's, is the reader's initiation, too, and the discoveries to be made are delightful. Rowling has conjured a fully realized world of magic, complete with centuries-old history and tradition, language, rules of conduct, games and the requisite battle between good and evil in which Harry and his new friends become involved, leading to tension, excitement, and mystery in this wonderful first novel. (Age 9 and older)

Ryan, Pam Muñoz. *Riding Freedom.* **Drawings by Brian Selznick. Scholastic, 1998. 138 pages. (0–590–95766-x) $15.95**
Charlotte Parkhurst is the first woman known to have voted in the United States. She did so in California on November 3, 1868, 52 years before women's constitutional suffrage was affirmed. And she did so posing as a man. Charlotte's masquerade wasn't just for the purpose of voting, however; it was the way she lived her life. Indeed, it wasn't until after her death in 1879 that "Charley," as she was known, was discovered to be a woman. Pam Muñoz Ryan's fictional story, based loosely on the life of Charlotte Parkhurst, will initially attract many young readers as a story about a girl and horses. As a child, Charlotte worked as a stableboy in the east for several years before moving to California, where she continued to drive stage and work on a ranch—always passing for a boy or young man. But Ryan always keeps Charlotte's female identity at the forefront of her storytelling, and in the context of an appealing adventure she demonstrates female ability and the injustice of laws that prevented women from voting, even slipping in a comment or two from Charlotte about the bravery of women who fought those laws without benefit of masquerade. An author's note at the end of the novel provides a brief summary of the real Charlotte Parkhurst's life. While the note does not provide full enough explanation as to why Ryan chose to set her fictional story in a slightly different time frame than that in which the real Charlotte lived (Charlotte's childhood has been moved from the early to the mid–19th century), it is nonetheless a welcome addition to the text of this engaging story. (Ages 8–11)

Rylant, Cynthia. *The Islander.* **A Richard Jackson Book/DK Ink, 1998. 97 pages. (0–7894–2490–8) $14.95**
As a boy, Daniel Jennings did not feel at home on the small island off the coast of British Columbia where he lived with his grandfather. He wanted to know all the things he was missing in the larger world. His grandfather's love was strong and certain, but it could not console this longing. Then one day Daniel sees a mermaid on the beach, glistening and beautiful and as shy as Daniel himself. She disappears quickly but later Daniel finds a key inside a seashell and he knows it is a gift from her. He never gives up hope of seeing her again but in the meantime the key—magical and mysterious—becomes Daniel's talisman. He wears it around his neck and whenever it vibrates it leads him without fail to something or someone in need, from an injured animal to a lost child. Over the years, with the help of the key, he begins to

feel part of the island—part of its natural life, and part of the small community of people who inhabit it. It unlocks his heart, and in doing so it leads him to a deeper understanding of what it means to be at home. Cynthia Rylant's sea-swept fantasy, told in the calm, centered voice of the adult Daniel, sustains an element of mystery as well as it unravels the secret of the mermaid, and the truth about Daniel's heart. (Ages 9–12)

Sachar, Louis. *Holes.* **Frances Foster Books/Farrar Straus Giroux, 1998 233 pages. (0–374–33265–7) $16.00**

In this age of gloom and doom in children's fiction, it's refreshing to find a truly funny book for kids. Sachar's over-the-top satire has depth, originality and loads of child appeal. Poor Stanley Yelnats is convinced he'll never get ahead in life due to a curse brought on his family by his "no-good-dirty-rotten-pig-stealing-great-great-grandfather." Falsely charged with the theft of a pair of valuable sneakers, Stanley is sent to a juvenile detention camp where he is forced, day after day, to dig a hole that's exactly five feet across and five feet deep. Sound grim? It is! But what makes this funny is Stanley's understated, deadpan description of the camp, the people in charge of it (Mr. Sir, Mr. Pedanski, and The Warden), the other delinquents (Zero, Zigzag, Armpit, X-Ray, Magnet, and Squid), and how their story fits together with the historical events which led to his family's infamous curse. The intricacy of the plot, eccentricity of the characters, and overall absurdity of the story reminds us of the novels of Ellen Raskin (*The Westing Game*; *Figgs & Phantoms*). Just beneath the surface of this entertaining tale, however, is a more serious statement about the enduring power of friendship and loyalty when the odds are stacked against you — curse or no curse. *Winner, 1998 CCBC Newbery Discussion.* (Ages 10–14)

Scrimger, Richard. *The Nose from Jupiter.* **U.S. edition: Tundra Books, 1998. 156 pages. Pbk. (0–88776–428–2) $7.95**

Norbert has been living in 13-year-old Alan's nose—yes, in Alan's nose— ever since arriving from Jupiter in his little space ship. When Alan talks to Norbert, people think he is talking to himself. Alan won't mention Norbert to the doctor, or to his parents. Even though they're divorced and his father lives far away in Vancouver, they still argue, and this would only make things worse. No, Norbert is a secret. That Norbert thinks of Alan's nose as an apartment with several rooms and a garage is more than people will be able to take—until Norbert decides to assert himself. This fresh, funny, punny, laid back story is a remarkable first novel by a Canadian author. (Ages 9–12)

Snyder, Zilpha Keatley. *Gib Rides Home.* **Delacorte Press, 1998. 246 pages. (0–385–32267–4) $15.95**

"On a dark, cloudy afternoon in the fall of 1909, a strange thing happened on the third floor of the Lovell House Home for Orphaned and Abandoned Boys. Something so downright mysterious that even firsthand witnesses could scarcely believe their eyes." Gibson Whittaker had returned-fairly well dressed and apparently healthy-carrying a handsome saddle. Why was he back? The last the boys or anyone there had seen of him about a year ago, Gib had been heading for adoption. Or had it been indentured servitude? That was something Gib had begun to realize could happen to boys who left the cruel punishments of the orphanage to be "adopted." No wonder he stayed on his guard at the ranch where Ty taught him to work with the horses. He and Ty got to eat with the family in the big house, but they knew their place. Gib had to wonder why the girl Livy kept watching him work with the horses, and he had good reason to wonder, as well, about what this family knew about his birth mother. Snyder's horse story is much more than that; it's no tall story, either, because it's based upon her father's childhood in a Nebraska orphanage and his experience of being "required to do a man's work when he was eight years old, beaten, mistreated." Her note in an afterword places some of the almost incredible elements of her gripping novel into a believable historic context. (Ages 11–14)

Wells, Rosemary. *Mary on Horseback: Three Mountain Stories.* **Illustrated by Peter McCarty. Dial, 1998. 53 pages. (0–8037–2154–4) $16.99**
Mary Breckenridge began the Frontier Nursing Service to provide medical care – and hope – for the people living in the rural Appalachian Mountains of Kentucky during the 1920s. She began with just a few nurses and her own passion and determination. Over the years, the Service grew as more nurses joined Mary and her dream of a hospital/clinic was realized. A few years later there were six such clinics, and many stories of lives that were touched and changed. Rosemary Wells tells three such stories in a work of short fiction for young readers that is deftly drawn from real people and events. Three compelling voices – a young boy whose father is injured in a logging accident, a 19-year-old nurse who comes from Scotland to join Mary's service, and a small girl who is grieving the death of her mother – chronicle events in the early history of the Frontier Nursing Service. Real-life events woven into the author's three first-person narratives with a storyteller's grace, so that each story is rooted in history but belongs as well to the imagination, where conversations and relationships among historical figures are fully realized. Black-and-white drawings by Peter McCarty open each story and are based on photographs taken for the Frontier Nursing Service by Mary Breckenridge's niece. An actual photograph of Mary Breckenridge and a brief biographical essay on her life follows the stories, and the author's acknowledgments provide the sources for the characters and events in this welcome book for young readers. (Ages 8–11)

Wolff, Virginia Euwer. *Bat 6.* **Scholastic, 1998. 230 pages. (0–590–89799–3) $16.95**
Effective use of multiple perspectives serves both to tell the story and tie theme into structure of this unusual and provocative novel set in 1949. The annual softball game each May between the sixth grade girls of Barlow and Bear Creek Ridge is the biggest event of the year in the two communities. But that year, 1949, something terrible happens during the game, and as the novel begins the girls from both teams have agreed to each tell their own parts of a story that stretches back to the start of the school year and farther in order to try to make sense of what happened. Each of the teams had a new player at the start of the school year. In Bear Creek Ridge, it is Aki, whose family has just returned to the community after years away, most of them spent in a Japanese American internment camp. The new player in Barlow is Shazam, an odd, out-of-synch girl who, it turns out, has been shuttled from place to place ever since her father was killed in the Japanese bombing of Pearl Harbor. The players on the two teams number more than 20, and Virigina Euwer Wolff has made them each part of a narrative in which the whole transcends the individual voice as the girls piece together why Shazam

viciously attacked Aki at the game. At the same time, the individual lives of the various girls are distinct, and in addition to exploring issues of race and prejudice, the narrative portrays the barriers between rich and poor among the many girls as well. Rich period details, such as the arrival of the first refrigerator for one girl and her family, heighten the reading experience of the novel. Younger readers may find it difficult to tell the many players apart despite these distinctions in their lives. There is a roster for each team at the beginning of the book and each speaker is clearly identified, but it is difficult to always remember which team she is on. What readers may discover as the narrative progresses, however, is that it doesn't really matter. They are all part of a larger community that is woven out of the truth of their collective voice. *Honor Book, CCBC Newbery Award.* (Ages 10–14)

See also: *Making Up Megaboy; Parcival; Seeing Lessons; Soft Rain*

Fiction for Teenagers

Baer, Edith. *Walk the Dark Streets.* Frances Foster Books/Farrar Straus Giroux, 1998. 280 pages. (0–374–38229–8) $18.00
Some of the changes in Eva's life are gradual, but most are sudden and drastic. Swastikas seem to appear everywhere, and there are signs on public benches prohibiting Jews from sitting on them. At school the curriculum and even the teachers change, and the way Eva is treated also changes. Eva's father can no longer operate his beloved bookstore. Her best friend and her family disappear. The community people who had celebrated her grandfather's birthday can no longer be counted upon for friendship. Arno becomes Eva's confidante, but their shared love of music and budding romance are continually threatened in one way or another. Arno's artist father has been placed in an asylum, and his stepfather has disowned him because he's Jewish. This compelling novel concerns a particular young teenager and her family, her first love, and how she was able to flee Germany. Chronicling local events affecting Jews in a small German town between January 1933 and July 1940, *Walk the Dark Streets* continues the autobiographical story Baer began in *A Frost in the Night: A Girlhood on the Eve of the Third Reich* (Pantheon, 1980). In that first work of autobiographical fiction, Eva's comfortable childhood as a cherished child and her family's life are carefully recreated within the general environment of growing dread that is fully realized in *Walk the Dark Streets*. Both novels are beautifully crafted and offer a perspective on the Holocaust not expressed in other novels for young readers. Baer came to the United States in 1940 when she was in her teens. (Ages 12–16)

Bauer, Joan. *Rules of the Road.* G.P. Putnam, 1998. 201 pages. (0–399–23140–4) $15.99
Sixteen-year-old Jenna Boller is a shoe professional. A whirlwind salesperson at Gladstone's Shore Store in Chicago, she can juggle a weary mom and her three fidgety kids, a sore-footed woman looking for relief and a hard-to-please man all at once and make them each feel special. There is nothing disingenuous about Jenna, however. Bad shoes can make people's lives miserable, after all, and she believes in knowing her product and taking care of her customers. Still, Jenna's not sure why Mrs. Madeline Gladstone,

retiring president of the Gladstone Shoe dynasty (176 outlets in 37 states) has singled her out. Mrs. Gladstone needs someone to drive her from Chicago to Dallas for the annual meeting of Gladstone's board of directors, stopping to check on various Gladstone Shoe Stores along the way, and she has chosen Jenna, with her six-month-old drivers license, for the job. Jenna is a witty, spirited young woman with a sharp sense for business, rocky self-esteem and a genuine passion for treating people right. As she and Mrs. Gladstone trek across the country in the older woman's Cadillac, Jenna must put all of her skills and knowledge about people to use as she builds a relationship with this imposing woman and then gets drawn into stopping a planned corporate takeover by Mrs. Gladstone's hard-hearted son that would change the service-oriented philosophy of Gladstone Shoe Stores forever. Joan Bauer's delightful comic writing shines in this outrageous, warm-hearted story. (Ages 13–16)

Burgess, Melvin. *Smack.* **U.S. edition: Holt, 1998. 327 pages. (0–8050–5801–X) $16.95**

Tar and Gemma are seemingly typical suburban teenagers, living on the outskirts of London, who decide to run away from home together so that Tar can escape his abusive father. Both feel that the adult world has failed them. In the nearby town of Bristol, they find a number of other young runaways, dropouts, and assorted cast-offs, living in abandoned buildings. Tar and Gemma are quickly accepted into this makeshift community of survivors who eke out a living by collecting public assistance, supplemented by shoplifting and prostitution. Like many of their peers, they are soon seduced by heroin and hooked into a marginal existence where they continually flirt with self-destruction. Their story, told from multiple first-person points of view, shows the the internal and external contrasts between two distinctive individuals who have made the same dead-end choice. Although the voice is fairly consistent throughout, the multiple viewpoints allow us to see Tar and Gemma develop fully as characters, with an amazingly non-judgmental tone on the part of the author. Originally published in Great Britain in 1996 with the title *Junk*, this ground-breaking young adult novel won the 1997 Carnegie and Guardian Awards in that country. (Ages 13–17)

Flake, Sharon G. *The Skin I'm In.* **Jump at the Sun/Hyperion, 1998. 171 pages. (0–7868–2392–5) $14.95**

Thirteen-year-old Maleeka Madison is always getting teased about the way she looks. "If it ain't about my color, it's my clothes." Maleeka can do something about the handsewn clothes she finds embarrassing. As long as she stays on classmate Charlese's good side, Char loans her fashionable outfits that Maleeka changes into each morning at school. But there's not much she can do about the color of her skin. No one has a problem with Maleeka being Black; after all, most of her classmates are Black, too. But plenty of them have a problem with Maleeka being *too* Black. "They don't say nothing about the fact that I'm a math whiz, and can outdo ninth graders when it comes to figuring numbers. Or that I got a good memory and never forget a single, solitary thing I read. They only see what they see, and they don't seem to like what they see much." Maleeka knows she deserves to be treated better, but there is a huge gap between knowing she deserves more respect and liking herself enough to demand it. A new teacher at her school, Miss Saunders, tries to help Maleeka see how beautiful she is both inside and out, but Maleeka is resistant to her efforts. In her opinion, Miss Saunders is butting into things that aren't her business, in spite of, or perhaps because of, the disfiguring birthmark on the teacher's own face. A stunning and courageous debut novel from Sharon G. Flake moves swiftly with dialogue finely tuned to the voices of contemporary African American teens as it explores issues of self-respect and self-esteem through the life of a creative and talented young woman who is learning to see herself in new ways. *Winner, 1998 CCBC Coretta Scott King Award Discussion: Author.* (Ages 12–16)

Fleischman, Paul. *Whirligig.* **Henry Holt, 1998. 133 pages. (0–8050–5582–7) $16.95**

"We can never know all the consequences of our acts. They reach into places we can't see. And into the future, where no one can." In a drunken moment of despair and self-pity, 16-year-old Brent tries to kill himself by crashing his car. He survives, but a young woman driving an oncoming car is killed. It is the young woman's mother who offers him a chance for some sort of redemption from his guilt and self-loathing. In her own grief, she is seeking to keep some part of her daughter Lea's caring spirit alive. She shows Brent a picture of a whirligig—Lea's favorite toy as a child. Put one up in the four corners of the United States, she tells Brent. Paint them in the image of Lea and write her name on each one, so that in some way she will continue to spread happiness. Brent travels across the country by bus to complete the task, his unskilled work improving with each new creation. He relies on help from the past in the carefully written notes left by another builder in the old book on whirligigs he bought. But Brent, too, is leaving notes for the future—messages that are open to interpretation in the form of each of the whirligigs he builds. Fleischman intersperses his narrative of Brent's journey with chapters that step into other people's lives at some future time, chronicling how each of the whirligigs has been viewed by someone whose life it has touched. In this way, the narrative as a whole moves back and forth through time like the blades of a whirligig spinning with the wind. But the story always returns to Brent's own journey as he gradually learns to trust both himself and others, and in doing so discovers his own strength and kindness, and the unending connections that give life its meaning. (Age 13 and older)

Gifaldi, David. *Rearranging and Other Stories.* **A Jean Karl Book/Atheneum, 1998. 148 pages. (0–689–81750–9) $16.00**

In "Jared," a teenager whose face has been badly burned in a fire struggles with anxiety and doubt as he contemplates an in-person meeting with a girl he has come to know well on the telephone. A 12-year-old boy involved in a joke that got out of hand, cruelly taunting a young man with a developmental disability, describes his own shame and the dignity of the young man's father who, with a simple gesture, offers him something beyond forgiveness in "Mr. Burrell." "The Driving Lesson" chronicles a teenage girl's pleasure and confusion as her relationship with her boyfriend becomes complicated by sexual exploration and her mother responds with an honest lesson in respect and hard-hitting truth. David Gifaldi's collection is comprised of stories at once subtle and striking. He writes about young adults for whom uncertainty, and sometimes pain, can be seen as not just part of the teenage condition but part of the human condition—struggle and transcendence in ways both small and large. His protagonists are drawn from the inside out—good kids who are distinctive, seen in situations that are individually unique, but all dealing with emotions and feelings that are universal: fear, self-doubt, anger, hope, resentment, shame, pleasure, confusion. While one story, "The Lords and Ladies of Coventry High," seems out of place with its over-the-top characterization of a Shakespeare-spouting teenage Romeo, the book as a whole is a series of finely crafted revelations—gifts of the heart for young adult readers. (Age 13 and older)

Grimes, Nikki. *Jazmin's Notebook.* **Dial, 1998. 102 pages. (0–8037–2224–9) $15.99**

Jazmin is a bright, introspective 14-year-old growing up in Harlem in the early 1960s who faces the harsh realities of her world with a poet's heart and soul. Living with her competent older sister who's little more than a teenager herself, Jazmin looks at the world with an endearing mixture of realism and optimism, which she expresses in a poem at the opening of each first-person chapter. In this short novel, Nikki Grimes slowly unfolds the complexities of an adolescent female character through her observations of everyday life, her memories of the past, and her hopes for the future. Anyone who knew only the superficial details of Jazmin's life would see her as an impoverished, neglected child; those of us who share her deepest thoughts and feelings, revealed in this slender volume, will see her as a fighter, a survivor and, above all, a gifted poet ready to make her mark on the world. (Ages 12–15)

Holeman, Linda. *Mercy's Birds.* **U.S. edition: Tundra, 1998. 198 pages. Pbk. (0–88776–463–0) $5.95**

Depression, alcoholism and the threat of sexual abuse are portrayed with senstivity and realism in this fine narrative by Linda Holeman. Teenager Mercy is the only member of her family who is working. Her mother sits in her room all day, the dreams she once had of opening her own bakery never even mentioned any more. Her aunt, who tries pathetically hard to please the people around her, still spends most of her time sitting in front of the tv, usually with a drink in her hand. The rent on the run-down house in which they are living is being paid by her aunt's boyfriend, who has a temporary job overseas. But there is no relief in that for Mercy. Barry—"B" she calls him in her head, unable to even say his name—frightens her with the things he has said, the way he used to stroke her hair, and she is terrified of what might happen once he returns, which could be any day now. She cut her once long, red-gold hair and dyed it black because of him, but she knows that won't protect her. The only bright spots in Mercy's life are her job in a flower shop, which she loves, and the tentative bond she is forming with a girl at high school who is persistent in her efforts to be Mercy's friend. When Mercy's mother has a complete breakdown and tries to kill herself, Mercy is sure that even these thin webs of hope will be destroyed, but in truth her mother's act of hopelessness is a turning point for them all as it forces Mercy and her family to disclose family secrets and reach out for help that was waiting all along, if only they could find the faith and courage to ask. (Age 14 and older)

Hughes, Monica, compiler. *What if...? Amazing Stories.* **U.S. edition: Tundra, 1998. 199 pages. Pbk. (0–88776–458–4) $6.95**

Fourteen short stories and two poems from a range of contemporary Candian writers comprise a collection of fantasy and science fiction imaginings that repeatedly invite readers to consider the unknown quantities of our lives today and of the future. Compiler Monica Hughes prefaces each story with a specific question that can easily be the launching point for students' own creative writing endeavors even as it introduces the piece that follows. "What if...the stars came out only once in a thousand years?" she asks as an introduction to Alice Major's poem "Star-Seeing Night." "What if...the moon were haunted?" is the question posed for Alison Baird's short story "Moon Maiden." The poems and stories themselves range from humorous to mystical to spine-tingling, and in addition to examining the unknown or unexpected, the collection as a whole has the undeniable effect of also inviting examination of where it is the human race may be heading. What if...we could make the future better? (Ages 12–15)

Jones, Diana Wynne. *Dark Lord of Derkholm.* Greenwillow, 1998. 345 pages. (0–688–16004–2) $16.00
The annual Pilgrim Parties are making most of the inhabitants of Blade's world miserable. Adventure vacations for offworld tourists, the Pilgrim Parties are a drain on their resources, and no one, from wizards to elves, thieves to trolls, demons to dragons is happy about them. But the offworlder Mr. Chesney has an age-old contract that seems impossible to break. So while he gets rich on Chesney's Pilgrim Parties year after year, farmland is ravaged, homes are destroyed, and the death toll mounts. All for the sake of giving the "pilgrims" a convincing show. This year Blade's father, Derk, has been chosen as Dark Lord, and Blade himself has been chosen to lead one of the pilgrim tours. Refusing is out of the question—they were chosen by Querida, High Chancellor of Wizards' University. The Dark Lord is responsible for overseeing the many facets of the adventures for offworld tourists, from managing marauding armies to conjuring up a demon. Derk seems an unlikely choice for such a job. He is an outcast from the wizard establishment, more concerned with his brilliant and original experiments than the traditional rules of conjuring. Derk has created pigs that can fly, horses that can talk and fly, carnivorous sheep and Friendly Cows (they go all moony eyed and slobbery with affection). And five of his seven children are griffins, each one a talented and distinct individual formed from the cells of lion and eagle as well as Derk and Wizard Mara, his wife. But what neither Derk nor Blade know is that Querida has chosen them based on the advice of the oracles as a means to end the Pilgrim Parties once and for all. A highly entertaining story with captivating characters and a page-turning plot is set in a world that is being exploited by one that sounds suspiciously like our own. There's no heavy-handed message here, however, just delightful satire for anyone who cares to find it. (Ages 12–16)

Paulsen, Gary. *Soldier's Heart: A Novel of the Civil War.* Delacorte Press, 1998. 106 pages. (0–385–32498–7) $15.95
There was no such thing as post-traumatic stress disorder at the time of the Civil War. The symptoms certainly existed, Paulsen notes in his foreword to this grim and moving novel, but there was no understanding among the majority of people as to what returning soldiers had experienced and how the trauma continued to affect many of their lives. Still, he notes, people knew they were different. "They were said to have a soldier's heart." Paulsen's story is based loosely on the life of a real person. He explains in an author's note that Charley Goddard was 15 in 1861, when he lied about his age to enlist in the first Minnesota volunteers. He died in 1868 at the age of 23, torn apart both physically and emotionally by what happened to him in the war. The fictional story Paulsen constructs to link those two events in the real Charley's

life is a tale of an innocent, unsuspecting boy's experiences on the cruel and unforgiving battleground of war. At first Charley is swept up in the excitement of going to war—marching in parade, the steamboat ride followed by the train ride east. He didn't like how much the other soldier's swore but it couldn't dampen his enthusiasm for the battles to come. Charley's excitement is soon replaced by horror and fear. *"Make it stop now!"* his mind cries out in the midst of his first battle, but of course it doesn't stop, not in that battle, and not in all that are to come. The encouragement and the praise of commanding officers is meaningless. Everything is meaningless but survival, and even that seems pointless at times. The details are realistic and brutal in this harrowing novel that leaves no doubt about the inhumanity of war. (Ages 13–16)

Pinkney, Andrea Davis. *Raven in a Dove House.* Gulliver Books/Harcourt Brace, 1998. 208 pages. (0–15–201461–6) $16.00
As soon as 12-year-old Nell says good-bye to her father after he's dropped her off at her aunt's house in the small town where he grew up, she realizes that things have changed. Her cousin Foley is different. He and his friend Slade have secrets, dangerous secrets. Nell hasn't been there a day before she's been drawn into their intrigue. Who could have imagined that a gun, a real one, would be hidden inside of the wonderful Dove House, the very doll house that had been a source of such pleasure during other summers? The very place where Nell had once been in charge of what happened has become a place of dread and danger, of a stark reality completely out of her control. Foley is out of control, too, and so is Aunt Ursa after a tragedy befalls the family and community. Nell holds on, and one of the people to whom she can still go, despite his new woman friend, is her quite, urbane father who has always seemed curiously estranged from his kinfolk. Strong characterizations and solid plotting earmark a contemporary novel about an African American family in a community that feels exempt from urban dangers, even when it isn't. (Ages 12–15)

Winter, Kathryn. *Katarína.* Farrar Straus Giroux, 1998. 257 pages. (0–374–33984–8) $17.00
Author Kathryn Winter's affecting portrait of a child caught up in the confusing and frightening conditions of war is based in part on her own experiences growing up as a Jewish child in Slovakia during World War II. Katarína is only seven years old in 1942 when her Aunt Lena fools the doctor into thinking Katarína has scarlet fever. The house is put under quarantine and Aunt Lena explains that no one, not even the Halinka Guards, can enter. When she is "well" again, Katarína is not allowed to return to school—Jews have been forbidden from attending. As a child living with an aunt who doesn't observe Jewish laws and customs and therefore has no sense of a Jewish identity, Katarína finds as little logic in this as she does in the later silence of her best friend, Eva, who is Catholic and who fails to answer any of the letters Katarína sends to her after Katarína's aunt marries and they move to the city. And Katarína wants to share her big news with Eva—she is Catholic now, too. Her aunt and new uncle's housekeeper has been teaching her prayers and the rosary; she has even attended mass. When Eva's aunt sends her to stay with a Catholic family in the country, Katarína fights loneliness and sadness but remains firmly convinced that her aunt will return for her just as she promised, unaware of the dangers that her aunt and uncle,

and she herself, are facing in a world gone crazy. It is this narrative's firmly grounded point of view in the mind of a child too young and too sheltered to put what is happening in her world into a context that in part makes this novel so compelling. At the same time, what can be read in and between the lines in the words and actions of the adults around Katarína affirms the gravity and the poignancy of the young girl's situation for readers, who will bring knowledge of the Holocaust to their understanding of the novel. The setting in Eastern Europe adds a layer of added interest as the seeds of future Soviet dominance in the region are sewn in the then-welcome arrival by adults around Katarína of the Russian troops as Slovakia's liberators from the Germans. (Age 13 and older)

Woodson, Jacqueline. *If You Come Softly.* **Putnam's, 1998. 181 pages. (0–399–23112–9) $15.99**

A quiet, beautifully etched portrait of a first love that is shattered by the racism, *If You Come Softly* traces the relationship of two teens whose lives intertwine for a short but life-changing time. Ellie is Jewish and white. Jeremiah is black. Both are from well-to-do families where it's sometimes hard to be yourself, and both are new students at Percy Academy. It was Jeremiah's father, a well-known African American filmmaker, who wanted Jeremiah to attend a private school. Jeremiah doesn't let anyone know who is father is, though, or his mother, an accomplished novelist. It's too hard being yourself—being accepted for yourself, if your parents fame precedes you. For Ellie, Percy was her own choice—made because she liked the sound of the name. "I knew it was a stupid reason to choose a school, but they all seemed exactly alike." Ellie lives with her parents in a large apartment that still echoes with the emptiness of her mother's leaving. It happened twice, and twice her mother returned, but the feeling of abandonment still haunts Ellie, even when she sits in the very same room as her mother harboring the secrets of her heart. One of those secrets is Jeremiah. They meet on the first day of school, and each makes the other feel right. But Ellie isn't sure how her parents would react to Jeremiah, and her heart can't risk finding out. For his part, Jeremiah takes Ellie home to meet his mother, who sees and understands her sons feelings. In his neighborhood, too, he has support, from a best friend whose mother is white and father is black. But he is hesitant to tell his father. "Thing about white people," his father tells him, "they don't know they're white. They know what everybody else is, but they don't know *they're* white." Jeremiah stays silent. Ultimately, however, it is not secrets and silence that separate Jeremiah and Ellie, it is the racism of our society, racism that makes a black teenage boy running with a basketball in a white neighborhood too quickly assumed as suspect, too quickly mistaken for a "tall, dark man" being pursued by the police. (Age 13 and older)

See also: *Bat 6; Blood on the Forehead; Bloomability; Fire, Bed & Bone; Holes; Las Christmas; Making Up Megaboy; Shakespeare Stealer; Victor; Wreckers*

New Editions of Old Favorites

Brown, Margaret Wise. *The Little Scarecrow Boy.* **Illustrated by David Diaz. Newly illustrated edition. Joanna Cotler Books/HarperCollins, 1998. 32 pages. (0–06–026284–2) $15.95**

The little scarecrow boy had wanted to accompany his father to the fields to make faces at the crows. "NO, No, little boy. You can't go. You're not fierce enough to scare a crow. Wait till you grow." Naturally the little scarecrow will not wait to be old enough to venture into the corn field. Of course he ends up safe and sound and on his way to breakfast, but not before he actually uses all six of his fierce faces. Clever uses of typefaces and sizes as well as loppity-looking scarecrows, sewn with button eyes, and sunshine- and garden-bright doll-like clothes, make this wonderful story come alive in exciting new ways. The paintings were created in watercolor, gouache, and pencil. (Ages 3–5)

Bryan, Ashley. *Ashley Bryan's African Tales, Uh-Huh.* **Atheneum, 1998. 198 pages. (0–689–82076–3) $22.00**

The 14 stories reprinted here were first published in one of these collections of folklore retold by Ashley Bryan: *The Ox of the Wonderful Horns; Beat the Story-Drum, Pum-Pum* and *Lion and the Ostrich.* Their original ochre and deep red illustrations adorn the pages of these tales: "Ananse the Spider in Search of a Fool," Frog and His Two Wives," Elephant and Frog Go Courting," "Tortoise, Hare and the Sweet Potatoes," "Hen and Frog," "Why Bush Cow and Elephant Are Bad Friends," "The Husband Who Counted the Spoonfuls," Why Frog and Snake Never Play Together," "How Animals got Their Tails," The Son of the Wind," Jackal's Favorite Game," "The Foolish Boy," and the two original title stories. Bryan's skill in finding the written cadence for each story and his affection for trickster, fool and hero alike make this a treasure trove in which to find some of his best-loved tales. Sources are printed at the end. (Ages 9–12)

Krauss, Ruth. *You're Just What I Need.* **Illustrated by Julia Noonan. HarperCollins, 1998. 32 pages. (0–06–027514–6) $14.95**

Krauss' marvelous text about imaginative play between a mother and very young child was first published in 1951 with the title *The Bundle Book.* Noonan's illustrations gently bring to life the game in which a child plays hide-and-seek under a blue blanket. "Can it be a bundle of laundry?" But the mother doesn't need a bundle of laundry, or a bundle of carrots, or any number of other things to which a giggling little hidden child has to say no. What does the mother need, anyway? "You. You're just what I need!" The warm, comforting text is timeless, and so is the hide-and-seek play between the red-headed mom and her toddler. (Ages 1–3)

Zolotow, Charlotte. *The Bunny Who Found Easter.* **Illustrated by Helen Craig. Houghton Mifflin, 1998. 32 pages. (0–395–86265–5) $15.00**

A beloved picture story first published in 1957 involves a nicely dressed bunny who wakes up from a long nap in the woods to find that he's all alone. He asks an owl where he will find other rabbits, but all the old owl knows is that rabbits are connected to Easter. The bunny sets off looking for Easter, thinking "it must be some place to the East." He finds a pool of water, sees a field of daisies, encounters a summer thunderstorm, notices autumn leaves, and enjoys a winter snowscape even though he's lonely. One day in spring he meets another bunny and forgets all about Easter for a while. Surrounded by a family of little new rabbits, the bunny understands "at last that Easter was not a *place* after all, but a *time* when everything lovely begins once again." He also begins to see why the old owl observes, "At Eastertime there are always rabbits." Craig's ink, watercolor and colored pencil illustrations perfectly complement the rabbit's quest to find those like him to share the wonders of all seasons. (Ages 3–5)

See also: *Adventures of Snowwoman; Circle of Days; Day Light, Night Light; Fourth Wise Man; Grassroots; Kid's Guide to Social Action; Max's Bath; Max's Bedtime; Max's Birthday; Max's Breakfast; Max's First Word; Max's New Suit; Max's Ride; Max's Toys; New Baby at Your House; Night Before Christmas; Sky Is Always in the Sky; Wake Up/Goodnight; Where Go the Boats; section on Folklore, Mythology and Traditional Literature*

Points of View

IBBY Regional
Children's and Young Adult
Literature Conference

sponsored by

United States Board on Books for Young People (USBBY)

with the
Cooperative Children's Book Center and
The Office of Education Outreach of the
School of Education, University of Wisconsin–Madison

Speakers: Nina Bawden, Anthony Browne, Virginia Buckley,
Joanna Cole & Bruce Degen, Floyd Cooper, Lois Ehlert,
Sarah Ellis, Jeffrey Garrett, Kevin Henkes, Nina Ignatowicz,
Keiko Kasza, Hector Viveros Lee, Julius Lester,
Naomi Shihab Nye, Katherine Paterson, Junko Yokota, and others

October 7–9, 1999

International Board on Books for Young People (IBBY)
Third Regional Conference

Madison, Wisconsin, USA

For conference details, contact Linda Shriberg (608/262–4477;
shriberg@soemadison.wisc.edu) or find information at
http://www.soemadison.wisc.edu/outreach on the World Wide Web.

United States Board on Books for Young People (USBBY) patron
members: American Library Association, Children's Book Council,
International Reading Association, and the National Council of
Teachers of English.

Appendix I
How to Obtain Books Listed in *CCBC Choices* and CCBC Publications

Obtaining the Books in CCBC Choices

The Cooperative Children's Book Center is not a bookstore. Please do not write or phone with the expectation of ordering the books in *CCBC Choices* from the CCBC itself.

Ask for these books at your public library, school library media center or bookstore. Be specific concerning the edition, noting the publisher, illustrator (if applicable) and ISBN (international standard book number) of the book you want to secure.

The CCBC can be of assistance by verifying up-to-date publisher and vendor addresses and phone numbers if you do not have access to the most recent annual *Children's Books in Print* (R.R. Bowker) or to regular information about the larger U.S. publishers from the Children's Book Council in New York City. Please contact the CCBC for address verification if you experience difficulty in locating any of the books recommended in *CCBC Choices*. We are aware that publishers of all sizes and in all regional locations change addresses and phone numbers frequently. The CCBC's public service hours, address and public service phone number are listed in a section at the end of this publication.

Book prices and ISBNs are cited for hardcover library or trade editions and for books which are also available or only available in paperback editions at this time. Binding information is provided for books available only in paperback. While the CCBC typically does not attempt to keep track of the paperback book field in any way, we do know that your purchase and use of hardcover books with young readers can often be a factor in whether or not these books ever become available in a paperback edition in years to come. The books we recommend that are available in paperback editions only often have unique content that cannot be found in other books for children. We encourage you to pay attention to these books, and to the announcement of future paperback editions of books that are currently available only in hardcover.

Addresses are provided for small publishers only. We recognize the challenge, the staff time and the cumulative financial obligation of small enterprises involved in responding to a wide variety of correspondence. We recommend that any queries sent to small publishers include a business-size, self-addressed, stamped envelope along with prepayment by check of the total amount of the order plus 15% for shipping and handling. CCBC experience with small/alternative publishers for more than 18 years underscores the observation that their books will no doubt be in print for a long time, maybe even longer than many of the books published by larger houses.

Obtaining CCBC Publications
CCBC Choices 1998

If you live in Wisconsin, send $3.00 or the equivalent in U.S. postage stamps to the Cooperative Children's Book Center, 4290 Helen C. White Hall, 600 N. Park St., Madison, WI 53706–1403 USA.

If you live outside of Wisconsn, send $6.00 to the Friends of the CCBC, Inc., P.O. Box 5288, Madison, WI 53705–0288 USA. You may also inquire about the rates for ordering copies of *CCBC Choices 1998* in quantity, and about the availability of earlier editions of *CCBC Choices*. Please do not phone the CCBC to ask for this information.

Regardless of where they live, current members of the Friends of the CCBC, Inc., receive a copy of this edition of *CCBC Choices* as one benefit of annual Friends of the CCBC, Inc., membership. To request a membership form, write to the Friends of the CCBC, Inc., at the address noted in the previous paragraph.

Other CCBC Publications

All CCBC publications *except* the two listed below are available free for postage and handling costs to Wisconsin residents.

Wisconsin residents are invited to send a self-addressed, stamped business envelope to receive a current list of CCBC Materials. Address this request to: Cooperative Children's Book Center, 4290 Helen C. White Hall, 600 N. Park St., Madison, WI 53706–1403.

The following CCBC publications can be purchased:

1) *The Multicolored Mirror: Cultural Substance in Literature for Children and Young Adults* edited by Merri V. Lindgren (Highsmith, 1991). Available from: Highsmith Press. Phone 1–800–558–2110 to inquire or place an order.

2) *Multicultural Literature for Children and Young Adults, Volume Two: 1991–1996* by Ginny Moore Kruse, Kathleen T. Horning and Megan Schliesman (CCBC, 1997). Available from the Friends of the CCBC, Inc. for $12.00 plus $3.00 for postage and handling. Write to Friends of the CCBC, Inc., P.O. Box 5288, Madison, WI 53705–0288 USA (prepaid orders only; no purchase orders). Also available from Publication Sales, Wisconsin Department of Public Instruction, P.O. Box 7841, Madison, WI 53707–784 for $12.00 + 5.00 postage and handling (prepaid orders only; no purchase orders). Phone 1–800–243–8782.

These publications are not available for purchase at or through the CCBC.

Appendix II
The Cooperative Children's Book Center

Vision Statement

All children and young adults deserve excellent literature that reflects their own experience and encourages them to imagine experiences beyond their own, that satisfies their innate curiosity, and that invites them to dream. We believe such literature fosters a fundamental understanding of themselves and one another, stimulates their creativity, and, most importantly, enriches their lives.

At the Cooperative Children's Book Center (CCBC), a library of the School of Education at the University of Wisconsin–Madison, we are committed to identifying excellent literature for children and adolescents and bringing this literature to the attention of those adults who have an academic, professional, or career interest in connecting young readers with books. The identity of the Cooperative Children's Book Center is grounded in literature for children and young adults. This is reflected in its collections, its role as a book examination center and research library, and its staff expertise in book arts, book evaluation, multicultural literature, alternative press publishing, and intellectual freedom. Within each of these areas, the CCBC is acknowledged as a leader and a catalyst for change. We are committed to fulfilling these roles by advocating and actively modeling a philosophy that embraces diversity, promotes understanding and respects the rights of the individual child.

The concepts of access and inclusiveness are vital to the discussion and evaluation of literature for children and young adults. These elements are also central to any discussion of the CCBC itself with regard to its collections and information services. Therefore, the CCBC seeks to expand both the means by which CCBC information is made available and the types of information to which users have access. We will be at the forefront in:

- collecting a wide range of contemporary and historical literature for children and young adults, including literature published by alternative presses and that created by current and former Wisconsin residents;
- encouraging awareness and discussion of issues essential to literature for children and young adults;
- advocating the First Amendment rights of children and young adults by: (1) providing Wisconsin teachers and librarians with in-depth information on literature whenever a minor's access to books is questioned, and (2) preparing Wisconsin teachers and librarians to respond to challenges to intellectual freedom;
- providing educational support for students in higher education and individuals with an interest in literature for children and young adults;
- shaping electronic means of access to and dissemination of information about literature for children and young adults, within the School of Education, across the university, throughout the state of Wisconsin, and beyond; and
- networking nationally and internationally with colleagues in related fields to create coalitions that recognize the importance of high-quality materials for all children and young adults.

The CCBC is a unique and vital gathering place for books, ideas and expertise. The CCBC vision for the future is the continued pursuit of excellence in literature for children and young adults by whatever resources are available, unwavering commitment to the First Amendment rights of children and young adults, and the establishment of a national and international network to connect all who share the belief that excellent literature can insure a brighter future for the world's children.

Purpose

The Cooperative Children's Book Center (CCBC) of the School of Education at the University of Wisconsin–Madison is a noncirculating examination, study and research children's and young adult literature library for adults. The purposes of the CCBC are: (1) to provide a collection of current, retrospective and historical books for children and young adults; (2) to provide Wisconsin librarians, teachers, students and others informational and educational services based on the collection; and (3) to support teaching, learning and research needs related to children's and young adult literature.

The CCBC is funded for these purposes by the UW–Madison School of Education and by an annual contract from the Wisconsin Department of Public Instruction/Division for Libraries and Community Learning. The CCBC was established in 1963.

Collection

The library collection contains review copies of newly published juvenile trade books, recommended children's and young adult trade books, historical children's books, contemporary and historical reference materials related to children's and young adult literature, children' and young adult books by Wisconsin authors and illustrators, and alternative press books for children.

The Dewey Decimal classification system is used to catalog all materials except the Alternative Press and Wisconsin Collections. Subject analytics are used extensively for card catalog access to reference materials. Author, title, illustrator, translator and subject access is provided for children's and young adult books and reference materials. Any known national award or distinction or selection tool recommendation is noted on the endpaper in the front of each children's and young adult title in the collection.

With the exception of the library's historical materials, most of the CCBC's holdings are in the University of Wisconsin–Madison's electronic library on-line catalog, MADCAT. In addition to the historical collection books, some alternative press materials, and some books published between 1990 and 1994 are still accessible through the library's paper card catalog only. Efforts to enter these items into MADCAT is continuing. Most of the CCBC records of books received before 1990 are entered in the WISCAT statewide database.

The CCBC collection is noncirculating.

Services

Reference assistance from a professional librarian/children's literature specialist is available most weekdays between 9 a.m. and 4 p.m. Reference assistance from student assistants is available to anyone on a walk-in basis on evenings and weekends, and at other times when a librarian is unavailable during the week. University students and faculty and Wisconsin librarians and teachers wishing to speak with a professional librarian/children's literature specialist are advised to make advance arrangments. Specialized reference assistance and children's literature consultation is also available by mail and phone to the above constituents anywhere in the state. Intellectual freedom information services are available to anyone serving minors in Wisconsin libraries and schools.

Tours and/or lectures are arranged as possible for university classes, library and school book selection groups, and public library system and school inservice groups coming to the Book Center.

Publications on selected children's and young adult literature topics are available along with selected award and distinction lists and annual CCBC Wisconsin-related literature publications.

Children's and young adult literature displays can be seen by walk-in library users. Monthly book discussions and annual award discussions apply literary standards and book evaluation techniques to new books and are open to any student, faculty member, librarian, teacher or other interested adult who reads some of the scheduled books beforehand, as are the annual awards discussions. Interested persons are welcome to contact the CCBC for a schedule or to indicate if information about a particular discussion is needed.

CCBC-Net is an electronic forum of the School of Education at the University of Wisconsin–Madison designed to encourage awareness and discussion of ideas and issues essential to literature for children and young adults. *CCBC-Net* is a community of individuals with an interest in children's and young adult literature extending across Wisconsin, the nation, North America and beyond.

CCBC-Net provides opportunities for guided discussions of contemporary children's and young adult literature, including multicultural literature, translated books, outstanding and award-winning books, and various themes and topics in literature. This unique listserv provides a forum for discussion of the book arts and book publishing for the young. Specific books to be discussed are announced in advance. To subscribe to *CCBC-Net*, inquire at the CCBC or send e-mail to *cdowling@ccbc.soemadison.wisc.edu.*

The CCBC's web site is at *http://www.soemadison.wisc.edu/ccbc/* on the Internet. Special features include a Book of the Week review by one of the CCBC librarians, links to recommended sites related to children's and young adult literature, and information about upcoming events at the CCBC.

Continuing education courses are taught throughout the year by the CCBC professional staff. As possible, the CCBC participates in statewide and regional conferences through the provision of book examination exhibits and/or leadership in scheduled sessions. The CCBC often co-sponsors conferences and workshops provided by UW–Madison Extension Programs.

Anyone interested in specific information is invited to visit the CCBC web site or write to request a current list of *CCBC Materials* or a copy of *The CCBC This Season*, a quarterly flyer briefly listing current CCBC on-campus and off-campus information and program services.

Governance

The University of Wisconsin–Madison School of Education is responsible for policies and funding of the Cooperative Children's Book Center. W. Charles Read is the dean of the School of Education. Assistant Superintendent Calvin Potter of the Division for Libraries and Community Learning/Wisconsin Department of Public Instruction administers the DPI contract that provides CCBC services for

Wisconsin libraries and schools. The School of Education dean, the DPI/DLCL administrator and the CCBC director comprise the CCBC Executive Committee.

The CCBC Advisory Board represents CCBC users on the University of Wisconsin–Madison campus and from libraries and schools throughout Wisconsin. Members of the 1998–99 Advisory Board are:

Claire Jandt (Chair), LMC Director (PreK–5), Franklin Elementary School, LaCrosse

Lisa Altreuter, IMC Director Holmen School District

Claudia Backus, Children's Services Coordinator, Waukesha County Federated Library System

Dolores Barabe, Library Support and Technical Services Coordinator Northern Waters Library Services Ashland

JoAnn Belanger, Elementary Library/Media Coordinator (K–6), Unified School District of Antigo

Malore Brown, Assistant Professor School of Library and Information Science, UW–Milwaukee

Kathy Champeau, Learning Facilitator/Reading Specialist Muskego-Norway School District

Chris Dowling, Network Administrator School of Education, UW–Madison

Joel Dworin, Postdoctoral Fellow School of Education, UW–Madison

Barbara Elleman, Distinguished Scholar of Children's Literature Marquette University, Milwaukee

Lance Ellmann, Federal Programs Consultant, Cooperative Educational Services Agency (CESA) #4, Onalaska

Lois Emberson, Media Specialist (K–5) Sauk Prairie Schools

Gayle A. Falk, Director Burlington Public Library

Suzanne Fondrie, Curriculum & Instruction Doctoral Program School of Education, UW–Madison

Sue Haertel, Reading/Language Arts Teacher, Marcy Elementary School Hamilton-Sussex

Dianne McAfee Hopkins, Associate Professor, School of Library & Information Studies, UW–Madison

Jacque Karbon, Reading Education Consultant, Wisconsin Department of Public Instruction

John Kean, Associate Dean School of Education, UW–Madison

Mary Keefer, Education Media Collection Coordinator, UW–Oshkosh

Nancy Kiefer, School Library Media Specialist, Chain O'Lakes Elementary School, Waupaca

Judith King, Director, Libraries, Techology & Communication Madison Metropolitan School District

Janelle Kohl, Director, Frank B. Koller Memorial Library, Manitowish Waters

Ellen Last, English/Language Arts Consultant, Wisconsin Department of Public Instruction

Mary McCarty, Elementary Library Media Specialist (K–5), Forest Glen Elementary School, Green Bay

Linda Pils, Multi-age Primary Teacher (1–2), Northside School, Madison

Kathy Prestidge, Director of Children's Services, New London Public Library

Jane Roeber, Youth Services Consultant Division for Libraries and Community Learning, Wisconsin Department of Public Instruction

Liz Strachan, Principal/Library Media Coordinator, Downsville Elementary School, Menomonie

Lysianne Unruh, Director Mt. Horeb Public Library

Kris Adams Wendt, Assistant Director/Children's Librarian Rhinelander District Library

Student Advisory Committee

A Student Advisory Committee was established in 1997 to provide the Cooperative Children's Book Center with direct input from School of Education students on the UW–Madison campus as to how the library can better serve their needs.

Members of the 1998–99 Student Advisory Commitee are listed below along with the program in which they are enrolled and their home communities:

Erica Cheung, Elementary Education
South Holland, Illinois

Joan Flynn, Elementary Education
Madison, Wisconsin

Suzanne Fondrie, Curriulum & Instruction
Doctoral Program
Eagle River, Wisconsin

Rachel Germain, Elementary Education
Vadnais Heights, Minnesota

Jessica Goldstein, Elementary Education
Swampscott, Massachusetts

Vivian Greblo, Elementary Education
Madison, Wisconsin

Sunny Hur, Elementary Education
Mount Prospect, Illinois

Kristin Ichishita, Elementary Education
Lincolnwood, Illinois

Sara Mattson, Elementary Education
Marshfield, Wisconsin

Emily Movall, Elementary Education
Thiensville, Wisconsin

Alison Shearn, Elementary Education
Chicago, Illinois

Jaimie M. Sherling, Elementary Education
Endicott, New York

Lesley Wagner, Curriculum & Instruction
Doctoral Program (Math)
Baltimore, Maryland

The Staff

In addition to Director Ginny Moore Kruse and Librarians Kathleen T. Horning and Megan Schliesman, the CCBC staff during 1998 included undergraduate and graduate students who helped carry out the daily responsibilities of assisting individuals on campus, in schools and in libraries who are working in many ways to meet the interests of all young readers.

The student staff during the creation of *CCBC Choices 1998* included graduate students Sheryl Boser, Elizabeth Dill, Laurel Maguire (1998), Jolen Neumann, Kathy Oker, Heidi Oliversen, Hélène Charmillon Pohl, Stephanie Steinwedel, and Nancy Wessling; and undergraduate students Marni Burton, Sara Cotton, and Dan Schuyler. Graduate students Corey Hansen and Latanya Richardson completed practicums at the CCBC during the fall of 1998.

Volunteers from the Friends of the CCBC, Inc., included professional librarian Sally A. Davis and professional librarian Tana Elias.

Public Service Schedule

The CCBC is open twelve months a year for public service to adults interested in contemporary or historical children's and young adult literature. The CCBC is open for public service 54 hours weekly during the Fall and Spring semesters: Monday–Thursday 9 a.m.–7 p.m., Friday–Saturday 9 a.m.–4 p.m.

During Summer School, the CCBC is open weekly Monday–Saturday 9 a.m.–4 p.m. During Intersession and University breaks, the CCBC is open Monday–Friday 9 a.m.–4 p.m. Phone 608/263–3720 to confirm the public service hours and to inquire about the availabilty of a professional librarian/children's literature specialist at a specified time. Extended public service hours can be arranged to accommodate campus course schedules as well as out-of-town users' arrivals and departures. Requests for extended service must be made more than two weeks in advance and will be accommodated if at all possible according to staff availability.

Appendix III
Cooperative Children's Book Center
Guidelines for Book Discussions

Look at each book for what it is, rather than what it is not.

- Make positive comments first. Try to express what you liked about the book and why. (e.g. "The illustrations are a perfect match for the story because....")
- After everyone has had the opportunity to say what they appreciated about the book, you may talk about difficulties you had with a particular aspect of the book. Try to express difficulties as questions, rather than declarative judgments on the book as a whole. (e.g. "Would Max's dinner really have still been warm?" rather than "That would never happen.")
- Avoid recapping the story or booktalking the book. There is not time for a summary.
- Refrain from relating personal anecdotes. The discussion must focus on the book at hand.
- Try to compare the book with others on the discussion list, rather than other books by the same author or other books in your experience.

All perspectives and vocabularies are correct. There is no "right" answer or single correct response.

- Listen openly to what is said, rather than who says it.
- Respond to the comments of others, rather than merely waiting for an opportunity to share your comments.
- Talk with each other, rather than to the discussion facilitator.
- Comment to the group as a whole, rather than to someone seated near you.

These guidelines may be reproduced as long as credit for their creation is given to CCBC librarians Kathleen T. Horning and Ginny Moore Kruse.

Appendix IV
The Compilers of *CCBC Choices 1998*

Kathleen T. Horning is a librarian and coordinator of Special Collections at the Cooperative Children's Book Center of the School of Education at the University of Wisconsin–Madison. For nine years she was also a children's librarian at Madison Public Library. She is the author of *From Cover to Cover: Evaluating and Reviewing Children's Books* (HarperCollins, 1997). She edited *Alternative Press Publishers of Children's Books: A Directory* and, with Ginny Moore Kruse, she coauthored *Multicultural Literature for Children and Young Adults, 1980–1990*, and with Ginny Moore Kruse and Megan Schliesman, *Multicultural Literature for Children and Young Adults, 1991–1996*. She was also a contributor to The *Multicolored Mirror: Cultural Substance in Literature for Children and Young Adults.* Katy is currently serving on the Américas Award Committee, under the auspices of The Consortium of Latin American Studies Programs (CLASP), University of Wisconsin–Milwaukee. She chaired ALA/ALSC's 1995 John Newbery Committee and served on ALA/ALSC's Notable Children's Books Committee and an earlier Newbery Award Committee. She also chaired USBBY's Hans Christian Andersen Award Committee which selected U.S. nominees for the international award in 1992. She served on the ALA/SRRT Coretta Scott King Award Committee and chaired ALA/ALSC's first Committee on Social Issues in Relationship to Materials and Services for Children. She also chaired the 1997 Mildred Batchelder Award Committee. Katy frequently lectures to librarians on issues in evaluating literature for children and young adults. She has a B.A. in Linguistics and a Master's Degree in Library and Information Studies, both from the University of Wisconsin–Madison.

Ginny Moore Kruse is director of the Cooperative Children's Book Center in the School of Education at the University of Wisconsin–Madison and a teacher of undergraduate children's literature and adult continuing education courses on and off campus. She is a former public school teacher, school librarian and public librarian. Ginny founded the award-winning CCBC Intellectual Freedom Information Services, and participated in developing the Charlotte Zolotow Award. She has chaired or served on many national children's literature award and distinction committees including the John Newbery, Randolph Caldecott, Mildred L. Batchelder, May Hill Arbuthnot, Laura Ingalls Wilder, Pura Belpré, Coretta Scott King, Boston Globe-Horn Book, and Teachers' Choices committees. She is currently national coordinator for the Jane Addams Children's Book Awards, and a member of two ALA book award committees: 2000 Caldecott Award and 2000 Pura Belpré Award. She chaired the *Book Links* Editorial Advisory Board during its first four years and served on the Freedom to Read Foundation Board, the ALA Intellectual Freedom Committee, and the USBBY Board. Currently she is an advisory board member for two new publications: *Parent's Guide* and *Riverbank Review.* Ginny is coauthor with Katy of *Multicultural Literature for Children and Young Adults, 1980–1990* and with Katy and Megan of *Multicultural Literature for Children and Young Adults, 1991–1996,* and she contributed to *The Multicolored Mirror: Cultural Substance in Literature for Children and Young Adults.* During 1996 Ginny received four formal acknowledgments of her professional leadership: Award of Excellence (Wisconsin Educational Media Association), Alumna of the Year Award (School of Library and Information Studies, UW–Madison),

Distinguished Service Award (Association for Library Service to Children, ALA), and the Intellectual Freedom Award (Wisconsin Library Association/SIRS). In 1997, she was the recipient of the ALA/AASL-SIRS Intellectual Freedom Award and the Hope S. Dean Memorial Award (Foundation for Children's Books). Ginny has a B.S. Degree in Education from UW–Oshkosh and a Master's Degree in Library Science from the University of Wisconsin–Madison.

Megan Schliesman is a librarian and administrator at the Cooperative Children's Book Center of the School of Education at the University of Wisconsin–Madison. Megan is coauthor with Ginny and Katy of *Multicultural Literature for Children and Young Adults, 1991–1996.* She compiled the bibliography *Poetry for All Seasons and Many Reasons: Selected Books for Children and Young Adults* (CCBC, 1996) and was co-compiler with Ginny of *Poetry for Children and Young Adults: Selected Resources* (CCBC, 1996). She currently coordinates the CCBC's annual compilation of books by Wisconsin authors and illustrators and books about Wisconsin, and edits the bi-annual *CCBC Resource List for Appearances by Wisconsin Book Creators.* Megan has served on the Charlotte Zolotow Award Jury and currently is serving on the 2000 John Newbery Award Committee. With Ginny and Katy, she co-teaches Educational Telecommunications Network (ETN) continuing education courses for librarians and teachers across the state, and she is an active member of the American Library Association. Megan oversees daily information requests received at the CCBC public service desk and manages the CCBC's book examination collection. She also coordinates and supervises the library's cataloging efforts. She has worked as a writer and editor on several publications in the Madison area and continues this work in various capacities outside the CCBC. Currently a member of the South Central Library System Board of Trustees in Wisconsin, Megan has a B.A. degree in English from UW–Whitewater and a Master's Degree in Library and Information Studies from the University of Wisconsin–Madison.

Tana Elias, who created the index for *CCBC Choices 1998*, is a librarian at Madison Public Library and a freelance researcher and indexer. Tana previously created the index for *Multicultural Literature for Children and Young Adults, 1991–1996*, and the 1997, 1996, 1995 and 1994 editions of *CCBC Choices*. She is also indexing the upcoming revision of the CCBC publication *On Wisconsin: Books about the Badger State for Children and Young Adults*. While a student reference assistant at the CCBC, Tana compiled *Children's Books by Wisconsin Authors and Illustrators and Children's Books About Wisconsin: An Identification Record of Titles Published in 1992* (CCBC, 1993). Tana currently sits on the Board of Directors of the Friends of the CCBC, Inc, and reviews books for *School Library Journal*. Tana has a B.A. in History from Hamline University and a Master's Degree in Library and Information Studies from the University of Wisconsin–Madison.

Appendix V
The Friends of the CCBC, Inc.

This membership organization sponsors programs to develop public appreciation for children's and young adult literature and supports special projects at the CCBC. Members of the 1998–99 Board of Directors are named in the Acknowledgments at the beginning of this publication.

Friends members receive invitations to events open only to the membership and to other opportunities for adults who share an interest in children's and young adult literature to meet with each other formally and informally. Members receive a quarterly newsletter with children's and young adult literature information as well as advance announcements about CCBC publications and services.

The Friends provide volunteer assistance at the CCBC, and hospitality for CCBC Advisory Board meetings and other special events. Friends provide other volunteer services on behalf of the CCBC, such as promotion and distribution of selected CCBC and Friends' publications and special editions of original notecards. The Friends provide funding for public lectures on the UW–Madison campus. The committee that selects the annual Charlotte Zolotow Award is comprised of Friends members.

Annual membership benefits include a copy of *CCBC Choices* and a limited edition publication of the annual Charlotte Zolotow Lecture. Membership is open to all.

The membership year runs from January through December. Dues paid after October 1st each year apply to membership for the next year. Membership dues are tax deductible to the fullest extent of the law. Individual membership categories are: Student-$9; Personal-$18; Sustaining-$30; Supporting-$50; and Patron-$100. Group membership categories are: Honor (2–5 individuals)-$75; Award (6–10 individuals)-$150; and Distinguished (11–15 individuals)-$250.

To join the Friends, send a check payable in U.S. funds to Friends of the CCBC, Inc., to: Treasurer, Friends of the CCBC, Inc., Box 5288, Madison, WI 53705–0288, USA.

Index

In keeping with the CCBC's emphasis on multicultural literature, this year's index intends to provide basic access to the ethnic background of the persons, fictional and real, portrayed in this year's *CCBC Choices* selections. Subject entries are as specific as possible, and include cross-references to point the reader to other groups of interest. For example, "Africans and African Americans" includes a cross-reference to "Tanzanians" and other culturally-specific sub-groups. For fictional works, the index includes groupings based on human and community relationships and themes, such as "Siblings" or "Friendship." Additional themes and subjects have been indexed with traditional and contemporary storytime, classroom uses, or reader's advisory in mind.

Entries for titles, book creators, ethnic backgrounds/origin, and relationships are interfiled, and arranged in letter-by-letter order. The filing arrangement ignores both cases, all articles (including those in Spanish), and all punctuation. Title citations for subject entries point only to the title's annotated entry, not for other locations in which the title may appear. Page numbers in italics refer to the page on which annotations for each title or author's work appear. For space reasons, only the main title was included in the index; bilingual books include entries under both English and Spanish titles.